EXPERIENCING RUPTU

THE ORDINARY AND UNE
GLOBAL MI

EXPERIENCING RUPTURES IN MIGRATION

THE ORDINARY AND UNEXPECTED JOURNEYS OF GLOBAL MIGRANTS

Editors:

Delphine Mercier, Víctor Zúñiga, Kamel Doraï, Mustapha El Miri & Michel Peraldi

Foreword by Roger Waldinger

Conclusion by Deborah A. Boehm

TRANSNATIONAL PRESS LONDON

2021

MIGRATION SERIES: 34

Experiencing Ruptures in Migration: The Ordinary and Unexpected Journeys of Global Migrants

Edited by Delphine Mercier, Víctor Zúñiga, Kamel Doraï, Mustapha El Miri & Michel Peraldi

First Published in 2021 by TRANSNATIONAL PRESS LONDON in the United Kingdom, 13 Stamford Place, Sale, M33 3BT, UK.
www.tplondon.com

Paperback
ISBN: 978-1-80135-022-8
Digital
ISBN: 978-1-80135-023-5

Cover Design: Nihal Yazgan
Cover Photo: Photo Boards, KZNTEn2r6tw, unsplash.com

Transnational Press London Ltd. is a company registered in England and Wales No. 8771684.

CONTENTS

ABOUT THE EDITORS AND CONTRIBUTORS

Deborah A. BOEHM, an anthropologist, is Professor of Anthropology and Gender, Race, and identity at the University of Nevada, Reno. Her ethnographic and collaborative work focuses on transnational Mexican families, U.S. immigration detention and deportation regimes, and the experiences of young people who migrate to the United States. She has been awarded an Andrew Carnegie Fellowship (2021-2023) to conduct publicly engaged research about U.S. immigration detention and the growing social movement to end it.

Robin CAVAGNOUD, a sociodemographer, is a Professor in the Social Sciences Department of the Pontificia Universidad Católica del Perú (PUCP) in Lima. Based on a qualitative approach to population studies and an analysis of individual and multi-generational biographies, his research interests are focused on the evolution of family livelihoods through the role of children and young people, and intergenerational relationships, in contexts of vulnerabilities.

Frédéric DÉCOSSE is a sociologist in charge of the National Scientific Research Center connected to the Labor Sociology and Economy Laboratory. His work focuses on temporary migration programs, the health of agricultural migrant workers, and the immigration struggle in the Mediterranean and in North America.

Kamel DORAÏ is a researcher at the CNRS (the French National Center for Scientific Research). He has been based at the French Institute for the Near East (IFPO) in Amman, Jordan, since September 2014, and in Beirut until 2021. He has been conducting research in Lebanon, Syria, and Sweden since 1996 on different refugee groups, collecting biographies, migration trajectories, and stories of urban mobility. He was based in the IFPO in Damascus (Syria) from 2006 to 2010. His work focuses mainly on asylum and refugees in the Middle East, new migrations and geopolitical restructuring in the Middle East, and migration and transnational practices within the Palestinian Diaspora. The comparative study of refugees residing inside and outside of camps as well as the analysis of their migratory experience and spatial practices provide an account of the refugees' socio-spatial dynamics in exile and of relations between the camps and their urban environment.

Mustapha EL MIRI is a Senior Lecturer in Sociology at Aix-Marseille University. His latest research revolves around migrations and their social effects in the Mediterranean basin. His most recent studies in the same field analyze the social qualification of migrants in their home countries undocumented migrants' beginning and integration modes, and the transformation of relationships at the border and during migration in transnational areas that are part of economic globalization (in the Hispano-

Moroccan case).

Alfredo HUALDE is a sociologist at the Colegio de la Frontera Norte in Tijuana. He is a tier-3 member (highest level) of Mexico's *Sistema Nacional de Investigadores*. His research focuses on the mobilization of knowledge in many industries at the Mexican border (electronic maquiladoras, aeronautics, software) and the role played by various actors and institutions in the recognition of this knowledge: educational centers, companies, and their own topics. His methodology prioritizes longitudinal perspectives, especially the study of professional trajectories.

Carolina KOBELINSKY is an anthropologist in charge of The National Center for Scientific Research with the Ethnology and Comparative Sociology, at Université Paris Ouest Nanterre La Défense. In her research, she focuses on migratory and asylum policies from an ethnographical approach. Her latest research revolves around the dead at the southern border of the European Union.

Hélène LE BAIL is a researcher in international relations and political sociology with the International Research Center at Sciences Po, Paris. Her work analyzes contemporary mobility to and from China, as well as Chinese migrants' forms of mobilization to Japan and France. Her most recent research focused on migration through marriage between China and Japan.

Ariel MENDEZ is a Professor of Management Science at Aix Marseille-University. Her work focuses on organizational dynamics while integrating institutional and time-based approaches. Her most recent research revolves around the re-structuring of work standards and skills involved in the globalization process, especially for skilled workers.

Delphine MERCIER is a sociologist (CNRS Research Director) at the *Laboratoire d'Economie et de Sociologie du Travail* (Institute of Labour Economics and Industrial Sociology) in Aix-en-Provence. Her areas of research are migration and international labour markets in the global South, globalization, free industrial trade zones in Latin America, Europe, North Africa, and the Middle East, international management systems (standards) and local governance in the face of environmental and global issues.

Michel PERALDI is a sociologist and anthropologist with the IRISS/CNRS/EHESS in Paris, where his work focuses on cities and migratory circulation, the emergence of transnational worlds in the heart of local society, and the economic, informal, criminal or legal forms of this emergence. He has also studied the "suitcase trade" and the loci of informal trade that represent its logistical "platforms": Tangier, Marseilles, Istanbul, and Naples. He has lived in Morocco for 10 years, where he has done ethnographic studies on sub-Saharan migration and a three-year study on Europeans who give their lives the shape of a migration journey.

Betsabé ROMÁN GONZÁLEZ is an associate researcher in El Colegio de Sonora, México, specializing in migrant children, teacher education, and children's social integration. She studies and documents the multiple back-and-forth movements of children between the United States and Mexico. She is member of Mexico's *Sistema Nacional de Investigadores.*

Cyril ROUSSEL is a geographer currently interested in the transformations of trans-border space and urban spaces in relation to an increased circulation of people and trades in the Middle East and the re-adaptation of these flows within a context of conflict. He works as a researcher with the CNRS and the French Institut for Middle East - *Ifpo* laboratory - in Irak (Erbil).

Roger WALDINGER, Distinguished Professor (Ph.D. Harvard, 1983) and Director of the UCLA Center for the Study of International Migration works on international migration: its social, political, and economic consequences; the policies and politics emerging in response to its advent; the links between immigrants and the countries and people they have left behind; the trajectories of newcomers and their descendants after migration. He is the author of over 100 articles and book chapters and eight books, among them, *A Century of Transnationalism: Immigrants and their Homeland Connections* (edited with Nancy Green; University of Illinois Press, 2016) and *The Cross-Border Connection: Immigrants, Emigrants, and their Homelands* (Harvard University Press, 2015).

Víctor ZÚÑIGA is a Professor of Sociology at Universidad Autónoma de Nuevo León, Mexico. He is a tier-3 (highest level) member of Mexico's *Sistema Nacional de Investigadores*. He holds a PhD in the sociology of education from Université de Paris VIII-Vincennes. He is co-editor (2005, with Rubén Hernández-León) of *New Destinations: Mexican Immigration in the United States*, New York: Russell Sage Foundation; and co-authored (2019 with Silvia E. Giorguli Saucedo) *Niñas y niños en la migración de Estados Unidos a Mëxico: la generación 0.5*, México, El Colegio de México.

FOREWORD

Roger Waldinger[1]

Today, proclaims the title of a best-selling textbook, is an *Age of Migration*; yet, it is also an age of migration control, as the people of the developed world want borders ever more stringently policed. States are indeed listening to their citizens, implementing policies designed to encourage the types of migrants of which voters approve – namely, the highly educated who arrive with skills reflecting the investments made by their home states – while shutting the door to the less fortunate – including the desperate refugees with nowhere else to turn.

Despite ever-increasing effort to strengthen the border, the citizens of the developed world often believe that their states' policies have failed. Things look quite different when the point of view shifts from that of the developed to the developing world; from this perspective migration controls appear all too effective. Doors to international trade in goods and services have massively widened, leading differences in international prices for goods to drop: a Big Mac bought in a developed country is not even twice the cost of the Big Mac purchased in countries at the 20th percentile of GDP. By contrast, differences in international *wages* have *grown* immensely, making gains to migration ever greater than before. Current wages ratios between numerous pairs of possible origin and destination countries (e.g., Vietnam and Japan at 1:9) are far higher than the comparable ratios that prevailed during peak years of mass migration around the turn of the 20th century. Although migration entails social and psychological costs deterring many potential movers, evidence indicates ample readiness to migrate. The Gallup poll estimates that 700 million people wish to migrate *permanently*: among them, 6.2 million Mexicans and fully *half* of the population of El Salvador, Haiti, and Ethiopia. Letting the world's poor move would appear to have immensely beneficial effects: according to one analysis, free migration could as much as *double* world income (Pritchett, 2006: 32). One need not go so far: if rich countries would let their labor force rise by a mere three percent, the gains to poor country citizens would exceed the costs of foreign aid by a factor of almost five (World Bank 2006: 5).

Thus, far from proving inept, as nativists and populists would charge, the rich democracies of the world do a remarkably good job of managing migration in a way that roughly approximates voters' preferences, facilitating cross-border movement by citizens of wealthy countries, while forcing people from the developing world to queue up for visas or climb over walls. And yet managing the flows in ways that proves politically acceptable is an

[1] Roger Waldinger, Department of Sociology, UCLA, Los Angeles, CA 90095, USA.

arduous venture, one that precious few governments pursue with success. While foreign people may not be welcomed, foreign workers are almost always wanted; as the pandemic revealed, without foreign-origin workers, essential services would come to a stop and the food on which the population depends would perish in the fields. Yet it is not simply a matter of business demand: despite the obstacles, migrants retain the capacity to shape their own destinies, moving across borders even when home as well as host states would prefer that they stay put.

Identifying the source of that capacity is sociological theory's key contribution to understanding the migration phenomenon: in essence, migrants can get around the barriers to migration – physical, financial, cognitive, affective, and even political – thanks to the one resource that they almost all possess: one another. The explanation is straightforward: social networks provide the mechanisms for connecting an initial, highly selective group of seedbed immigrants with a gradually growing base of followers from back home. The contacts linking veterans and newcomers rest on social relationships developed prior to the migration decision, most importantly ties of kith and kin, in which trust is taken for granted; connections of this sort provide the confidence needed to hold networks together and make them function as conduits for the flow of resources needed to move and get started in a strange place. Over time, migration networks lead to qualitative changes in both home and host societies, facilitating movement. In the home society, the propensity and capacity to emigrate increase due to feedbacks from the place of destination: whether involving the sending of remittances, the return of migrants for stays of longer or shorter duration, or investments in housing and land, signal after signal yield a demonstration effect, providing hard evidence of the gains to be made by displacement. Meanwhile in the host society, veteran immigrants consolidate their standing in the workplace, gaining access to inside information about hiring needs and acquiring skills that they can transmit to referrals who learn on the job. The settlers' deeper, more secure implantations diminishes the costs they bear when providing information and support, while simultaneously increasing the benefits that new migrants gain from the settlers' help. A growing population base also provides the basis for activities and institutions that build bridges linking immigrant ego-centric networks that would otherwise be disconnected: thus, the activities and institutions that arise to service immigrants' everyday needs – whether related to commerce, legal status, spirituality, leisure – generate weak ties that link newcomers to persons that they would never have known had they stayed home. And in turn, as immigrant communities emerge, the social and psychological costs of migration diminish even as the benefits grow. Thus, once implanted, migrant networks provide a long-standing stimulus to migration, counteracting states' efforts to control movement across their borders.

Thus states' efforts at closure come into tension with migrants' social capital; the latter lacks the power to undo controls, but still makes for significant and persistent breaches in the gates. And yet scholars look with increasing skepticism at explanations emphasizing migrants' social capital. It betrays a preference for the social – not an unusual vice among sociologists or anthropologists. It tends to emphasize the mutually supportive aspects of migrants' connections, as opposed to the exploitative, highlighting the ethnic safety net, as opposed to the ethnic cage (Rosales, 2020). A particularly influential line of attack contends that social capital theory ignores the potential for market-based forms of solving the everyday problems associated with migration from one country to another. In many instances, the migration industry – an "ensemble of entrepreneurs, firms, and services…chiefly defined by financial gain (Hernandez-Leon, 2013: 26) – does a superior job, yielding lower costs, greater efficiency, and more reliable results than can be achieved through the mobilization of family, friends, and community contacts.

Social capital theory has yet another deficit, placing too much emphasis on the stability of homegrown connections, which can never be fully reproduced in the new place where the migrants land. Immigrants from any one hometown are almost always a numerical minority in the environments they enter, whether within the workplace or outside it; their connections invariably extend to others who are socially proximate in the new environment, but emanate from home society communities that are distant from one another. In moving across borders, moreover, migrants both produce and experience globalization, with the result that the new context exposes them to people who would be unknowable had they stayed home. In addition, rupture can be cause or consequence of migration: countless migrants have left home precisely to break unbearable ties; and even if rupture were not at the origin of the move, the options available in the migratory context often provide reasons to cut the tie, whether to family, homeland friends, or broader ethnic community. Thus, as David Trouille has argued in his ethnography of Latino men in Los Angeles, migrant sociability and commitment to a shared experience is not a given, but rather an accomplishment resulting from migrants' active collaboration. "Social tying", as Trouille describes, means that migrants don't simply recreate urban villages that reproduce conditions back home; rather, they "re-create ties and identities lost through immigration in a manner that [makes] sense emotionally, but [is] well-suited to their new environment (Trouille, 2021: 12)."

The superb collection of ethnographies that the reader will find in the pages to follow provides yet further insight into the ways in which movement across state borders represents a creative accomplishment. With cases selected from around the world – the Middle East, North Africa, Latin America, North America, and Europe – the chapter in this book demonstrate that migration is undertaken not only against states and their bureaucracies, but in tension with and possibly in opposition to migrants' closest associates – precisely the people whom social capital theory paints as the font of the resources that make migration possible.

Consider, for example, the fascinating story of a Moroccan immigrant, Reda, told by Mustapha El Miri, one that highlights the intersection of history and individual biography. The relevant history is that of North African migration to France: it began as a labor migration, recruiting single adult males who circulated between France and North Africa, leaving families behind; then, in the mid-1970s, when workers were no longer wanted, switched to a system in which spouses and children could reunify with fathers residing in France, albeit one in which the state sought to progressively hinder the opportunities for family reunification. Thus, when it came time for the family to reunite with a father residing in France, the constraints of French migration law required that someone be left behind and Reda was left in Morocco to fend on his own, with ties to his family on the other side of the Mediterranean steadily attenuating. Reda did have access to migration-relevant social capital, but *not* in the form of resources made available by immediate close ties: as El Miri shows, Reda's France-residing relatives were unwilling to help, an example that demonstrates how the detailed, biographical approach brings out the contingencies underlying so many aspects of social life. Reda did have an alternative, in the form of migration smuggling: emerging to circumvent state controls, smuggling is a hybrid institution, belonging to the migration industry and yet building on contacts and reputations developed through years of transporting migrants. Smuggled into Spain as an undocumented immigrant, Reda found work in agriculture: entering a world in which fellow workers were similar, but none personally known, he did not benefit from pre-existing social ties – as social capital theory would insist – but rather engaged in the type of proactive, social tying that Trouille found among Latino migrants in Los Angeles. In Spain, Reda learned that employers at once disliked immigrants as people all the while valuing immigrants as workers. That lesson, in turn, triggered another adaptation, as Reda developed a sort of split personality, acting as a Moroccan farm laborer at work, but when in public trying to hide his legal status by adopting the dress and behavioral codes of the Spaniards around him. Here we see the capacity for individual agency and innovation, at variance with the emphasis on social reproduction inherent in social capital theory. The next and final stop in Reda's trajectory was France, made possible through the weakest link in the chain of migration control, namely marriage migration. Reda connected to a France-born spouse of Moroccan background via a matchmaker, an experience that highlights the blurry boundaries separating social capital and the migration industry: the matchmaker depends on ties to a particular ethnic community – and thus can be considered an aspect of community migration social capital; yet she provides connections on a fee for service basis – and thereby exemplifies the migration industry. And thus we see how institutional change and individual action converges. On the one hand, the matchmaker is an institution made possible by the emergence of new actors who want to remain within the ethnic community and yet gain freedom from the preferences of their closest connections. On the other hand, Reda and his spouse are the actors making make the self-conscious step of going the matchmaking route: as users of a for-profit service they gain options unavailable had they decided to rely solely on the resources made possible by mobilizing social capital to pre-existing, interpersonal ties.

Thus, this case of a single, individual adds significant nuance to more conventional analyses: migration controls impede but can't fully stop migrants motivated by the significant gains to be moving from poorer to richer countries. A mature migration stream, like the Moroccan, can generate migration-relevant social capital that facilitates movement, but those resources are not always available and certainly not on the terms that later movers would prefer. Though raised in a particular environment, whose norms they have absorbed, migrants are not oversocialized but rather capable of innovation, in turn finding the weak chink in the armor of migration control and taking advantage of a migration's maturity to opt for weaker, rather than, stronger forms of ethnic social capital, thus gaining further degrees of freedom.

Many other, similarly penetrating insights are to be find in the chapters of this scintillating volume. Thus, Helene LeBail's study comparing two middle-aged Chinese female migrants, one to Japan and the other to France, shows how these seemingly most constrained of migrants nonetheless find a way to make globalization work for them and their families, at once cracking open resources that can be transmitted from the rich societies where they settle to their needy families in China but also using the protections found in their new homes to gain additional degrees of personal freedom. If "social tying" figures in El Miri's chapter it takes an even more salient form in Cyril Roussel's study of a Kurdish refugee, who careens around the Middle East and Europe in an eventually successful effort to find asylum for himself and his family. Here, we see migrant creativity at its most acute: if anyone should be trapped it should be Sardar, the protagonist of this story, at once caught in a tangle of potentially deadly national, ethnic, and tribal rivalries and simultaneously unwanted in the places that could give him refuge. But Sardar finds more than one way out, inventing, via the activation of distant ties, an entirely new identity for himself and his family as Kurdish Jews, thus opening the door to resettlement in Israel. Later, finding life in the Jewish state not to his liking, he somehow secured a path that eventually led to settlement in Switzerland. In a way, Zuniga and Roman-Gonzalez's chapter, profiling the lives of three child migrants, is a case study in the hard face of the nation-state: these children belong to the "Great Expulsion", the wave of Mexican immigrants and children of Mexican immigrants who have crossed back into Mexico in reaction to the ever-more repressive environment in the United States, only for the children to find that they are strangers in a country in which they nonetheless hold citizenship. Here, we also see the limitations of social capital theory, which provides insight into circumstances characterized by social reproduction, but is far less useful for explaining a fundamental change, such as this wave of "return migration". But the children are caged, neither by the policies of the Mexican and US governments, nor by the expectations of their Mexican relatives and teachers; rather, they find innovative ways of responding to the duality of life as "American Mexicans". Furthermore, the U.S.-born among them can look forward to the critical juncture point that will appear when they reach majority, at which point they can opt for continued residence in Mexico or head back to the United States as full-fledged, status citizens. While that decision will surely to be affected by state policies and the expectations of family, friends, and community members, the trajectory to be followed by these "American Mexicans" is not predetermined but rather a matter within their scope of action.

Of course, these summary remarks just provide a teaser of the lessons to be learned in the pages to follow. Reading the pages to follow will also provide a casebook in the biographical approach to the study of migrant lives, a perspective too infrequently taken in the English-language literature but one, as the chapters in this book so clearly demonstrate, that provides new and badly needed insight.

References

Hernández-León, Rubén. "Conceptualizing the migration industry." In *The migration industry and the commercialization of international migration*, pp. 42-62. Routledge, 2013.

Pritchett, Lant, 2006. Let their people come: Breaking the gridlock on global labor mobility. Brookings Institution Press.

Rosales, Rocio. 2020. Fruteros: Street Vending, Illegality and Ethnic Community in Los Angeles, Berkeley, CA: University of California Press.

Trouille, David. 2021. Futbol in the Park: Immigrants, Soccer, and the Creation of Social Ties. Chicago: University of Chicago Press.

World Bank. 2006. *Global Economic Prospects.* Washington, DC: World Bank.

INTRODUCTION

Víctor Zúñiga, Kamel Doraï, Delphine Mercier, and Michel Peraldi

The *Groupe de Recherche Internationale* (GDRI), sponsored by several European and Latin American institutions, started its collective work in 2012 with one purpose: to analyze the emergent forms of international migration in the contemporary contexts of globalization. The first meeting was held in Guatemala, City in 2012; a year after, the group continued its work in Amman. The third meeting was held in Tokyo in 2014; this was the opportunity to invite new participants who were working on Asian countries. Finally, in 2015, the last seminar took place in Madrid. Throughout this time, participants from North Africa, Middle East, Latin America, Asia, and Europe were developing the outline of this book. During this time, in some sense, part of our work was inspired by the fruitful conversation made by Cohen and Sirkeci (2011) about Mexican and Kurdish migration processes during the first decade of XXI century.

As a result of these meetings - and four years of continuous exchanges, scholars participating in the GDRI recognized that the contemporary emigrant/immigrant's journeys that they were documenting (from the United States to Mexico, from France to Morocco, from China to France, from Kurdistan to Israel/ Switzerland, from Lebanon to Syria/ Gulf States/ Germany, from Bolivia to Argentina, from Nigeria to Morocco/France) demonstrate the unexpected within the ordinary. The ordinary in our research is people seeking work in other countries, Palestinian refugees looking for asylum, professionals pursuing better working conditions, children following their families, women seeking marriage, political guerrilla members trying to protect their families, Central African immigrants seeking for their families, and so on. However, in the midst of those stories, the unexpected always plays a role, because gender, politics, job networks, international legal arrangements, and/or family duties, fear, motherhood, and even love are intermingled at every stage of the journey.

All of these conditions are materialized in what we finally chose to call *the migratory experience* (objectively and subjectively undergone by international migrants, today). The novelty of the approach developed by the various authors of this book is thus rooted in the adoption of a point of view that seeks to address both the experience of migrants and the resources/constraints of migratory spaces within a single perspective (Séhili & Zúñiga, 2014). As Emmanuel Ma Mung (1999) argues, migration must be considered from the point of view of autonomy, which combines two dimensions: expertise and empowerment. It is therefore a matter of giving priority to an analysis from the migrant's point of view, without neglecting the specific circumstances in which the mobility occurs (i. e. the meso-level contexts privileged in Cohen and Sirkeci's analysis, 2011). The plurality of situations observed whether through the multiplicity of geographical and cultural spaces included in this work, or through the reconsideration of the distinction between voluntary and forced migration, also underscores the distinctiveness of this approach.

This book aims to portray migratory experiences, documented in the form of biographical narratives. We are interested in the dynamic aspect of migration, which effectively becomes a complex trajectory, made up of stages, returns, and circulations and no longer simply, as in the industrial era, a bipolar exile (there and here). In these complex and dynamic movements, many trajectories become bifurcations, by which we mean shifting fates. In these stories we found paths, events, and bifurcations, all combined together, in terms of biographical construction based on accumulated experiences. These narratives are both very banal and very unusual journeys, portraying a new international human globalization. They are simultaneously stories of barriers to be crossed in chaotic situations interspersed with peaceful events in quiet contexts. These journeys reveal not only the weight of migration policies, but also the certification policies implemented and developed by various countries. This tension is present throughout all of the narratives, between assigned fates, bifurcations, adventures, mobilizations, careers (Freitas & Godin, 2013; Martiniello & Rea, 2014). Individuals break free from local norms and at the same time that these norms are maintained and sometimes even more prevalent in their universe of arrival or circulation. Human beings move and travel for different reasons, so this book recounts life stories. Finally, through these stories we will discover that making these journeys personal has a decisive influence on the way in which migration is perceived (Shinozaki, 2012). What emerges as important in these stories is not so much the migration as the bifurcation. Sayad (1999) describes what sociology becomes when we study the sociology of migration: it is the sociology of bifurcations, the sociology of subjugation. This book presents itineraries, social logics of mobility; the routes become the analysts. If statistics record regularities, the personal approach captures specificities that produce meaning and contribute to a reinterpretation of current forms of mobility.

The contributors to this book recognize the value and heritage of Thomas and Znaniecki's approach (1918): migration is a geographical/biographical route that includes continuities and bifurcations. Hence, life stories constitute the most powerful method that social scientists have available to understand human movements in space, decisions over time, and the agency of social actors crossing international borders (Tripier, 1998). In addition to this, the authors acknowledge the contribution of the sociology of work in this sense: the accumulation of experiences of working in particular settings develop hard, soft and tacit skills (Polanyi, 1966; Star & Strauss, 1999) that allow people to be innovative according to their personal and cultural backgrounds. The accumulation of migratory experiences becomes both a process of knowledge and learning across which migrants manage their trajectories and minimize contextual constraints. As Waldinger (2006) pointed out, the history of international migrant's strategies showed that, for facing and solving their problems, migrants utilize their own resources, that is, their own accumulated experiences. Finally, in this book, contributors demonstrate what Boehm and colleagues (2011) explained: "Migration is inherently characterized by rupture—a break, change, distance, division—and it necessarily includes the everyday: even in, during, or perhaps because of cases of acute disruption, social life persists. Paradoxically, rupture is often situated within or occurs alongside the mundane… "(p. 1). In the same vein, Sayad (1993) points out: "Is there any need to recall that all emigration is a rupture, a break with a territory and thus with a population, a social order, an economic order, a political order, a cultural and moral order?" (p. 407). In the stories collected by GDRI members, one can see how intermingled the everyday (i.e., the ordinary) is with ruptures, bifurcations, and the unexpected.

The book is divided into four sections. The first section discusses the migrant pathways where family issues are at the heart of the narrative. The second section gathers stories where migrant children and teenagers are the protagonists of border-crossing events. The third section focuses on migratory journeys where people seek to escape undesirable conditions of exploitation, patriarchal control, political ties, or poverty. The fourth section gathers the stories of professional migrants who move between countries in an attempt to improve their professional careers. In each section of the book, the authors highlight the micro-events and meso-events of each singular documented case, demonstrating what is ordinary alongside the unexpected plights that explain the bifurcations and the migrant's agency. The final section of the book offers methodological and theoretical reflections and discussions inspired in those migratory stories told in each chapter. In this section, Deborah Boehm will show how it might be useful to focus on singularities in order to gain a better understanding the multiplicity of contemporary forms of migration.

References

Boehm, D. A., J. Meredith Hess, C. Coe, H. Rae-Espinoza & R. R. Reynolds. 2011. "Introduction: Children, Youth, and the Everyday Ruptures of Migration", In: Cati Coe, Rachel R. Reynolds, Deborah A. Boehm, Julia M. Hess & Heather Rae-Espinoza, eds., *Everyday Ruptures: Children, Youth and Migration in Global Perspective*, Nashville TN, Vanderbilt University Press, pp. 1-19.

Cohen, J. H. & I. Sirkeci. 2011. *Cultures of Migration. Global Nature of Contemporary Mobility*. Austin: University of Texas Press.

Freitas, A. & M. Godin, M. 2013. "Carrieres migratoires des femmes latino américaines dans le secteur de la domesticité a Bruxelles." *Revue Européne des Migrations Internationales* 29 (2). 1-20.

Ma Mung, E. 1999. "La dispersion comme ressource", *Cultures et conflicts* 33-34: 89-103.

Martiniello, M. & A. Rea, A. 2014. "The concept of migratory careers: Elements for a new theoretical perspective of contemporary human mobility". *Current Sociology*, 62 (7): 1079-1096.

Polanyi, M. 1966. *The Tacit Dimension*. London: Routledge & Kegan.

Sayad, A. 1999. *La Double Absence*, Paris: Éditions du Seuil.

Séhili, D. & V. Zúñiga. 2014. "Une lecture des migrations au prisme des savoirs et des ressources", *Migrations Société*, 26 (153-154): 87-94.

Shinozaki, K. 2012. "Transnational dynamics in researching migrants: self-reflexivity and boundary-drawing in fieldwork" *Ethnic and Racial Studies* 35 (10): 1810-1827.

Star, S. L. & A. Strauss. 1999. "Layers of Silence, Arenas of Voice: The Ecology of Visible and Invisible Work", Computer-Supported Cooperative Work: *Journal of Collaborative Computing* 8: 9-30.

Thomas, W. I. & F. Znaniecki.1918. *The Polish Peasant in Europe and America. Monograph of An Immigrant Group. Vol. 1*. Boston: Richard G. Badger, The Gorham Press.

Tripier, P. 1998. "Une sociologie pragmatique", In W. I. Thomas & F. Znaniecki, *Le paysan polonais en Europe et en Amérique, récit de vie d'un migrant*, Paris: Nathan.

Waldinger, R. 2006. "Transnationalism des immigrants et présence du pasée", *Revue Européenne des Migrations Internationales* 22 (2): 23-41

PART ONE

MIGRANT FAMILIES AND THEIR RE-CONFIGURATION

CHINESE MIGRANT WOMEN CREATING MEANINGFUL LIVES DESPITE VULNERABLE STATUSES

Hélène Le Bail

In 2012, it had been nearly twenty years since Ma Li had come to Japan through a marriage arranged by a matchmaking agency. She had divorced six years earlier, but she still lived in the same village as her former husband: "Only the strongest women stayed in the region; the others have left. It takes a strong woman to travel that far to get married." In 2015, eight years after she left for France, Wang Hong returned to China for the first time to see her mother and her son. "I am 54 years old. My mother is 86. Thanks to her, I am strong. For my family in China, I have been successful. In addition, I succeeded alone, without any support."

The Meeting

Ma Li and Wang Hong[1] followed feminine migratory routes, the first as a wife, the second through one precarious employment situation after another: nanny, housekeeper, personal services. The parallel between their two stories aims to highlight the common logic to the two migratory routes, which explains the strong feminization of migratory flows since the 1980s: cross-border marriages and worker mobility, whether or not through legal channels, supporting the domestic work and personal care. The stories of Ma Li and Wang Hong's lives illustrate the "globalization of reproductive work," the constraints and power relationships generated by the structure of the labor and marital markets, and allow us to analyze the ability of people to choose, to negotiate, to change their trajectory, at each step of the migration experience. To this end, the stories covering ten to twenty years of these two people's lives are subject matter that contributes to a nuanced understanding of migration experiences. To avoid a simplified opposition between the description of victims (of gendered inequalities) and actresses (of global transformations), these life stories show us how the power relationships between men and women, migrant and sedentary, host society and foreigner, are constantly redefined.

Ma Li's story was compiled between 2011 and 2013. Two semi-structured interviews took place at her place of employment and at her home in 2011 and 2012, in the town of Shōnai, located in the Yamagata Prefecture in the northwestern part of the main island of Japan. The interviews were supplemented by informal discussions during meals, meetings with her friends, emails exchanged in 2013, and the reading of her professional blog. Wang Hong's story consists of a long, semi-directed interview that took place

[1] Names have been modified.

in Paris in June 2015 at her place of employment, which is supplemented by numerous informal meetings at her home, and during meetings and activities linked to the NGO program that she works for today.

Independent Migration of Chinese Women in French and Japanese Environments

Since the 1990s, the trend towards the feminization of international migration has been confirmed with two particularly interesting characteristics: first, this feminization is observed in particular in the case of migration to wealthier countries and, secondly, it concerns more and more women who migrate alone (outside of family reunification). According to the figures published by the UNDESA Population Division in 2013, when the entire migrant population is taken into account, men remain overall more numerous than women. More specifically, there are more men among migrants aged 0–49; however, among migrants over 50, women are more numerous. However, if only wealthy destination countries are considered, women are proportionally more numerous from the 30–34 age group and above. On the contrary, in developing countries, men are still more numerous except for the over-65 age group (UNDESA, 2013). In addition, in some wealthy countries such as the United States, immigrant women have been more numerous than men since the 1930s. The major difference that has marked recent decades is that, of these migrations of women, the share of migrations for family reunification is in decline, while a larger proportion of women migrate alone. In 2006, the UN Population Fund published a report with an updated look at this feminization. During the first half of the 2000s, more than 60% of Filipino and Sri Lankan migrants were women; more than 75% of Indonesian migrants were women; in Spain, more than 70% of Latin American migrants were women (UN Population Fund, 2006). They either came to work in the care sector to do domestic work, with more or less formal contracts, or to get married in a wealthier country.

In this way, the feminized flow is mainly visible in wealthy countries and corresponds to a growing number of women migrating alone, as was the case for these two Chinese women, whose trajectories toward two wealthier countries (i.e. France and Japan), are analyzed in this paper.

In France, according to the 2014 census, 59% of Chinese immigrants (foreigners born abroad) were women.[2] The number of admissions to resident status also indicates an overrepresentation of Chinese women as compared to Chinese men, but three-quarters of these are students, a category of Chinese residents we will not be considering in this chapter. In the early 2000s, several surveys highlighted the emergence of new points of departure to France from northern China, and the overrepresentation of

[2] Taken from the detailed census data published in 2017 by INSEE: "Etrangers-Immigrés en 2014," published online on 06/29/2017: www.insee.fr.

women among these migrants (Cattelain, 2002; Pina-Guérassimoff et al., 2002; Gao & Poisson, 2005). For the Chinese coming from Zhejiang province, which is the historic home region of the Chinese in France, the distribution skewed in favor of men in 2005 (54% men and 46% women); however, for the three northeastern Chinese provinces, the new hotbeds of international migration, the distribution clearly favored women (71% women, 29% men) (Gao et al., 2006). The large proportion of women among the new migration flows from China, including undocumented migration to France, follows a complex logic that pertains to both the context of departure and the opportunities identified in the countries of destination (Xiang, 2007). On the one hand, men are less affected by the unemployment and precariousness that has been on the rise since the 1990s; on the other, information flows spread the idea that the labor market in France was more favorable to women: textile workshops (until the early 2000s in Paris), beauty (nail salons) and massage salons, as well as nanny and domestic work. Qualitative surveys confirm that migrant women from these Chinese regions often hold so-called "women's jobs" (Lévy & Lieber, 2009; Pina-Guérassimoff, 2010; Lévy, 2012).

In Japan, the Chinese, who represent a population of more than 600,000, are today the largest population of foreign residents. Since the 1980s, a significant number of people from China, mainly women, entered Japan on a spouse visa.

Since the early 1980s, bi-national marriages involving a foreign woman saw a rapid increase, moving from less than 5,000 per year in 1980 to about 20,000 in 1990, and more than 30,000 in the early 2000s. In contrast, bi-national marriages between a foreign man and a Japanese woman increased slowly and plateaued at around 8,000 per year in the early 2000s. Of these marriages between foreign women and Japanese men, Chinese women have made up the largest group since the mid-1990s. The number of marriages between a Chinese woman and a Japanese man was less than 1,000 per year in the early 1980s, rising to more than 12,000 per year in 2009.[3] For many, these marriages are made possible because of meetings arranged through international wedding agencies or by relatives. The women migrate to Japan after marriage, which entitles them to a spouse visa. The increase of cross-border marriages is a worldwide phenomenon (Johnson Hanks, 2007; Palriwala & Uberoi, 2008; Schaeffer, 2012), which has become a social phenomenon in Asian countries (Constable, 2003; Hsia, 2007; Cheng, 2013; Fresnoza-Flot & Ricordeau, 2017). A rapid rise was observed in the 1990s and 2000s in South Korea (13.6% of all marriages in 2005), Japan (6.1% in 2006) and Taiwan (27.4% in 2004). The proportion of these marriages is particularly high when considering that in these countries, foreigners represent less than 2% of the population. Certainly, bi-national weddings are favored due to the growing presence of Chinese residents in Japan, but a

[3] Japanese vital statistics data taken from the official platform: http://www.estat.go.jp

detailed statistical analysis combined with interviews with the local authorities allow us to confirm that, in peripheral regions, Chinese women have almost exclusively immigrated as a result of commercially arranged marriages. It is therefore rare to find mixed couples who met in Japan before marriage. For example, in 2006 in the town of Mogami, in Yamagata Prefecture, where I conducted my survey, there were 96 foreign residents (1% of the population), including 75 wives (Chinese, Korean, Filipino, and Brazilian), one husband (U.S.), and 20 female Chinese trainees (Le Bail, 2017).

In France, as in Japan, typically female Chinese migration journeys exist, but through different means: women migrate through paid work in one case, and through marriage on the other. But despite these differences, their life stories highlight the similarities in their journeys; that is, women making choices and creating their own lives.

Life Story: Stage One

Departure: The Burden of Social Norms and the Call of Opportunity

Ma Li migrated to Japan in the early 1990s on a Japanese "spouse" visa. At the time of her departure, she had been working for the Meteorology Bureau in Beijing for five years. Ma Li migrated first and foremost to escape from her parents. Her older brother had left Beijing for Hainan, and she was left living alone with her parents, who pressured her to marry a man who had graduated from college. The concern for the family's image took precedence over all other factors. Ma Li had actually gone to college, but her friends were from rather modest backgrounds and none were considered to be a "good match." To escape this pressure, Ma Li planned to go to Japan to continue her studies. But her father was not reassured by the perspective of his daughter going to Japan as a student. Ma Li was very motivated to go to Japan and showed interest when a friend of her mother's mentioned the possibility of marrying a Japanese man. For Ma Li's parents, having a Japanese husband, that is to say, a husband from a wealthier country, would clear the path to a higher social status for the family. Leaving to get married in Japan was a sign of success and of financial stability, while going to Japan as a student would have forced Ma Li to do odd jobs, which would have relegated her to a lower social class.

Wang Hong's story is different. Before she left for France, she and her husband had been separated for long time. They had one son, whom she raised alone. She never received any financial support from her husband to support their son's education. She worked in a small textile factory as a dressmaker and did not have enough money to send her son to university. Although her son was already twenty-two years old, her main motivation was to provide for his future. In her company, more qualified dressmakers often received offers to work elsewhere, but she did not. In her case, moving to another Chinese city was not a viable solution, as her wages would not be higher. Wang Hong considered her salary to be too low. She was growing older and would not be able to continue working in her profession forever, so something had to change. But Wang Hong had no specific training, and people aged 40–50 struggled to find work. When she spoke to her son about the possibility of emigrating, he did not like the idea. He told her she was going to need a lot of money in order to leave, and he did not see where she would find it. Wang Hong also discussed it with her sister, who asked her how much money she would need. When she announced that she would need 80,000 yuan, her sister was astonished, because she knew that Wang Hong had no savings and wondered how she would be able to pay back such a large amount. But her sister, despite her misgivings, agreed to lend her 30,000 yuan, and her older brother agreed to lend her 20,000. She still needed 30,000 yuan. With no other options, she spoke to her frightened mother who told her: "What's gotten into you? Why do you want to go that far away? It's so expensive; it must be a scam." It was a colossal sum, but Wang Hong assured her mother that she knew many people who already traveled to France and had no problems there, and that everything had gone well. Her mother agreed to help her and gathered the rest of the money that Wang Hong needed.

Now let us return to Ma Li's story. She contacted a Japanese marriage agency that arranged meetings with Japanese men in the early 1990s. The Tokyo-based agency organized the Japanese men's stay in China. During the session she attended, the Japanese men were all from the same rural area of Shōnai. On the Chinese side, the women dealt with an intermediary, a kind of non-formal agency. There was nothing in writing: no signature, no contract. She recalls that four women found a husband during the week of meetings organized by the agency in Beijing. During that week, the women met with several candidates, and Ma Li met with three or four men. Once an agreement was reached, the marriage was held in Beijing. Ma Li even remembers that she attended the first ceremony where two women got married. A few weeks later, she was married at a second wedding ceremony.

Wang Hong, who left ten years after Ma Li, did not receive much information before her departure either; instead, she placed her trust in her broker.[4] She knew that she was leaving for France, but she did not choose the destination, her broker did. Wang Hong had no specific opinion on the choice of her destination. When the smuggler suggested that she go to France, she asked some relatives for their opinions, but she did not have many people to rely on; as was the case for many Chinese at the time, she had little information about the world beyond their borders. Wang Hong was able to gather a little information from a friend who told her that France was a country in the European Union, that it was a quiet country; a relative told her that it was possible to earn 700 euros per month, which was the

[4] Wang Hong uses the term shetou: this is a common word in Chinese used to refer to people who provide assistance in applying for visas and crossing borders.

equivalent of a year's salary in China. Wang Hong also learned that it was possible to be a nanny there. With just this limited amount of information, she decided to leave for France. Wang Hong knew of a friend's friend who took care of children in Paris; she contacted the husband who had stayed behind in China. He told her that his wife would meet her at the broker's appointed place and time, and that she could follow her. On the day of the broker's appointment, the friend came to pick up another woman in the group; Wang Hong followed and took a taxi with them. The woman took them to see another Chinese woman who worked as nanny and whose employers were absent. The two Chinese women who had taken care of her made a series of phone calls to find housing for her and find her a job. One of the women she contacted, who lived in the 13th arrondissement of Paris, said that she could help. In this way, Wang Hong was able to find a dormitory for five euros per night when she arrived in France. Wang Hong found everyone she met to be friendly, and she followed the advice that was given to her.

Life Story: Stage Two

The Start of the Immigration Experience: The Question of Exploitation

Ma Li felt abused by her Japanese husband and by the marriage agency. They had showed her pictures of shopping centers in Tokyo that led her to believe that she would live in a modern urban neighborhood. They told her that the wages were three times higher than they really were. Her husband had told her that his mother was a sweet woman. She did not know that her husband had paid the agency somewhere between three and four million yen for the marriage. During a fight, she learned the truth and saw the contract that her husband had signed with the marriage agency. She felt as if she had been sold to him. Her mother-in-law seemed hold her responsible for the cost of the marriage. A portion of the three million yen paid to the Japanese agency was supposed to be sent to her family in China, but her parents never received it. Her husband did not want to make trouble at the agency and she was not able to speak to them in Japanese. When she arrived in Japan in 1993, she was the first Chinese woman in the town. Three other Chinese women arrived later, also believing that they would live in a city. The feeling of having been cheated was stronger for Chinese women who came from large cities because when they married, they lost their urban resident status and rights in China;[5] they thus experienced a strong decline in social status in moving to a rural area. Ma Li's husband was violent, and she filed for divorce in 2006. The post-divorce period was financially difficult for her. In addition to her regular employment, she also worked at a bar that employed Filipino

[5] This refers to the *hukou,* a household registration system in China. In the 1990s, having an urban *hukou* was a real privilege.

hostesses. Despite her divorce, she stayed in the village for her children, but as she recalls, few women remained there. Today, Ma Li believes that men who seek a foreign wife must have issues; they either have behavioral problems or family troubles. Her husband was violent and completely under his mother's influence. In her opinion, the Chinese women who agree to these marriages are strong and do not accept these overbearing mother–son relationships. These strong women often end up divorcing and have no desire to be bound to anyone ever again. This makes relationships extremely difficult.

Three days after her arrival in France, Wang Hong was offered a job by a Chinese woman. It entailed taking care of three children for a monthly salary of 800 euros. Wang Hong promptly accepted, satisfied with the salary. She would be the nanny for three children aged 3, 1 and just a few months old. The family lived in a one-room apartment; counting Wang Hong, this meant that 6 people shared this small space. The parents did not provide her with a key, so she could not go out during the day. When the woman from the 13th arrondissement called to find out how she was doing, Wang Hong told her that the situation was not good. The woman offered her a job with a different family with three children who paid 750 euros. Wang Hong left her first employers after just a few days. However, at the end of her first month with the second family, she was only paid 700 euros. Her employer assured her that this was the amount that had been agreed to and, after checking, Wang Hong discovered that the intermediary had lied to her about the salary. The Chinese woman who had served as her intermediary had asked her for a fee of 100 euros for finding her a job, which was refundable within the first fifteen days if she was not satisfied. Wang Hong only stayed three days with the first family, but the intermediary refused to refund her the fee, arguing that she had already spent it. Wang Hong insisted, crying, telling her that it had been difficult to leave the country, that she was in debt and had little money left. The intermediary told her that she only had 80 euros, and Wang Hong agreed to waive the last 20 euros. Wang Hong paid the fee again for the second family.

Wang Hong worked for the second family for three years and almost completely paid back all the money she had borrowed. When the job came to an end, she returned to Paris' 13th arrondissement to seek a place in the dormitory, and contacted other Chinese women from her home region to look for work. One of her relatives, a woman who had flown to France with her, set up a meeting for her at Porte d'Ivry, in Paris, and took her to an area near the Porte Dorée metro station, saying "we work here." Wang Hong did not understand what she meant until another woman gave her two condoms. Wang Hong was confused. She fled home when the first car approached. She thought about the situation all night long and finally decided to return the next day. This time, she met two women she knew who told her not to worry, that they were there for the same reason, and that there was no reason to be ashamed. Wang Hong found them very friendly. They taught her all about the job and told her that the woman who had brought her there initially should have explained it to her. For example, she needed to know that she should never allow the client to bring her back to her spot in his car, to avoid being stopped by the police. These two women, as well as others who worked in the neighborhood, explained a lot of things about how she should work. Later, the woman who had initially brought her to the neighborhood asked her to pay a commission. The woman asked Wang Hong to lend her 500 euros, but Wang Hong knew she was referring to the introduction fee. Another woman who overheard their conversation told the intermediary that she was asking for too much. Wang Hong offered her 200 euros, which the woman accepted and pretended it was a loan, promising to pay her back. A few weeks later, Wang was mistreated by a customer and she decided to quit, despite her financial needs. With the help of a non-profit organization, she filed a police report to arrest this dangerous client.

Life Story: Stage Three

Family and Professional Success: Leveraging Migratory Expertise

For both Ma Li and Wang Hong, migration allowed them to transfer values or goods to their children and gave them a sense of accomplishment. Ma Li, who lives in a rural area in Japan, says that when her children were young, her in-laws told her that it was unnecessary to teach them to speak Chinese; she very much regrets not having stuck with it, because she wanted to give them a window to the outside world. On the other hand, the Japanese family hoped that the children would not leave and would instead stay in the village. Ma Li found the Japanese family very backward (*luohou*). When her sons were young, they were ashamed of their mother and asked her not to speak during school meetings. Today, they recognize that she fought hard to give them the best education possible and taught them to make sacrifices. In her opinion, Chinese mothers make their children their priority and push them to succeed, much more than the Japanese women in her region. In 2012, Ma Li's eldest son was accepted to a very good public university in Tsukuba, thanks to her constant encouragement, and she felt that her son's Japanese father was not able to appreciate the value of that encouragement.

Wang Hong's first objective after her arrival in France was to reimburse her debts. After two months, she managed to save 1,000 euros, which she sent to her sister, who was able to reassure all her creditors that Wang Hong was indeed earning money. Her second goal was to send money to her son, but she was afraid that he would spend it foolishly. Instead, she sent the money to her sister. Her mother told the sister: "You must be very careful with her money; she works hard to earn it." Wang bought an apartment for her son and paid for his wedding, which she was not able to attend. In 2015, she also paid for her son and daughter-in-law to travel to France.

In addition to their children's success, for these women, migration was also the opportunity to gain professional experience related to their skillful management of their migratory know-how. Upon her arrival in Japan, Ma Li worked in a supermarket for five years. After her divorce, her financial situation was unstable and, as mentioned before, in the evening she worked as a hostess in a bar. In the region, this type of employment was typically held by Filipinas. Her situation became stable in 2009 when she was appointed head of intercultural relations for the municipality. Her job was to organize welcoming activities and to oversee relations with foreign residents, in particular with migrant wives and Chinese apprentices working for local companies (the program allowed apprentices to work in Japan for up to three years). She enjoyed the job very much, as it required strong interpersonal skills and an understanding of migration trajectories. At the beginning, she still took particular care of women who arrived as a result of a marriage; they often came from China's northeast provinces and in particular from rural areas. Over time, women arriving through marriage became rarer: in her area, there have been no new arrivals in five years. The Japanese classes have closed; there were only a few women left who came to see her for personal problems, or for questions about their children's education. As part of her job, Ma Li created a blog in Japanese to promote Sino-Japanese exchanges and help the Japanese to better understand their foreign neighbors. Unfortunately for Ma Li, women migrating through marriage became more rare in the village, and even the number of Chinese trainees declined, so her job was not renewed in 2013. Finding herself unemployed again, she was offered training as a caregiver by the Labor Office.

In France, Wang Hong decided to focus on learning to speak French. She was able to find French employers who let her do housework without an employment contract. Through one of her employers, she was able to obtain a permanent contract as a caregiver for an elderly person that allowed her to apply for legal status in 2014. Despite the low salary, she enjoyed the job: she liked to chat with her client and cook for him. Around the same time, a program from the NGO Doctors Without Borders, which works with female Chinese sex workers in Paris, contacted her. They sought a health prevention facilitator who shared the same experiences with the women in their program: migration, illegal immigration, and sex work. From a community health approach, their aim was to recruit a peer, someone whose migration experience could be used to improve the quality of the Health Prevention Program. Wang Hong was unsure whether to accept, as she had just been able to straighten out her immigration status through her permanent job, and she knew that working for Doctors Without Borders would be much more difficult. A French friend encouraged her to accept the job offer, telling her that it was an excellent opportunity, that it would be an interesting job, a way to help many others, instead of just helping one person. Wang Hong decided to accept the job that was created on her arrival. The main focus of her work was to conduct interviews with and hold health prevention workshops for female Chinese sex workers. She had to create the position from scratch, implementing new working methods and, most importantly, she had to earn the other women's trust. She knew some of them already, so she would need to increase her professional credibility, so that the other women would be able to understand her change in status and not be afraid that she would break the rules regarding confidentiality. As many of the women were from the same part of China as Wang Hong, they could fear that rumors would spread about them to their families back home, since they shared many personal things during their discussions with the social worker. However, Wang Hong's professionalism was recognized, and she now plays a very important mediation role between the beneficiaries of the program and the rest of the NGO team, allowing for deeper communication, as she understands the migrant women's sacrifices, their way of thinking, and sometimes even how to comfort them.

Discussion: Globalization of Reproductive Labor and Migration Through Marriage

According to Nicole Constable, "the most striking migratory pattern of the late twentieth and early twenty-first centuries is of young women from poorer parts of the so-called Global South or Third World who provide intimate labor—as caregivers, cleaners, cooks, nurses, sex workers, entertainers—for those in and from the wealthiest parts of the Global North or First World" (Constable, 2014, p. xi). Indeed, the increase in migratory flows related to the fact that migrants (especially women) provide domestic and care work is well documented by the international institutions (UN Population Fund, 2006) and by researchers in different disciplines (such as Parreñas, 2001b; Ehrenreich & Hochschild, 2003). Through the two stories shared here, we aim to expand this perspective and, following in the footsteps of authors such as Pei-Chia Lan (2008) and Eleonor Kofman (2012), include in this field of study the case of women who migrate through marriage. Transnational wives follow a similar logic of migration and, in their country of residence, take on the roles of caregivers, cleaners, cooks, nurses, sex workers, and entertainers; because, even in migration, these tasks are performed, whether or not they are paid activities (Beneria, 2007). Migration through marriage can be seen as one of the aspects of the "striking migratory pattern" referred to by Constable above, and may be analyzed as a type of migration for labor (Piper & Roces, 2003; Le Bail, 2017). In order to create connections between the migratory circuits of work and family that are often analyzed separately (Kofman, 2012), we prefer to use here the term "reproductive labor," rather than care labor or intimate labor, the terms most often utilized. Reproductive labor covers actions and interactions that sustain people on a daily basis at the intergenerational level. It covers a wider set of activities than care work and intimate labor: it involves maintaining community ties, children's socialization and emotional support (Parreñas, 2012). Futhermore, the study of Chinese female migration also allows us to expand the analysis beyond the "young women" evoked by Nicole Constable in the previous quote, because the Chinese women discussed about here are often older than other migrant women (we will discuss this later on).

As mentioned in the introduction, the analysis of female migration, whether it concerns domestic workers, caregivers, wives, or sex workers, tends to be divided between interpretations insisting on, on the one hand, the forced nature of migration, with a view of migrant women as victims, and a focus on the renewal of patriarchal norms and inequalities between men and women; and, on the other hand, interpretations that emphasize migrant women's agency, their exploitation of migratory resources and their increased autonomy. The problematic interplay between these two perspectives is sometimes found in the work of a single author. The need to account for these two different realities is not new. In the early 1980s, in an article on the emerging forms of independent female migration in the 1970s–1980s, Mirjana Morokvasic (1984) already insisted on the need to consider both constraints and agency in migration routes.

Through the two stories provided here, we position ourselves in the continuity of these works by observing how the economic, normative, and administrative constraints are, at every point along the journey, counterbalanced by the women's agency, autonomy, and the formulation of individual projects, and by observing how migrant women are able to give a meaning to their migration project, even in situations of high vulnerability. The stories have been divided into three stages, in order to encourage a discussion that focuses on three points. First, far from approaching the subject in terms of human trafficking or forced marriage, departure is often a personal project, taking into account family constraints and aspirations. Second, the forms of exploitation and abuse are multifaceted in the case of isolated and vulnerable migrants but remain negotiable. Third, the female migration project and its success are very broadly defined within the broader framework of the family, but do not exclude the search for personal accomplishment.

Departure: Social Pressure or Personal Project?

The migration of women has long been studied through the lens of family reunification (the wife leaving to join the husband who has migrated before her, or who has come back to marry in his country of origin). Female migration is not often seen as an individual choice, but as the result of a familial logic. In the light of the increasing number of women who migrate independently, most official statements and analyses carried out by international organizations and NGOs focus either on exploitation and trafficking, in particular in cases of cross-border marriages and sex work,[6] or

[6] One text that is representative of this tendency is the Palermo Protocol, a protocol supplementing the UN Convention against organized transnational organized crime, whose aim is to prevent trafficking in persons, especially women and children (2001). This protocol approved and officialized the representation

on survival strategies and therefore, on the feminization of the economy of survival. These analyses certainly express an important reality, but they tend to ignore the wide range of situations and in particular, of migratory trajectories that are initiated and sought out by migrant women. The stories of Ma Li and Wang Hong highlight how these projects come to fruition and are individually formulated before being negotiated with the family. This certainly does not mean that these migration projects are completely independent from considerations related to the inequality between men and women, women's precarity, and social norms around marriage and parenthood in the society of origin. In the case of the migration of women from regions without a history of international migration, many studies ascribe the importance of male/female inequality and the women's precarious status to the emergence of migration flows (Pina-Guérassimoff, 2010; Lu, 2012 ; Angeloff & Lieber, 2012). The same factors are also described for other countries experiencing a feminization of departures, such as Vietnam (Grillot, 2013) and Mexico (Schaeffer ,2012).

Sometimes, rather than a question of survival, the aim of female migration is to attain a certain social status in order to escape family pressure and the impression of social failure. Wang Hong indicated that her primary motivation was her son, to whom she wanted to give as much as other families are able give their children; she wanted to be able to buy him an apartment so he could get married under the best possible conditions. She expressed her feeling that the stagnation of their socio-economic situation were related to her separation from her husband, and to the father's lack of contribution to their son's academic success. She seemed to be seeking reparation for the difficulties caused by her separation and the failure of her marriage. For Ma Li, the social pressure that led her choose a cross-border marriage was the norm of marriage: her parents and entourage made her feel that it was not only time for her to get married (she was approaching 30), but also that she needed find a husband who met their expectations. For Chinese women, the choice of a cross-border marriage allows them to combine their social obligation[7] with an aspiration towards upward social mobility. In the research carried out in Japan and elsewhere, the difficulty of marrying or remarrying in China is a recurring argument heard from Chinese migrant wives (Le Bail, 2012). Among the purported obstacles to finding a suitable partner for marriage in China are their advanced age, divorced status, or single motherhood. According to Japanese statistics, in 2005, the average age of Chinese women married to Japanese men at the time of marriage was 31.7 years of age, that is to say, higher than the average age of Japanese women, which was 29.4 years of age in 2005[8] (Ministry of Health, Labor and Welfare,

---

of migrant women as victims of human trafficking.

[7] Statistics of marriage rates in China are a social norm indicator: in 2005, only 2% of women were still unmarried in the 30–34 age group and only 0.2% of women were single at 50 years old. See Guilmoto, 2012.

[8] The average age for Korean wives is much higher (35.6 years old), contrary to that of Filipino wives (27.9

2006), and higher than the average age of marriage for women in China, which was 23.5 in 2005 (Guilmoto, 2012). The proportion of Chinese women whose marriage to a Japanese man was a second marriage was around 43.4%, meaning that nearly one in two women was divorced or widowed (Ministry of Health, Labor and Welfare, 2006)[9]. Moreover, according to the JOIN network, which supports foreigners in the Niigata Prefecture of Japan, 90% of foreign wives had a dependent child in their country of origin.[10]

The profile of Wang, in France, overlaps with that of Chinese women migrating to Japan through marriage. Most of the Chinese women who migrate alone to France are divorced or separated, have dependent children, and are considered too old to marry or remarry. They seek a job in sectors of activity where many new and younger internal migrants work (Lévy 2015). Thus, parental responsibilities and the stigma of being divorced or separated often explain the choice of migration for these women.

But this choice also is that of an individual adventure embedded in the forces of globalization, as in the market for marriage and domestic work. As with many of the other migrants, Ma Li and Wang Hong had few options that would allow them to complete their migration project. Far from traditional migration networks and far from large-scale networks of organized crime, they were pioneers in their families and entourages in terms of migration. They used intermediaries who understood the needs of the labor markets in their destination countries: in France, this meant the division of labor within the Chinese population, where domestic work is delegated to migrants who do not have a social network; in Japan, this meant the more or less official initiatives in favor of the immigration of wives in peripheral regions most affected by depopulation (Le Bail, 2013). Ma Li and Wang Hong took advantage of migration opportunities in countries with very restrictive migration policies. They sought to "'deal with it' rather than to defy the order which makes the borders more impermeable for them [women] and their search for work" (Morokvasik; 2010).

Scales of Exploitation, Denunciation, and Negotiation

Both stories highlight how precarious administrative status and isolation are sources of vulnerability. In Japan, as in many other countries, foreign spouses are dependent on their husband or wife for the renewal of their resident status. In France, as is the case everywhere else, undocumented workers accept working conditions that do not conform with the applicable laws. In both cases, the language barrier and the absence of networks of trust mean that migrants are dependent on the people in their entourage. Exploitation, understood as taking advantage of someone unfairly due to a

---

years old).

[9] The re-marriage rate is also high for Korean women (41.4%) and very low for Filipino women (12.5%). "2006 Statistics on Marriage", op. cit.

[10] Field notes, winter 2012.

power relationship, is present in these stories and takes on various forms, sometimes on a very small scale: they are abused by the marriage agency (which takes advantage of both migrant women and their husbands), parents-in-law, family-employers, and by other migrant women. Ma Li and Wang Hong do not deny the forms of exploitation and violence that they have been the victims of. They are able to identify, analyze, and negotiate them, even in situations of multifaceted vulnerability.

Despite the loss of human and social capital during migration, the ability to withstand hardship and to negotiate is quickly recovered with experience. Ma Li denounced her husband's violence as well as her mother-in-law's reasoning that turned her into a good ("she was expensive") and initiated a divorce procedure. Wang Hong refused to accept her first employer's practices and negotiated better working conditions with the second. She negotiated the introduction fees requested by her Chinese "friends," and took legal action when she was abused by a client while doing sex work.

Taking into account the extended duration of the migration experience, over a period of ten or twenty years, is one way to avoid creating an opposition between the reality of the power relationships that constrain migrants and their ability to renegotiate these relationships at each step. The long time frame allows us to avoid judgments that promote "the construction of migrant women as victims of trafficking. This implies that women are not considered as subjects of their own history, but as objects" (Guillemaut, 2006).

"Success:" For One's Family and For Oneself

Studies on women migrating alone emphasize the responsibilities and family ambitions at the center of the women's migration projects. Thus, the field has been enriched by embracing the concepts of "transnational motherhood" and a "care chain" that can be found in the studies of Filipino women who hold a central place in migrating processes (Parreñas, 2001a). In the case of Chinese migrant women in France, Florence Lévy's studies of migrant men and women from northern China to Paris confirm the specificity of female migration. Far more than men, women choose to leave in order to ensure their parental role (pay for children's studies, purchase an apartment for their children) and remotely maintain their educational and emotional role (Lévy, 2015, pp. 406-408).

Whether there are children who are left behind in the country of origin or children born through cross-border marriages, the success of the migration project often depends on ensuring socio-economic mobility for these children. In the case of Chinese wives in Japan, many women arrived in the rural or peripheral areas of Japan with the feeling that they had taken a social step backwards. Moreover, marriage and motherhood involve a loss of mobility, which runs contrary to the idea of a cosmopolitan adventure. The correspondence between marriage and mobility toward more prosperous areas (Davin, 2008), in other words strategies of hypergamy, are ultimately disappointing. Women feel trapped in rural areas, with conservative, even backward, families. Faced with a sense of failure, the migration project is then reformulated on a new time scale, that of the next generation. The children's success is a continuation of the migration project: gaining social mobility—in particular through academic success—and spatial mobility out of rural areas.

The value of migrant mothers' dedication is not only demonstrated through external analyses, but it is also found in interviews. For women who experience a social downgrading or take part in highly stigmatized activities, there is a need to legitimize their choice of migration, both for others and for themselves. In addition to undervalued domestic work, occupations such as bar hostess or sex worker are highly stigmatized. Commercially arranged marriages are sometimes presented as a form of prostitution, an economico-sexual exchange which, combined with migration, could imply either exploitation or slavery. The figure of the mother who sacrifices everything for her children is one way to respond to these stigmatized representations of the migration journey. This figure allows for the simultaneous expression of the various forms of exploitation, the sacrifices made during the migration, and offers a way to speak about the women's determination and agency. Also, in the selected citations used to introduce this chapter, Ma Li and Wang Hong insist on the fact that their trajectory is that of a strong woman.

The language used by these women in giving meaning to their migration, as well as all of the works studying transnational motherhood, tend to see the mothers' migration as a sacrifice. The stories shared here also evoke this motherly "sacrifice." However, leaving one's family behind and discovering a new culture are also elements of freedom and personal development. Migration through marriage is initially a long-term project, in theory a permanent migration. For undocumented Chinese migrant women, the project of departure is often reevaluated and reformulated in the light of their experiences. Ma Li and Wang Hong's stories are those of women who have chosen to accept work that highlights the experience they have gained through their migration journey and gives them a new social status. They work for either the municipality or for a well-known NGO and have become role models for other migrant women. Beyond the specific cases of these two women, the meaning that is ascribed to migration varies according to a woman's concrete and symbolic aspirations, but it is always reformulated through adaptation to the conditions of migration.

Finally, the study of independent female migration in the sector of reproductive work confirms the need to combine the analyses of relationships of specific forms of power and violence with the analysis of agency. In political and activist spheres, this means that it is important to consider migrant women not just as victims of the labor markets' overall exploitation of their labor force (in other words, of the new international division of reproductive work), but also as the agents of their own stories, in order to better support them in their migration projects.

References

Angeloff, T. & M. Lieber, eds. 2012. *Chinoises au 21ème siècle. Ruptures et continuités.* Paris: La Découverte.

Beneria, L. 2007. "Paid/Unpaid Work and the Globalization of Reproduction." GEM-IWG Working Paper. http://pds19.egloos.com/pds/201011/11/71/beneriapap.pdf

Cattelain, C., ed. 2002. *Les modalités d'entrée des ressortissants chinois en France.* Paris: Direction de la Population et des Migrations, ministère de l'Emploi, de la Solidarité et de la Cohésion sociale (non publié).

Cheng, I. 2013. "Making foreign women the mother of our nation: the exclusion and assimilation of immigrant women in Taiwan." *Asian Ethnicity* 14 (2): 157–179.

Constable, N. 2003. *Romance on a Global Stage.* Berkeley: University of California Press.

Constable, N. 2014. *Born out of place. Migrant Mothers and the Politics of International Labor.* Berkeley: University of California Press.

Davin, D. 2008. "Marriage Migrations in China: The Enlargment of Marriage Markets in the Era of Market Reforms." In Rajni Palriwala and Patricia Uberoi eds, *Marriage, Migration and Gender.* New Delhi: Sage Publications India pp. 63-77.

Ehrenreich, B. & A. Russell Hochschild, eds. 2003. *Global Woman: Nannies, Maids, and SexWorkers in the New Economy.* New York: Macmillan Books.

Grillot, C. 2013. "The Fringes of Conjugality On fantasies, tactics and representations of Sino-Vietnamese encounters in borderlands." PhD thesis, Vrije Universiteit.

Guillemaut, F. 2006. "Victimes de traffic ou actrices d'un processus migratoire?" *Terrains & travaux* 10: 157-176.

Guilmoto, Ch. Z. 2012. "Skewed Sex Ratios at Birth and Future Marriage Squeeze in China and India, 2005-2100." *Demography* 49: 77-100.

Hsia, H. C. 2007. 'Imaged and Imagined Threat to the Nation: The Media Construction of the 'Foreign Brides Phenomenon' as Social Problems in Taiwan.' *Inter-Asia Cultural Studies* 8 (1): 55–85.

Fresnoza-Flot, A. & Gwenola Ricordeau, eds. 2017. *International marriages and marital citizenship: Southeast Asian women on the move.* Abingdon and New York: Routledge.

Gao, Y. & V. Poisson. 2005. *Le trafic et l'exploitation des immigrants chinois en France.* Genève, Bureau International du Travail.

Gao, Y., F. Lévy, & V. Poisson. 2006. "De la migration au travail. L'exploitation extrême des Chinois-e-s à Paris." *Travail, genre et sociétés* 2(16): 53-74.

Johnson-Hanks, J. 2007. "Women on the Market: Marriage, Consumption, and the Internet in Urban Cameroon." *American Ethnologist* 34(4): 642-658.

Kofman, E. 2012. "Rethinking Care through Social Reproduction: Articulating Circuits of Migration", *Social Politics* 19(1): 142-162.

Lan, P. C.. 2008. ""Migrant Women's Bodies as Boundary Markers: Reproductive Crisis and Sexual Control in the Ethnic Frontiers of Taiwan." *Signs: Journal of Women in Culture and Society* 33(4): 833–861.

Le Bail, H. 2012. "Femmes chinoises dans les campagnes japonaises: négociation de la modernité", in Tania Angeloff and Marylène Lieber, eds. *Chinoises au 21ème siècle. Ruptures et continuités.* Paris: La Découverte: 139-156.

Le Bail, H. 2013. "Skilled and unskilled Chinese migrants in Japan: context and perspectives". Working papers, Cahiers d'Ebisuhttp://www.mfj.gr.jp/publications/nouveautes/les_cahiers_debisu_no_3/index.php.

Le Bail, H. 2017. "Marriage Migration or Labour Migration ? Crossborder Marriages between China and Japan." *Critical Asian Studies* 49(2): 226-243.

Lévy, F. 2012. "The Migration of Women from Northern China: A Gender-oriented Choice?", *China Perspectives*, 2012(4): 43-51.

Lévy, F. 2015. *Entre contraintes et interstices, l'évolution des projets migratoires dans l'espace transnational. Une ethnographie des migrants de Chine du Nord à Paris*. PhD thesis. Paris, EHESS.

Lévy, F & M. Lieber. 2011. "Sex and Emotion-Based Relations as a Resource en Migration: Northen Chinese Women in Paris." *Revue française de sociologie* 52, English supplement: 3-29.

Lu, M. C-W. 2012. 'Transnational Marriages as a Strategy of Care Exchange: Veteran Soldiers and Their Mainland Chinese Spouses in Taiwan.' *Global Networks* 12: 233–251.

Ministry of Health, Labor and Welfare, 2006. "2006 Statistics on Marriage. Special report of the Population Vital Statistics." http://www.mhlw.go.jp/toukei/saikin/hw/jinkou /tokusyu/konin06/index.html.

Morokvasic, M. 1984. "Birds of Passage are also Women." *International Migration Review* 18(4): 886-907.

Morokvasik, M. 2010. "Le genre est au cœur des migrations." in Jules Falquet and alii, *Le sexe de la mondialisation. Genre, classe, race et nouvelle division du travail.* Paris. Presses de Sciences Po: 105-119.

Palriwala, R. & P. Uberoi, eds. 2008. *Marriage, Migration and Gender*, New Delhi: Sage Publications India.

Parrenas Salazar, R. 2001a. "Mothering from a Distance: Emotions, Gender, and Intergenerational Relations in Filipino Transnational Families." *Feminist Studies* 27(2): 361 – 390.

Parrenas Salazar, R. 2001b. *Servants of Globalization: Women, Migration and Domestic Work.* Stanford, CA: Stanford University Press.

Parreñas Salazar, R. 2012. "The reproductive labour of migrant workers." *Global Networks* 12(2): 269-275.

Pina-Guerassimoff, C., E. Guerassimoff & N. Wang. 2002. *La circulation des nouveaux migrants économiques chinois en France et en Europe*. Paris. Ministère de l'Emploi, de la Solidarité et de la Cohésion sociale, drees/mire (non publié).

Pina-Guérassimoff, C.. 2010. "Migrantes, femmes, mères: les Chinoises… des "nouveaux oiseaux de passage" en Europe ?" *Espaces, Populations, Sociétés:* 471-484.

Piper, N. & M. Roces, eds. 2003. *Wife or Worker?: Asian Women and Migration*. Lanham: Rowman & Littlefield Publishers.

Schaeffer Amaya, F. 2012. *Love and Empire: Cybermarriage and Citizenship Across the Americas.* NY: NYU Press.

UNDESA (Department of Economic and Social Affairs) - Population division. 2013. "International Migration 2013: Age and Sex Distribution." http://esa.un.org/ unmigration/documents/PF_age_migration_FINAL_10.09.2013.pdf.

UN Population Fund. 2006. "State of World Population 2006. A Passage to Hope: Women and International Migration." http://www.unfpa.org/publications/state-world-population-2006#sthash.ZHGQ5UPV.dpuf.

Xiang, B. 2007. "The Making of Mobile Subjects: How Institution Reform and Outmigration Intersect in Northeast China." *Development* 50(4): 69-74.

CONFLICT AND MIGRATION FROM IRAQ: BUILDING A LIFE IN EXILE AMID THE TWISTS AND TURNS OF A DRAMATIC HISTORY

Cyril Roussel

Migration from the Middle East has not always received as much media coverage as in recent years (2015–2016). Yet a continuous flow of emigration towards Europe, North America, and Australia essentially began in the 1970s and 1980s. It mostly involved urban elites leaving countries led by regimes that were repressive towards them, like in Iran after the Islamic Revolution, Turkey after the military dictatorship, or Iraq in the time of Saddam Hussein. Opponents to these regimes became political refugees, some of whom formed the embryos of future diasporas in the West. Here we have chosen to present one of them, who was threatened as a Kurd (a group persecuted in the Middle East following their fight for the recognition of their identity) and at the same time as a political activist and member of the Communist Party.

Like many refugees, Sardar has been living in Europe for years. He settled in Lausanne, Switzerland and worked as a translator with the cantonal authorities, helping asylum-seekers who chose to move to that country to continue their life far from the tumult of the East, and the wars and "identities" that have become "murderous" (Maalouf, 1998, p. 216). The stories of people exiled from war-torn countries are generally epic, and always dramatic; Sardar's story combines many elements that show the ingenuity of some of the migrants wanting to reach the Western democracies, the only territories in which they can imagine living. The length of his journey is also an important factor to take into account, showing that no migratory strategy is ever guaranteed in advance, despite the perception that people may have in the arrival country. His journey shows migrants' ability to adapt to situations of obstruction, as well as the fragility of such constructions. It helps us to gain a better understanding of why many remain stuck in the first country of asylum that they enter, that is, in the immediate proximity of the countries that they wish to leave, as it is so difficult to reach Europe.

Sardar is a translator. Today, he is fluent in French, as he arrived in francophone Switzerland in the late 1990s. His main strength is being able to move from Arabic to Turkish via the two main Kurdish dialects, which he speaks perfectly as mother tongues: Sorani and Kurmanji. We will not dwell on his knowledge of Hebrew, which is of no use to him in his daily work. Therefore, he is able to detect where people are from when speaking with them, particularly when dealing with Kurds, with a high degree of accuracy. This ability to switch from one language to another is due to his background, as he spent a long time in a multicultural environment where Kurds, Turks, and Arabs coexisted: Northern Iraq. An educated man whose university studies in Mosul were conducted in Arabic, he possesses a considerable linguistic and intellectual capital. His migration experience enabled him to improve his linguistic knowledge during his time in Turkey and even allowed him to learn a new language, Hebrew. Yet this was not the decisive factor in his migratory journey. Sardar's migration story highlights the opportunity, even the unpredictability—if not randomness—involved in building one's journey, even though this person possessed a largely satisfactory cultural and financial capital. Despite his intellectual capital, his journey was also shaped by family resources and local mutual support (friendships and political network), which helped to resolve situations that might have seemed insoluble at first.

The Meeting (Methodology and Justification)

I began studying Iraqi Kurdistan when I was living in Amman, Jordan. My plan was to continue researching Syrian migration when civil war broke out, suddenly cutting me off from my area of interest, although it was so close. I had been drawn to the unique situation of the Kurds in the Middle East and on several occasions, had had the opportunity to travel to Syrian and Kurdish areas. Yet in Iraq, where the situation had evolved more in their favor, I had no contacts. I therefore ventured into this new area by setting up a research program designed to help understand the socio-spatial dynamics underway in a proto-state in the making: the autonomous region of Iraqi Kurdistan.

Every other month, I flew to Erbil, the capital of the autonomous region, and gradually built up a network of acquaintances there. In 2012, when I was working on clandestine cross-border passages between countries in the region (Syria, Turkey, Iraq, Iran), the daughter of a Kurdish friend told me about the case of one of her relatives. He was living in Switzerland and had traveled all over part of the Middle East in the 1990s in the hope of finding a way to reach Europe. I was told that what he had apparently managed to do, after several years of waiting and being in transit, was completely different from the usual journeys of the Kurds I had been able to interview until that point.

I met Sardar a few months later in Iraqi Kurdistan and invited him to work with me on research assignments about human smuggling networks in the border areas between Iraq and its neighboring countries. His experience, knowledge of the region and points of passage across the border, as well as his connections made him the ideal person to work on this research topics. During our various journeys in Kurdish territories, he gradually told me the whole story that a few years earlier had taken him from the small city of Akre, in Northern Iraq, to the shores of Lake Geneva. Iraqi migration to Switzerland was not unusual in itself, but the steps along his journey certainly were, as was the way he had managed to seize opportunities to travel from one place to the next.

Firstly, Sardar is a perfect example of migration by political activists and opponents to the established authorities in that part of the world. He faced a double threat: first as an activist in the Kurdish rebellion against the Ba'athist authorities in Baghdad, and then as a Communist in Kurdistan, which had become autonomous (in 1991) but was dominated by traditional Kurds who aimed to be equally hegemonic (PDK, for the area he hails from).

Next, Sardar's case illustrates a journey that was admittedly complicated, not to mention risky and dangerous, but which eventually worked out in the end: it is the story of a successful journey at a time when many Kurds have not managed to reach Europe. The success of this journey must be understood as a series of steps, which the migrant had never thought would occur in his previously calculated strategy. It may be that Sardar's experience provides new insight into Kurdish migration, which did not usually follow this route. We think that these pioneers, these adventurers, took journeys that could open up new paths in migration, new perspectives for others who may come in the future. Thus, although his journey may seem unusual (although we are not claiming that it is),[1] it still sheds light on some migrants' ability to map new migratory routes by going "off the beaten path."

Lastly, the choice to use Sardar to illustrate this section is also due to the unusual nature of his journey. Indeed, after spending time in Turkey, a standard stage in the Iraqi migration process, Sardar remained in transit in Israel for a long time. Although he is non-practicing, Sardar was born into Muslim family and posed as Jewish in order to enter Israel. This change of identity and circumstances is remarkable to us, particularly in an area where religious affiliation is sometimes the factor that opens up migration opportunities. Sardar's migratory trajectory is unusual in the sense that it intersects with that of members of another community, one that has also been extensively persecuted during other periods of history: the Jewish community. This interaction of identities raises a question in migration studies, which generally present networks structured around transnationalism (transnational family), diasporas, or communities in the narrow sense.

Having worked in the Middle East since the late 1990s, I have long been interested in the migration of populations in situations of marginality, be it cultural, political, and/or economic. Some of these populations, when they find themselves socially, economically, and therefore politically marginalized, can feel relegated to the margins of the state system and attempt to circumvent the constraints suffered and perceived through migratory movements. Building an alternative "space of freedom," expanded by

[1] I was not able to investigate in Israel or in Iraqi Kurdistan to find out whether Sardar's journey was a quasi-unique case, or if other Kurds, like him, had followed the same itinerary and adopted the same strategy in order to leave Iraq.

migrations, can prove to be the result of collective strategies used to respond to contexts of severe constraints. This was the case with the Druze in Syria (Roussel, 2011). In some of my earlier work, I demonstrated that community resources could easily be mobilized in order to build a space of substitution through migration, enabling these groups to overcome political and economic restriction on a national scale. However, the case that I have chosen to present here goes beyond the scope of migration built on a community's own resources. Yet at the same time, it does not call it into question since Sardar, a young Iraqi Kurd, also used community resources along his journey: what makes his journey unusual, as we will see, is that although Sardar relied on a community at a crucial time for his journey's success, it was not his own original community, as is generally the case.

Context

As a non-Arabic, non-Turkish, and non-Persian population, the Kurds have experienced an eventful history, which we will briefly review in order to gain a better understanding of the overall context. Being Kurdish is often an "offense" in the Middle East (Sammali, 1995). Therefore, the Kurds are generally represented as a "persecuted group," generally with the added issue of political engagement by some in the struggle against repressive regimes. Doubly threatened by their nationalist fight and their political engagement, many Kurds, be they from Iraq, Turkey or Iran and Syria, have been and still are a target for the respective central authorities of the countries in which they have settled.

Kurdish history, since the end of the Ottoman era (1918/1923),[2] has been punctuated by dramatic events involving episodes of political marginalization, bloody repression, mass slaughter and exodus, as well as deportation, sometimes organized. In an almost permanent struggle that lasted from the end of the First World War through 1991 against a central state that denied them any right to cultural or political autonomy (let alone national independence at that time), the Kurds often had to adapt their survival strategies to include a parameter that had become recurrent: violence. In Turkey, between 1925 and 1938, there were no fewer than thirty Kurdish revolts (Boulanger, 2006, p. 43); the guerrilla reprisals in the 1980s triggered unprecedented migratory movements both within the country and to Europe following repression from Ankara. Thus, throughout the 20th century, the frequent, violent repression by the central authorities often resulted in migratory movements of varying durations, whether to Turkey, Syria, or Iraq.[3]

---

[2] From the 19th century onwards, the Turkish Ottomans attempted to challenge the autonomous status that the Kurds had enjoyed for several centuries. The centralization of power in Istanbul, encouraged by the decline of the Empire under pressure from the West, provoked Kurdish uprisings that were immediately suppressed.

[3] In Iraq, the Sheikh Mahmud Barzanji uprisings (1920s) ended with the leader and his partisans

The Kurds present in Iraqi territory were also subjected to a policy of violent assimilation. Struggling against the various regimes that followed in Baghdad, they fought to resist the Arabization policy and the triumphant Arab nationalism of the 1960s. During this time, their contemporary guerrilla warfare, although it had originally begun as far back as the 1920s, resumed. In this context of permanent rivalry with the central authority, Iraqi Kurdish fighters would withdraw into the border mountains as an effective guerrilla strategy when threatened. Coming from a mountain background, the leader of the Kurdish guerrilla after the Second World War, Mullah Mustafa Barzani, is an excellent example of this. A native of the Barzan Valley, this historic leader of the rebellion against the regime in Baghdad—accompanied by his Peshmerga—spent many years in the mountains north of Iraq on the Turkish and Iranian border, a zone called "Kurdistan" by Kurdish nationalists. These guerilla movements were built around military leaders who in some cases launched political parties. In Iraq in the 1980s, all Turkish fighters were tied to partisan organizations that one by one entered into conflict in order to impose their own hegemony (1990s).

This context of highly politicized, permanent violence in Iraq, in which Kurds were constantly fighting a central authority that they deemed repressive, is an important part of Sardar's story. The rivalries between local political parties were also decisive factors in this context, as we will see in the next section. Although Sardar did not leave Iraq directly because of the war, we must admit that the context in which he found himself at the time was steeped in a conflictual dynamic created by the civil war between actors in a struggle for supremacy.

Sardar's family life played an important role at the outset of his journey and in its transitional phases. His biological family as well as his political "family" (the Communist Party) provided resources that played a decisive role in his departure from the country, enabling him to leave in good conditions without being arrested. Leaving an authoritarian country in which one is wanted by the authorities or threatened is generally the first main difficulty faced by political activists, sometimes requiring them to resort to risky and expensive underground strategies.

Finally, we must stress the importance of the periods of transit in the two countries where he spent time: Turkey and Israel. Each time, the local context played an important role in the migrant's experience, in his desire to stay for

fleeing to the mountains and then to Persia. In 1947, General Barzani took refuge in Iran with his men following the failure of the Iraqi Kurd nationalist movement, which opposed Baghdad. After that, he spent eleven years in exile in the U.S.S.R. The guerrillas' failure in 1975 prompted 180,000 Kurds to leave for Iran and over 200,000 to leave for Southern Iraq. The Anfal genocide in the 1980s caused the death and deportation of hundreds of thousands of people to Iran. Finally, the "great exodus" following the Gulf War (1991) led many Iraqi Kurds to move to Turkey and Iran, escaping repression by the Iraqi Army. In addition, during the enforced Arabization of the southern part of Kurdistan, there were episodes of deportation of the Kurdish populations to Southern Iraq, where many were massacred (1960s–1980s).

a while or leave. These transit periods, which he had not planned for in the case of Israel, gave him the means to continue on his journey to another place that he had not previously intended.

Story of a Migrant's Life

The Iraqi Period: From Militancy to Exile

Sardar's political engagement was to be a decisive factor, as it forced him to leave the country to avoid being arrested, as was the case for many young activists in the Middle East.

Sardar is Kurdish first, Iraqi second. Like many other young Iraqi Kurds of his era, he shared the feeling that their future had been stolen by Saddam Hussein and the Ba'athist regime, which promoted an ideology that promoted "Arabic-ness" over other regional identities. When he was a child, all the men in his family were Peshmerga in the PDK's army; they fought the central regime and many of them went into exile in Iran when the Kurdish rebellion collapsed following the Algiers Accords in 1975.[4] Born to a family of traders in a small city in the north of the country called Akre, he studied in Mosul in the 1980s. In this period of distant war between his country and Iran, young Sardar became a student at Mosul University—one of the main hotbeds of intellectual activity in Iraq, along with Baghdad—and joined the Communist Party. On the Kurdish political scene, the Communist Party was a rival to the PDK, the historic Kurdish party founded by Mullah Mustafa Barzani, the leader of the struggle for Kurdish national liberation. The leadership of the PDK was taken over by his son Masoud after his death. At the time, the Communist Party was seen as a party of intellectuals, mainly from urban, educated backgrounds; its progressive ideology was similar to that of the other main historic Kurdish party: Jalal Talabani's PUK, also a less conservative party. In this regard, he did not fit in well with the PDK, which was more traditional and archaic in its respect for tribal and clan traditions. Communists could not accept this in the name of their class struggle.

The local context is important in understanding political trends. Akre is located within a large rural and tribal area, but in Akre itself, the "city-dwellers" do not belong to any tribe. The city is an administrative center and a distinct town–country split divides both space and society. In the city, some of the middle-class families traded with people from the surrounding countryside and acted as intermediaries with the major neighboring cities (Mosul, Erbil). The others were civil servants. The Akre region was more a fiefdom of the PDK, which was powerful in the countryside and also in the

[4] On March 6, 1975, Iraq and Iran signed the Algiers Accords, which brought an end to the border dispute in the Shatt al-Arab region (southern Iraq). For Turkish fighters, this event marked the end of Tehran's logistical support for their guerrilla movement against Baghdad. Mustafa Barzani's men then went into exile in Iran.

city. A small part of the population at that time stayed loyal to Saddam's regime, generally out of self-interest, and served in the intelligence services or in the army. In these conditions, the Communists were a marginal political force and occupied an uncomfortable position between being a pro-PDK force and a pro-regime force. The CP was nonetheless established in the city, the only territory not held by the tribes. In 1984, when Sardar joined the party, it was through a friend, who was himself a member of the Iraqi CP. He entered as a militant member along with his group of friends, a total of six people. Together, they were in charge of distributing leaflets against Saddam Hussein's regime all over the city of Akre, after nightfall.[5] Sardar was 16 years old at the time. The following years provided him an opportunity to increase his political activity and strengthen his local political network, which as we can see was not structured around the family nucleus but rather around bonds of friendship. After becoming a student in Mosul, in 1986, he became particularly active against the regime in place; as time went by, he even surrounded himself with new activists whom he recruited, to the point that between 1986 and 1988, he managed a group of around twenty people. An active member in the Akre branch, from then on Sardar also opposed the local leading lights of the PDK, who frowned upon political competition.

Sardar was 20 when the war with Iran ended. Due to his political activism, he remained directly threatened by the Ba'athist regime's intelligence services. In 1988, he was called up to the national army to be a soldier. He was fortunate that the country was no longer at war. He went to Najaf, in the South, for his military service; he would be sent back to Mosul in 1989, in a garrison close to his region of origin. The new war looming in Kuwait was already causing desertions. In 1990, as Saddam Hussein was preparing to invade Kuwait, Sardar (aged 22) refused to enlist in the army and instead joined the Communist Kurdish guerrilla in the Akre mountains with all of his friends from the Akre cell. In early March 1991, when Saddam Hussein had been defeated by the coalition and withdrew from Kuwait, the Kurdish Peshmerga from all parties attacked the Iraqi Army's positions everywhere in order to liberate their region: the Communist movement was at the forefront of the insurrection, sometimes ahead of the Kurdish nationalists from the traditional parties, as was the case in Sulaymaniyah. At that time, the Communist fighters thought it was possible to overthrow Saddam Hussein's regime in Kurdistan. The regime's army retreated to the south of the Kurdish mountains in order to reorganize. Part of Kurdistan was liberated by the Iraqi Army. Many Communist cells and movements met there and sought to

[5] In the 1980s, the Iraqi Communist Party suffered greatly under the repressive dictatorship of Saddam Hussein's regime. Its activities were closely monitored, and the party was banned. The Communist Party had more freedom in Iraqi Kurdistan than elsewhere in the country, where the intelligence services were merciless. Several cells of Communist activists operated in the Kurdish zones in rebellion against the central authorities. In the Kurdish mountains, some of their members were Peshmerga and military camps existed. In March 1991, the Communists played an important role in the Kurdish insurrection against Saddam Hussein following the attack on the country by coalition forces dominated by the United States.

merge.

After 40 days of freedom following the Kurdish insurrection, the Iraqi Army returned. The repression was terrible. Around 1.5 million Kurds left the country, either for Iran or Turkey, depending on how close they were to the border. Fearing the use of chemical weapons, as the army had done in 1988 in Halabja, the young fighters from Sardar's region led their families to safety in Turkey. The exodus was long and arduous: nearly a week's trek through the mountains. In order to spare his family the terrible ordeal of the camps, Sardar used his political networks to house them in a Kurdish village in Turkey near Şırnak and went off to fight in Iraq. A month-long exodus in Turkey allowed him to form contacts with members of the PKK, the Kurdistan Workers' Party, which was fighting the national army in Turkey for Kurds' rights. There were strong relationships between Communist Kurds and Kurdish PKK members, as both parties had Marxist-Leninist allegiances. In the summer of 1991, after new Kurdish uprisings in the Kurdish towns of Iraq despite them having been recaptured in April, the Iraqi Army retreated to Kurdistan (in July) and imposed an embargo on the Kurdish region (in October). Protected by Operation Provide Comfort and the "no fly zone" created by the West, the refugees could return home, but economic and sanitary conditions were difficult. The double embargo that hit the region (as the entire country was also under an international embargo) drove tens of thousands of Kurds into exile abroad (to Europe in particular) during the 1990s. Although the armed forces were no longer present, the regime's intelligence services remained active in Akre.

The following year in Kurdistan, which was now effectively autonomous, Sardar was still an active CP member and took part in creating a cultural center in Akre and starting a newspaper. The Communist Party's Akre branch became a powerful political network that opposed the PDK locally. But the PDK's desire for power was not compatible with the CP's political activity. Pressure from the PDK soon led to tension and confrontation. On a Kurdistan-wide scale, the PDK and the PUK—the other major party that arose from the Kurdish rebellion in the 1970s—began to take military action against each other in 1994, triggering a civil war in liberated Iraqi Kurdistan that would last for three years. The CP, which had placed itself under the protection of the PUK's Peshmerga, was threatened. Locally, the PDK prevented Communists from continuing their political activities. Sardar decided to leave Akre in 1995. He took refuge in the mountains again, but he was wanted by the PDK, which sought to arrest him, as he was suspected of maintaining ties with the PKK and the PUK, which had joined forces in the inter-Kurdish war. He was soon informed by family members, who were themselves PDK members, that his name was on the party's intelligence service's lists. He therefore decided to go into exile in order to avoid prison.

The Turkish Period: Transition to a Third-Party Country

Crossing the border between Iraq and Turkey was Sardar's first problem. In order to leave the country, he needed a laissez-passer from the Kurdish militia in the sector. As a wanted man, he risked arrest by the PDK forces, which at that time already controlled the entire western half of Iraqi Kurdistan, on the border with Turkey. But Sardar was from a family with ties to the PDK. One of his cousins, a member of the party's intelligence in Akre, was able to provide him with the precious permit that could only be obtained at the central office near Erbil. Between family members, arrangements were always possible. He was allowed to leave the country under the false pretext of marriage to a Kurdish woman from Turkey. For his family, Sardar's departure abroad was a good way to keep everyone happy and give him the chance to rebuild his life in Europe, far from intra-Kurdish politics. On June 1, 1995, he left Iraq through the only border-crossing point with Turkey, Ibrahim Khalil, and went to Silopi, the first Kurdish township on the Turkish side. He brought his passport, so the crossing was entirely legal, following border agreements between the de facto Iraqi Kurdish authorities and the government in Ankara.

He then decided to leave for Ankara, where he owned a *pied-à-terre.* He traveled was by bus. He met up with an old acquaintance, his only contact in the Turkish capital, a Kurd from Bardarash who was a friend from Mosul University. He would stay there for a year before finding a way to continue his journey. Yet when Sardar first arrived in Ankara, his idea was to reach Europe as soon as possible. For Iraqi Kurds, Turkey is very often only a country of transit, but first they must find the means to leave. To this end, Sardar saw two solutions, those used by most of his countrymen who followed the same path: either marriage to a Kurdish woman in Europe who would provide him with a visa, or illegal entry via Greece or Italy, by boat.

Initially, he moved to his friend Hikmat's apartment in Ankara, which was used as a waiting place for Iraqi Kurds. Hikmat had married one of his cousins who lived in Canada and was waiting for the paperwork that would enable him to fly to North America. Sardar knew that he needed to find $8,000 in order to try his luck with the smugglers, but he had another idea in mind, which a family member had suggested: going to Israel. To do this, he devised a plan, although he was well aware that it was unlikely to succeed. This idea must be understood in the context of the multicultural environment in which many Iraqi Kurds lived. Most cities of Kurdish origin are a melting pot of religious identities (Muslim, Christian, Jewish, syncretic minorities) and/or ethnic identities (Kurds, Arabs, Turks). In Akre, a large Jewish community had left its mark, and many Kurdish residents still had ties to Jews from Iraq who had made their *aliyah*[6] to Israel, most of them in the early

[6] This is a Hebrew term referring to the act of a Jew immigrating to Israel.

1950s.[7] In Sardar's family, his aunt, a Muslim, had married a Jew from Akre in the 1940s. Of course, the husband had to convert to Islam. But this meant that Sardar had cousins whose father had been Jewish, and they still had proof of this in the form of birth certificate-type documents. At first, on the advice of one of these cousins, Sardar decided to contact the Israeli Embassy in Turkey, claiming that he had Jewish origins through his father. Of course it was a ruse, because he was actually going to present his uncle's documents, not his own father's. However, this was in vain since his mother needed to be Jewish for him to have any hope of obtaining certificate to prove his invented Judaism. However, the embassy suggested contacting his supposed family (an imaginary family, of course) in Israel in order to try and put together an application. Although the plan failed, a small window was left ajar.

Faced with this stumbling block, Sardar took a series of odd jobs in Ankara. He needed to survive. He improved his Turkish language skills and managed to find jobs quite easily. He spent several months working at a printing press and distributing newspapers. Kurdish smuggling networks offered him a chance to leave for Europe illegally, but he immediately refused. Since his first attempt at the Israeli Embassy, Sardar had kept this tiny flame of hope alive. To do this, he mobilized his family in the country. His brother, who in the meantime had met the members of a Jewish delegation on a trip to Akre, was able to make contact with Abdullah, an ex-Akrawi (resident of the city of Akre) of Jewish origin, who had lived in Israel since 1948. He agreed to act as an intermediary between Sardar's Kurdish family and Israel, especially with all the bureaucracy at the Jewish migration office (Jewish Agency) in Tel Aviv. The only way to bring Sardar to Israel would be to invent a false identity for him, via a Jewish family from Kurdistan who, in exchange for payment, would agree to make a false declaration that he was a member of their family who had remained in Iraq.

This was at the start of the winter of 1995. The process Sardar has chosen was expensive and took time. His family had money, but the clock was ticking; time was not on his side. Once again, the context in Iraqi Kurdistan was not favorable: civil war was raging between Kurdish partisans; Saddam Hussein's army was an ever-present threat; Kurdistan, under an embargo, was economically exhausted. Under these conditions, many Iraqis chose to emigrate. It was an costly process. Other people seemed to know about the migratory route via ex-Iraqi Jews, and families with whom to negotiate were not easy to find. In the spring, Sardar's Turkish visa expired, and he began to lose hope. He decided to try the illegal route like many of his countrymen, whom he met in growing numbers in Ankara, even in the flat that he was still occupying, which provided a safe haven for candidates in exile like him. In

[7] Ostracized by the Iraqi State after the plan to split Palestine and create a Jewish State in Palestine was announced, nearly all of Iraq's Jewish community (around 120,000 people) left the country between the end of 1949 and 1952, following the rescue operation (or evacuation operation) Ezra and Nehemiah.

early 1996, there were up to sixteen people living in the home's three rooms at any time. After saving up several thousand dollars, Sardar left for Istanbul and embarked on an illegal crossing over the Greek border. The group of migrants was arrested by Turkish guards, who only released them after extracting a bribe of 300 dollars each, threatening them with expulsion to Iraq.

Finally, the situation was resolved. His brother managed to find reliable intermediaries to allow him to connect with a Jewish family in Israel who was originally from Dohuk (a town in Iraqi Kurdistan) and agreed to carry out the procedures to "repatriate" Sardar. The operation ended up costing around 6,000 dollars and after a few weeks, he received his new "false" papers, although they were genuine for the authorities, in the form of a permit to immigrate into Israeli territory as a new citizen. On April 15, 1996, Sardar flew to Tel Aviv Airport.

The Israeli Period and an Eye on Europe

Sardar arrived in Israel under fairly difficult conditions. He experienced discrimination due to his status as a new arrival. He felt foreign in this society, which he did not understand and which was very community-oriented. He was not familiar with its conventions or its language. He describes this period of his life as perhaps one of the most painful, although paradoxically he seemed to have made it—legally at least. This phase of his life was above all marked by distance from his family, who was still in Iraq, a country that continued to suffer from armed conflicts. On the shores of the Mediterranean Sea, Sardar would endure the death of his mother from a distance, in isolation and with a terrible feeling of powerlessness. That year, he had a difficult time integrating, finding a network of friends, rebuilding a life in this country of exile: he experienced a period of genuine depression.

Economically, daily life was not easy either. For the first six months, he lived on social security benefits in a country that had a high standard of living. Then he tried to break out of the benefits system and build a more dignified existence for himself. He took a series of odd jobs, as is often the case, and managed to find employment at a hotel. The manager trusted him and offered him an interesting job that was far from degrading. A certain solidarity grew up between them: his employer was an Iraqi Jew. For Sardar, it was an opportunity to enter the network of Iraqi Jewish immigrants, many of whom lived south of Tel Aviv, between the capital and Ashkelon, in the city of Ashdod. He socialized through this network. After growing close to his employer's family quickly, he even received a marriage proposal from a daughter of the family living in the United States. For a migrant, this was obviously an ideal opportunity to build a new life in America; especially since the potential in-laws were wealthy. Against all logic, Sardar declined the proposal. He had only one thing in mind: to bring his family over from Iraq and keep them safe. After ten months or so, he managed to "buy" passage for his sister and three brothers, along with their relatives, for around 10,000 dollars, using the same type of scheme he had used for himself. He helped them to settle in Kiryat-Malakhi, a village near Ashdod.

Life in Israel did not agree with Sardar. He was looking for something else. Over a year after arriving in Turkey, in summer 1997, he took a flight to Germany with his Israeli passport in his pocket. He aimed to settle there. He first applied for asylum in Europe in the city of Nuremberg as an Iraqi Kurd. His application as a political refugee was accepted and he waited for his new papers. That is when his family members, who had only just arrived in Israel three months before, told him they were unable to feel at home in that country and all wanted to go back to their own country. The civil war had just ended between the Kurdish parties. Sardar returned to Israel in November 1997: he traveled as an Israeli because, due to his early departure, he did not have time to wait for his asylum procedure in Germany to be finalized.

The return to Israel was a challenge and a disappointment. He went back because he did not want to see his brothers and sisters start from scratch again by returning to Kurdistan. He had worked so hard, invested so much, for nothing. But at that point, he was the one taking initiatives for the rest of the family. He knew Israel; he had learned Hebrew; he had a network. Soon, he found a job in the Ashdod area. It was a major farming area that employed many people. Sardar worked for ten months as a fruit and vegetable distributor for a wholesaler in the region who owned several cold storage units. He lived with his relatives in the village. It took ten months for him to save up enough money for the seven people to buy plane tickets to Europe. On August 21, 1998, after a few days in France and the Netherlands, they arrived in Switzerland. Sardar applied for asylum for a second time there, in a country outside of the European Union. He has lived there ever since, is married, and has two children.

Life in Switzerland is pleasant, but he has no job security. He has been a contract worker for years. Achieving professional recognition as a newcomer to a country is another struggle that is equally difficult (see the chapter by Ariel Mendez). As living conditions in Iraqi Kurdistan improved, Sardar considered moving back to Erbil; in particular between 2010 and 2014. There was "business to be done" and opportunities for the most resourceful. He has stayed in touch with the Kurdish parties. When war began again, his hopes were shattered.

Theoretical Discussion

Sardar's journey, which was so unusual due to the route taken, shows how important it is for a migrant to have a powerful mutual support network and a good deal of success, or even luck. Moreover, Sardar's story also shows that migratory plans, even when poorly thought out because they are made urgently and in a hurry, can still work out... but at a high cost. It took a chance encounter to resolve things for him (his brother meeting the members of a Jewish delegation in Akre) when he was in Turkey, with no possible way of continuing on his journey, as well as a high degree of family implication (financial help, mutual support). For a successful migration, family is an essential resource, as this journey demonstrates. Having been helped to escape from a "tight spot" in Turkey, the migrant felt indebted, as his family had helped him out of a "tricky situation." He in turn mobilized the resources he had accrued during his migratory experience in order to help his family to leave Iraq. He took responsibility for the group by playing the role of decision-maker and taking them to Switzerland with him. Sardar's journey shows that this is a collective undertaking, even if it was not originally planned as such. Although this may resemble the gift and counter-gift mechanism in Marcel Mauss' theory, here it seems that the context of war should not be overlooked. The "duty" of wanting to take your relatives away from danger is clearly formulated here, highlighting the emotional aspect in the decisions made by the primo-migrant, who we must remember had already left Iraq fearing for his life. "It was my duty to get them out of there. In Iraq, you never know what will happen to you; anything can happen. I wanted to give them the option to leave the country. I had managed it thanks to my brother... I couldn't leave them like that" (extract from an interview, Erbil, Iraqi Kurdistan, February 2015).

Sardar's journey was spread across several years: June 1995–August 1998. This particularly long time frame shows the difficulties that Eastern migrants had in crossing the borders of Europe, even back then, though this comes as no surprise. This long time period above all demonstrates the uncertainty inherent in this type of journey; the way space–time can close in on the migrant, plunging him into a waiting period over which he almost never has any control, so to speak. Sardar experienced this in Turkey, in particular. He hesitated between several possible ways of leaving this country of transit and ending his interminable wait. Fumbling, hesitation, and uncertainty were integral to that unique stage of this migratory journey, for the migrant knew very well that the place he had reached could have been the end of the line. An obstacle would mean returning to Iraq, back to his starting point, and therefore, in the case we have just discussed, immediate imprisonment. It is also particularly important to analyze the Israeli episode. In Israel, where his story could have ended, he was again plunged into a very different socio-cultural context where he was unable to rebuild his life. Here, although paradoxically he had more agency over his own destiny than ever before, he was operating within a temporality that was still beyond his control, due to his desire to look after the rest of his family. This forced him to leave Germany and return to the Holy Land for another period of nearly a year. Ultimately, the migrant was faced with very diverse contexts and yet his journey was divided between temporalities that he seemed to endure rather than control.

This example also shows that migratory journeys are the result of choices that may appear more or less judicious to the outside observer, but which clearly reflect each migrant's personality. In the case we have just seen, a more individualistic migrant than Sardar might have chosen the unique opportunity to go to America when the possibility arose, through the intermediary of a marriage proposal as mentioned above. This may or may not seem like a rational decision depending on the goal in mind. When Sardar decided to leave Germany after his refugee status had been accepted and his papers were in the process of being issued, the choice that he made—to join his family in Israel—was to be decisive later on, as he lost any chance of returning and completing this process in Germany and the rest of the European Union. Ultimately, journeys are simply the result of a series of choices that have met with success or failure and have opened or closed doors. Switzerland thus offered him a second chance. The waiting periods, which we have referred to as "temporalities" in the stages of the journey, can therefore be analyzed as a shortage of solutions or a series of failed attempts to continue his journey. Sardar being stuck in Turkey—after he had failed to exit the country illegally via Greece, and this strategy was the last solution after a fruitless attempt to obtain false papers at the Israeli embassy—is a good example of this.

Finally, it is important to look at the role of identity in the migration process. Put extremely concisely, what we have just described here is the story of a Kurd who emigrated to Europe via Israel by posing as a Jew. Sardar's journey was not built on an intrinsic identity component—a kind of emigration vector—that would have provided him with a unique resource, as is often the case in the Middle East, with community-based migratory networks (Middle Eastern Christians for example). The Kurds, unlike the religious minority groups in the region (Alawites, Druze, Ismailis, Yazidis, Sabeans, Shabaks, etc.), do not form an enclosed confessional community focused on preserving their distinctive identity, nor do they form a community group unified around a shared identity. They share cultural elements with their Arab and Persian neighbors and are themselves made up of various religious and linguistic groups. The main networks of solidarity which are generally used as a resource in Kurdish migration are invariably political or familial, and even geographical in the sense of a feeling of belonging to a geographical tribe, located in a territory (a village, a city, a sector): being from Akre in our specific case. Perhaps this lack of a strong community structure is what has prompted some Kurds to pass for Jews in order to benefit from the resources specific to that community, which has a high degree of solidarity. In any event, this ability to harness a community resource that the migrant does not naturally possess is part of their migration know-how. As he is fundamentally atheist, although born to a Muslim family, the religious resource is one type of resource that Sardar does not possess. Opportunistic and pragmatic, he did not hesitate to blend in with a temporary adopted community in order to acquire the means to continue his journey.

This example shows that migration resources are acquired, for although Sardar, by birth, did not have the community resources to emigrate to a country within the migratory field, his journey was nevertheless dotted with identity resources that enabled him to bounce back. His greatest strength was his ablility to connect to community networks outside those of the Kurds. Being a Muslim Kurd does not enable a person to move around easily, unlike other Eastern groups that have more opportunities. Two essential episodes illustrate this: the connection with the delegation of Iraqi Jews in Akre, which allowed him to leave Turkey; and the Iraqi Jewish network in Ashdod, which allowed him to work in Israel and bring family members there from Iraq. Thus, this account shows how community boundaries can be porous and vague, and how a particularly skillful migrant can use this to construct his own exile strategy. Even though he could not rely on the resources of his own community, Sardar was able to resort to a purely community-based process in order to leave Turkey, the red zone of migration from the East.

This account sheds light on the complete migratory path of an activist who had to leave a warring, authoritarian country enduring historic ruptures in the form of repeated conflicts. It helps us to understand the seemingly rational or irrational choices made by a migrant who, during his migratory journey, endlessly sought to adapt and re-mobilize new resources in order to carry on. Lastly, it gives visibility to all those "uncalculated" moments, those chance occurrences of life in the difficult context of exile, along with the periods of waiting that are unwanted and usually suffered: periods when all hope seems lost. This is quite far removed from the idea of migratory know-how possessed by the migrant before his departure. It is also far removed from the established strategies that are often presented in diaspora or transnationalism studies. The migratory journey appears here as a series of phenomena that are not necessarily strung together following a logic that is planned in advance or understood as predefined, but one in which chance occurrences, opportunities, and choices are combined in a fairly random way.

References

Maalouf A., 1998. *Les Identités Meurtrières*, Paris: Gresset.

Roussel C., 2011. *Les Druzes de Syrie. Territoire et mobilité*. Beyrouth: Presses de l'Ifpo. http://ifpo.revues.org/1860

Sammali J., 1995. *Etre kurde, un délit ? Portrait d'un peuple nié*. Paris: L'Harmattan, Collection Comprendre le Moyen-Orient.

FROM FAMILY DISPERSION TO ASYLUM-SEEKING: PALESTINIAN REFUGEES IN LEBANON AND SYRIA

Kamel Doraï

In 2011, when the Syrian crisis began, many families gradually left Syria to seek asylum in neighboring countries. Palestinian refugees in Syria were gradually been caught up in the conflict and some of them were forced into exile. While most neighboring countries closed their borders very rapidly to this group of refugees, Lebanon adopted a more flexible approach (Doraï & Al Husseini, 2013). More than 50,000 Syrian Palestinians have found asylum in Lebanon. The geography of this exile is singular. Lebanon is one of the countries in the region where the legal status of Palestinians is most precarious. More than half of the Palestinians in Lebanon still live in one of 12 refugee camps, where socio-economic conditions are very difficult. This polarization of Palestinian migration from Syria to these areas may, however, be explained by the historical ties between Palestinian refugees in both countries (Doraï, 2015). Forced migration related to the current conflict in Syria is based on forms of mobility developed since the 1948 exodus *(Nakba* in Arabic).

This chapter is based on the story of Umm Maher, a native of Haifa, whose family has been scattered—like many Palestinians—at a regional level. While the majority of Palestinian refugees in Lebanon come from northern Palestine and have settled directly in the nearest country, some families have experienced more complex trajectories. Thus, refugees did not all arrive directly from Palestine to Lebanon in 1948. Some headed North of Palestine, staying inside Palestinian territory to join relatives. The West Bank was a first step for Palestinian families, especially the city of Nablus. The exodus dispersed families in several host countries while the Israeli border was closed to the return or even the crossing of refugees. Palestinians suffered long journeys trying to gather families that had been divided between several countries. But for the vast majority, exile meant a permanent state of dispersion. Perceived as a constraint, resulting from a forced exodus, this dispersion can also be considered a resource following Emmanuel Ma Mung (1999). Multiple internal and international forced displacements, as well as mobility and circulation for family reasons, contribute to the emergence of a space of cross-border mobility. From being a constraint, dispersion becomes a resource that is available in different contexts, not only to establish matrimonial ties but also to facilitate access to asylum space in case of conflict. The trajectory of Umm Maher, the leitmotif of this chapter, echoes the experience of many Palestinian families that were built in exile and dispersion.

As many writers have pointed out since the mid-1990s (e.g., Richmond, 1994), rather than opposing the so-called "forced" migrations with those considered "voluntary," the migration trajectories developed in Umm Maher's close social sphere demonstrate instead the continuities between different forms of migration and their articulation in time. In relation to other Palestinians in Lebanon, Umm Maher is a rather sedentary person. The mobility of her children, their spouses, and also relatives who circulate, is organized around her. Some settle at her house temporarily or with her relatives in Tyre. This relative immobility, which can be qualified as a form of local anchoring, is central to the structuring of the mobility of her relatives. This experience also allows for the discussion of the notion of rupture in migratory trajectories. The time frame of migration allows us to consider forced mobility from a longer time perspective. This long-term perspective shows how long circulations need to develop and consolidate, alternating periods of distancing and reactivating with specific events (weddings, conflicts, etc.).

This chapter is based on interviews conducted since 1999 in the region of Tyre in Southern Lebanon. The story of Umm Maher was collected for the first time at this date. The evidence gathered focused on her journey of exile and that of her family, her settlement in Lebanon, and the consequences of the wars on her experience. This narrative was then contextualized in the long term through multiple and regular stays in the area since then. The recent outbreak of the Syrian crisis in 2011 allowed me to analyze the current migration situation through the observation of the Palestinian mobility that I have studied since the mid-1990s, which led me to follow the path of families split between Lebanon and Syria. More recently, I did two series of surveys in the Palestinian camps and informal gatherings around the city of Tyre, and more particularly the camp of Al Buss. Both surveys were conducted in December 2013 and May 2014 with 25 families.[1] Following Benezer and Zetter's findings (2014), one aim of this chapter is to explore the role of social networks in terms of constraints and opportunities during asylum-seeker and refugee journeys. These surveys over the long term have allowed me to observe a new migration trend in the region. Palestinians in Lebanon have long been more affected by conflict. Many experienced forced displacements, while Palestinians in Syria were one of the most stable groups. The conflict that began in 2011 has dramatically changed this reality. Today, Lebanon hosts the majority of Palestinian refugees from Syria who are fleeing war in Syria.

---

[1] These surveys were conducted as part of the ANR MOBGLOB. I would like to thank Jaber Abu Hawash for the valuable assistance he gave me to select Palestinian families from Syria and giving me the proper contextual elements to understand the local issues of the presence of this new group of refugees in southern Lebanon.

Conflicts, Displacement, and Secondary Migration: Some Contextual Elements

The Forced Displacement of Palestinians Since 1948

In most cases, the exodus of Palestinians in 1948 did not take a single, direct route but counted many migration stages. The complexity of migration patterns is related to five main factors: (1) the progressive advance of troops from the future State of Israel, who gradually pushed Palestinians into neighboring countries; (2) the mode of transport used by refugees: trains and boats more often took refugees directly outside of Palestine, while other, slower, means of transport, like cars or walking, forced many stops along the way; (3) policy distribution of refugees implemented by international organizations and by local authorities in host countries, which often kept refugees from settling where they wished; (4) the housing and job opportunities offered to the Palestinians who arrived without resources; and (5) previous knowledge of the host region and the presence of relatives there.

The period from 1948 to 1956 is characterized by a significant dispersion of the Palestinians. This geographical dispersion is related to the nature of the exodus. The hasty and unorganized departure of the refugees resulted in the dispersion of families that did not all leave together. The exile was first thought to be temporary. Refugees headed to the closest safe areas, without taking the time first to gather together and get organized themselves in their host countries. Some were temporarily settled in border areas close to their region of origin, others in transit camps set up by the international community. Some were hosted by their families, as was the case of Umm Maher. It was only after 1956, when Israel completely closed its borders and became a permanent part of the regional environment, that refugees tried, for those who had the possibility, to rebuild family ties from before 1948 that the brutality and rapidity of the exodus had destroyed.

Settlement, with family reunification at the local level, was strained by the multiple displacements due to the successive conflicts in Lebanon since 1975. Forced mobility became an integral part of the lives of Palestinian refugees in Lebanon. Umm Maher and her family had to repeatedly flee the fighting, but without being able—or willing—to leave Lebanon. Syria was involved in the Lebanese conflict. As a result, it was not considered a safe space for most Palestinians at the time, as relations between the Syrian authorities and the Palestinian Liberation Organization (PLO) were very poor. During the war, Umm Maher's family became internally displaced and sought refuge in informal gatherings in different locations in Lebanon. The conflict was of such intensity that family networks played only a minor role. Palestinians acquired a culture—or an experience—of forced mobility during conflicts, which would be re-utilized in other contexts in the future.

The Lebanese civil war that began in 1975, and the Israeli invasions of 1978 and 1982, would result in a significant displacement of the population.

More than 170,000 Palestinian refugees were forced to flee in 1982. This included most of the population residing in the invaded areas occupied by Israel. The Israeli invasion was accompanied by significant material destruction (Schiff, 1995). The War of the Camps was a direct continuation of the Israeli invasion of June 1982. It began in 1985, just after the withdrawal of Israeli troops and expanded into West Beirut and the Tyre area, where Palestinians and Lebanese Shiites lived together. It took place in several phases of more or less intensity. The total blockade of some Palestinian camps alternated with periods of fighting and bombing. One major objective of the War of the Camps was to reduce the presence of the Palestinian population in the areas populated by Shiites around the city of Tyre and some districts of Beirut. Civilians were prime targets for the *Amal* militia. They were driven to pressure the PLO, resulting in significant population displacement. The War of the Camps is still very present in the Palestinian consciousness. The current Syrian conflict led to new forced displacement of Palestinian refugees at a regional level.

Umm Maher: the History of a Family Dispersed Across a Region

The story of Umm Maher, a Palestinian refugee who arrived in Tyre (southern Lebanon) in the mid-1950s, though a singular one, is similar to many other trajectories that led to the dispersion of many Palestinians throughout all the countries in the region. Following the 1948 Exodus, Umm Maher's family found itself spread across 3 countries; one of her sisters moved to Amman, in Jordan, while the other was in the Neirab camp near Aleppo, in Syria.

Umm Maher was born in 1944 in Haifa. She was forced to leave in 1948 when she was only four years old. She was able to narrate her exodus, even if she was not able to remember the exact facts. She first left with her grandmother, two sisters, father and his wife to her aunt's house. Her mother had died when she was very young. Her stepmother's family lived in Jordan, which is why she did not go to Lebanon during the war of 1948. When she arrived in Irbid, north of Jordan, her father went back to Palestine to look after his business, and to earn a living. He had left all his money behind. He and her stepmother never came back; they died in Palestine. Umm Maher was taken in by a Christian monastery, where she lived for three years. At that point, her paternal aunt came to get her and took her to a refugee camp called Askar, in Nablus. As she was an orphan, she was put in a school in Nablus, and later in Jerusalem until 1955.

In 1955, her grandmother, who was taking care of her, wanted to see her son, who had fled Haifa and found asylum first at the Lebanese border in a village called Rmeich, further north in Tyre. During their vacation, they went to see him, crossing first through Jordan. They stopped in Syria to see one of her other aunts who was in the Mezzeh camp in Damascus. They stayed in Syria for two or three months. They then headed towards Tyre, to the Al

Buss camp. During their stay in Tyre, her grandmother, who was 90 years old, passed away and was buried there. As Umm had no living parents, she stayed with her uncle. He was very poor. Sometimes he did not even have enough money to buy flour. Since she was his niece, he took care of her. Four years later, in November 1959, when she was fourteen, she married her cousin and settled in Nahr al Samir, right next to the camp.

Her two other sisters would experience similar trajectories that led one to settle in Jordan, her first country of exile, and the other to find refuge in northern Syria. Though Umm Maher's family moved to Tyre in a small informal group, the family grew. In a difficult socio-economic context, the Palestinians tried to reconstruct their society in exile. Relatives gradually came to live near the house where Umm Maher and her family settled. Palestinian refugee camps tend to grow by becoming integrated into the economic activity and their urban environment (for a history of refugee settlements in Lebanon, see Sfeir, 2017). Though these areas remain marginalized and segregated, they are now part of the fabric of life in major cities in the Middle East. Economic activity, daily mobility, the presence of new migrants, and strong political and cultural significance for Palestinian refugees, are the various elements that characterize the refugee camps today as urban settlements. Due to demographic pressure, most of the camps have informally extended beyond their boundaries. Nahr al Samir is actually an informal extension of the Al Buss camp located at the entrance to the city of Tyre. Some of the families who lived in the camp left to build larger houses outside the camp. They settled nearby on empty land along the *Al Samir* river. Other families who arrived later and wanted to join their relatives in the Al Buss camp could not find any available housing, so they settled in informal housing near the camp. Family networks play a central role in the development of the settlement spaces in Lebanon.

The story of this family is characterized by the dispersion of three sisters at a regional level. The successive conflicts, especially the wars that tore Lebanon apart from 1975 to 1990, made it difficult to travel between the family's different areas of settlement in Syria, Lebanon, and Jordan. This period was one of intense internal displacements of Umm Maher and her close family. Her husband was imprisoned by the Israelis in the Al Ansar camp, and some of her children were wounded. The family was forced to flee repeatedly to safer areas inside Lebanon. These repeated experiences of forced mobility fostered a culture of asylum that would be mobilized later to host family members fleeing the Syrian conflict in 2011.

Lebanon and Syria: A Space for Mobility that Developed in the 1990s

The period that followed the end of the Lebanese War was characterized by the reconstruction of relationships between Palestinian families living in different countries. Safer conditions allowed people to travel between Syria and Lebanon once again. The location of the Palestinian refugees in Lebanon played a central role as a reception area for Palestinians traveling from Syria. Umm Maher's sister visited her relatives in Lebanon. Later, two of Umm Maher's sons married two of their maternal cousins living in the region of Aleppo. The second generation of refugees helped to rebuild family ties despite the dispersion and the conflicts. Both sisters came to Lebanon and settled in the Palestinian cluster. Following their move, their mother came to Lebanon several times, strengthening ties between the two branches of the scattered family.

Family relations between the sisters who lived in Lebanon and their relatives in Syria remained strong, supported by frequent visits. The second generation, born in exile, strengthened these ties through marriages between the two branches of the family in the 1990s and early 2000s. Umm Maher's sister tells of the relations between the two branches of the family:

> We did not choose to be separated when we were young. In Irbid [a city north of Jordan], we all lived together in my grandmother's sister's son's house. My sister [Umm Maher] who had lived for a while in a boarding school in Jerusalem joined us. I was the oldest; they had only younger children. I did the cleaning at home. They gave us a room and we lived there. I spent all day at home, and the night I went to sleep with my grandmother and my sisters. When I was 12 years old, they told us that we have to leave and live with our father's family that was scattered throughout Syria and Lebanon. My cousins, children of my father's uncles, lived in Syria. One of my uncles wanted me to marry his son. We went to Syria with my sisters and my grandmother. I told them I did not want to marry my cousin. I did not like him. I told them I wanted to go to my aunts, my mother's sisters, in Aleppo. I decided to go to Aleppo myself. My sister went to Lebanon. I stayed in Aleppo alone until 1955. I got married in 1958 and settled in Syria, in the region of Aleppo.
>
> I did not see my sisters until 1982. We didn't keep in touch. I had small children and my husband was poor. It was the same for my sister in Lebanon. One of her sons was wounded and lost his hand, others were injured. In 1982, when I heard what had happened, I went to visit them. At the time it was easier to cross the border then it is today [1999]. Now it is difficult. When my son was in the Syrian army,[2] he spent time in Beirut, and I went to see him in Barbir.[3] I just went with my Palestinian ID. After that, it became more difficult to travel between the two countries. Syria allows us to go to Lebanon, with all the facilities, but Lebanon does not let us in. It started becoming difficult to travel around 1996, I think. Palestinians from Lebanon can easily go to Syria, but the opposite is difficult. My daughters were married in Lebanon. I want to go and see them when they give birth to their children. But it is difficult because the Lebanese do not let us in.
>
> I decided to have my two daughters marry here in Lebanon. One of my sister's sons lost his hand, the poor thing. My younger sister [Umm Maher] lived through the *Nakba,* which was difficult. I really wanted to my daughter to marry her son, because they had experienced a difficult situation. I love her son. I saw him when he was younger, when he lost his hand in 1982. Then when I saw my older daughter in Tyre—the one who married first—I thought it would be good if her

---

[2] Palestinians in Syria had to join a special unit of the Syrian army.

[3] One of the districts in Beirut where the Syrian army was stationed.

> sister also lived in Tyre. That way my oldest daughter would not be alone. A girl cannot be alone like that.

As a result, these matrimonial alliances between Tyre and Aleppo would continue. One of Umm Maher's granddaughters, born in Lebanon, married one of her cousins in Syria. In this way, the next generation took over and the relationships between the two families are strengthened, but this time it was due to a young woman who left Lebanon to live in Syria. The familial ties were consolidated across generations.

Alongside this strengthening of family ties through matrimonial strategies, relatives came to southern Lebanon to work as seasonal workers, as did many Syrian workers at the time. Despite the obstacles Lebanon enacted to limit the entry of Syrian Palestinians into its territory, such as those mentioned by Umm Maher's sister, there was still some movement of migrants/refugees between the two countries. It was always possible, though difficult, to obtain an entry visa for family reasons. Other Palestinians entered Lebanon illegally. It must be recalled that until 2005, Syria's military occupied much of Lebanese territory, and traffic at the border was very heavy. For some Palestinians in Syria, seasonal work in Lebanon represented an additional source of income. For example, Mohamed, a member of Umm Maher's extended family, went to Lebanon in 1999 for a few weeks to find work. He stayed with one of Umm Maher's sons. These migrations, for both family and economic reasons, helped to create a dense cross-border space of circulation. These families hosted relatives and facilitated their insertion on the local labor market.

In July and August 2006, Israel bombed Lebanon, destroying local infrastructure throughout the country. The South was particularly affected. Part of Umm Maher's family sought temporary refuge in Syria. Umm Maher's two daughters-in-law, who were Palestinians from Syria, tried to take their family to safety in Syria during the conflict. They left Tyre by car and headed towards the northern border. However, they were not allowed to cross the border, as the Syrian authorities refused entry to Palestinians from Lebanon during the war. Only the two sisters were allowed to enter Syria, because they had their Syrian Palestinian identity documents. Their husbands and children were registered as Palestinians from Lebanon. Legal constraints thus limit refugees' mobility. In these particular situations, family support networks are unable to play their role.

The Syrian Crisis: Re-mobilization of Family Migration Networks

The Syrian Conflict: Towards a New Exile for Palestinians

The conflict that began in 2011 pushed Palestinians in Syria back into a stateless situation and forced them to seek asylum abroad. The Syrian conflict left Palestinians in Syria in an ambiguous situation, oscillating between individual forms of protest and more structured opposition movements to the regime and to some parts of the Palestinian leadership (Napolitano, 2012). In 2018, a total of 120,000 of them fled Syria, according to UNRWA figures, heading mainly to countries in the region (Lebanon, Jordan, Turkey, Egypt) as well as Europe.[4] However, in Lebanon, this number decreased from more than 50,000 in 2015 to 31,000 in 2018, due to re-emigration, mainly towards European countries or a return to Syria.

This movement of refugees, largely overshadowed by the scale of the Syrian crisis, raises many questions about the status of refugees who are forced to leave their country of first settlement to seek asylum in another, outside of any framework of international protection (Bastaki, 2017). Unlike UNHCR, the UNRWA has a limited mandate of protection. As explained by Jalal al Husseini:

> The fact that Palestinian refugees have benefited from the humanitarian services of an agency, UNRWA, dedicated exclusively to their basic needs for more than sixty years has not yet filled this vacuum of protection. Although its relief, health and education activities have played a protective role in conflict, they do not replace the political and physical protection activities covered by UNHCR's mandate. (2015)

This displacement is an extension of other forced Palestinian migrations in the region and calls into question the asylum policies implemented by the states in the region (Doraï & Al Husseini, 2013). In countries bordering Syria, the relative closure of the border to Palestinian refugees contrasts with the welcome of Syrians, which is related to the specific and unique position of the Palestinian question in the region. The treatment of Palestinian refugees from Syria makes it possible to develop a more holistic view of the selectivity of migration policies in the Middle Eastern countries in a context of crises. In the field of forced migration, there is confusion between legal categories (refugees, asylum seekers, etc.) and those of the migrant experience (Zetter, 2007). Palestinians, although recognized as refugees in their country of registration, find themselves in a singular situation when they cross an international border. They remain stateless and deprived of formal protections. Lebanon, like some other Arab countries in the region, is not a signatory to the 1951 Geneva Refugee Convention. The category of "refugee"—with the exception of Palestinians who are recognized as refugees in the state where they have permanent residence—does not exist as such (Zaiotti, 2006).

Cross-Border Circulation and Asylum-Seeking

The migratory space developed by the Palestinians between Syria and Lebanon was mobilized again, this time more extensively, with the outbreak of the Syrian crisis. When hostilities began in Syria in early 2011, circulation between the two countries increased. Palestinian refugees from Syria left for Lebanon for many reasons: to escape the fighting in their area of residence,

[4] www.unrwa.org/syria-crisis (accessed 01/02/2018).

to access health care, or to escape a tense situation. As long as it was possible for them to circulate between the two countries, very few Palestinians decided to settle "permanently" in Lebanon. They moved back and forth regularly between Lebanon and Syria. The restrictions imposed by the Lebanese authorities regarding access to education, health, or the labor market, as well as the high cost of living, pushed Palestinians not to settle permanently Lebanon but rather to consider Lebanon as a temporary sheltering space. The escalation of the conflict in Syria and in particular the attacks on the Yarmouk camp in Damascus in December 2012 changed the situation radically. As long as the conflict lasted, a return to Syria was no longer an option for Palestinians, who how settled "for the long term" in Lebanon, in a highly constrained legal and socioeconomic context. In December 2013, a family originally from the Yarmouk camp had planned to go back to Syria in light of the many socio-economic difficulties they had faced since their settlement in Tyre; but in May 2014, this option was no longer possible. The destruction of a large part of the Yarmouk camp, the siege to which it is subject, and fighting between different factions and the Syrian regime completely destroyed their hopes of return. The temporary shelter turned into a search for asylum in time.

Like their counterparts who had settled in Lebanon decades before, just over half of the recently arrived Palestinian refugees from Syria were concentrated in one of the 12 existing refugee camps. Others settled in neighborhoods or rural informal settlements where there was a strong Palestinian presence. The geography of the Palestinian presence in Lebanon was not significantly modified by the new arrivals, with the exception of new settlements in the Beqaa Valley, which is close to Syrian border and a first stopping point for those who left Damascus by the main road that connects it to Lebanon. There was a densification of populated areas by Palestinians and a polarization of migration towards the outskirts of the main Lebanese coastal cities. This geography of asylum is based on the existing family relationships between the two groups in Lebanon and Syria. When the conflict escalated, the first Palestinians who sought refuge in Lebanon were those who had relatives there.

From Aleppo to Tyre

The region of Aleppo, home to Umm Maher's sister and her family, was not affected by the conflict at the start of the Syrian revolution. It was only after several months that the first family members went to Lebanon to find temporary refuge there. At this stage of the conflict, they sought to protect themselves from the fighting. The situation on the ground changed quickly and it became safe once again, so the family members decided to return to Syria. Until 2013, it was fairly easy for Palestinians to travel between the two countries. Umm Maher said that her family did not want to lose their jobs or interrupt their children's education. They also feared for their belongings and property in Syria. At that time, it was mostly women who sought refuge in

Lebanon, while the men remained in Syria to work.

It should be recalled that Palestinians in Lebanon are one of the most underprivileged communities in the Palestinian diaspora (Chaaban et al., 2010). Palestinians in Syria who sought refuge in Lebanon faced the same discrimination that Palestinians in Lebanon faced. After the Israeli invasions of 1978 and 1982, which destroyed much of the Palestinian infrastructure and forced the PLO to leave the country, Palestinian refugees were marginalized from the socio-political scene. This stigmatization of the Palestinian population in Lebanon was translated spatially by their high concentration in camps, more than 65 years after their exodus. These spaces are marked by the informality of housing and the lack of public infrastructure.

It was only when the situation deteriorated significantly and became unsafe that an increasing number of refugees stopped their movement between the two countries to settle in Lebanon long-term. The mobility restrictions imposed by the Lebanese authorities subsequently helped stabilize them in their second home country, for fear of not being able to return if they visited Syria, even for a short period. As they faced a protracted conflict, and with Palestinians in Lebanon having limited resources, the situation was very difficult for families that were unable to host relatives on the long term, as was demonstrated in the Shatila camp in Beirut (Abou Zaki, 2015). Mohamed, who had come to seek a better future in Lebanon in 1999, returned once again following the conflict in Syria. He tried to find a job. He also needed a medical treatment. He settled at Umm Maher's son's home. His family in Lebanon tried to help him, contacting a non-profit organization they were in touch with to help reduce the cost of his medical treatment. Tensions arose when the organization did not—or could not—afford to cover his medical fees. The situation was also fraught because the Syrian Palestinians in Lebanon could receive UNRWA assistance, which the Palestinians of Lebanon were not entitled to. Labor market tensions were also significant. Palestinians in Lebanon were confined to low-skilled and low-paying jobs. The influx of Syrians—and to a lesser extent of Palestinians from Syria—tended to increase competition in certain labor market segments, such as daily workers in the construction and agriculture sectors.

Due to these multiple challenges, as well as internal tensions within the family related to Mohamed's attitude, which was disapproved of by several family members, he was forced to leave Umm Maher's informal settlement. Family solidarity is fundamental when welcoming new refugees, but it is constrained by the limits that are inherent to the socioeconomic context the Palestinians live in. These networks of solidarity are not free of tension, and this can limit their impact in the long term. Another limitation is their inability, in some cases, to mitigate the effects of the legal constraints imposed on refugees. Starting in 2014, it became almost impossible for Palestinians to enter Lebanon from Syria. Umm Maher's family members were unable to find asylum in Lebanon, as the situation in the region of

Aleppo deteriorated sharply due to the fighting between the central government, the opposition, and the Organization of Islamic State.

The family was once again unable to come together because of a conflict. Umm Maher's sister, though she came to find temporary refuge at the start of the conflict, ultimately decided to return to Syria to stay close to her children and grandchildren who had stayed behind. Today it would not be possible for her to return to Lebanon if she wanted to get an entry visa.

From Settled Refugees to Precarious Asylum-Seekers

The absence of a legal framework for Palestinian refugees who are forced to leave their country of habitual residence (e.g., Syria in this case), as well as the specific legal treatment of Palestinian refugees by states in the region, raises the problem of secondary migration during conflict (Erekat, 2014). Secondary migration is often analyzed in the literature through the resettlement of refugees outside their area of first asylum to Europe or North America (e.g., Hein, 1993). The Palestinian case, despite its specificities, raises the question of refugee status and secondary mobility. The refugee status of Palestinians is linked to their country of residence. When they leave their country of residence, they do not fall under the mandate of the UNHCR and can only access limited humanitarian assistance provided by the UNRWA. Conflict tends to transform Palestinian refugees into asylum-seekers, and most of the time they are seen as illegal migrants in their country of temporary residence. As they are stateless, they cannot even seek the protection of their country of origin. The singularity of the Palestinian experience is related to the non-resolution of the Arab-Israeli conflict, to their stateless status, and their exclusion from the 1951 conventional asylum system. To what extent can this experience be considered unique in the field of social sciences research? As Michael Kagan (2009) notes, the "plight of Palestinian refugees offers lessons for others, and the norms and knowledge developed from other refugee situations offer a great deal for Palestinians." The Palestinian experience is very instructive since it sheds light on the question of cross-border mobility in the context of protracted conflicts. As protracted conflicts develop in the Middle East (Iraq, Syria, Yemen), the Palestinian experience can help us to understand and analyze the mobility of other refugees.

Since 2012, a growing number of family members from Syria began to seek temporary asylum in Tyre and were welcomed by their relatives. Some moved back and forth as long as the situation in Syria was relatively safe. Because they had close relatives in Lebanon, it was easier for them to obtain a visa until restrictions were established, than it was for Palestinian refugees without family ties. The establishment of a mobility system based on transnational family networks has facilitated the movement of Palestinian refugees from Syria. The forced dispersion of Palestinian refugees since 1948 has been turned into a resource in times of conflict. An expertise of migration has been built up over the years by different family members, with different mobility practices (marriage, visits, circular labor migration, etc.). These networks also facilitate access to economic opportunities and accommodation. Access to local resources is also facilitated, and ties are reactivated with family members living in third countries, such as the Gulf States or those in Northern Europe. Some family members attempt to resettle on their own with the help of family networks in countries like Sweden, Germany, or the United States. This raises the question of the role of transnational networks in shaping forced migration.

Since the mid-1990s, there has been growing interest in the relations between refugees and transnationalism (Shami, 1996; Al Ali et al., 2001; Wahlbeck, 2002). Studies of refugees' transnational activities have contributed to a more comprehensive analysis of the role of previous migration in shaping migrants' networks, bridging forced and voluntary migration. Black comments: "Focusing on the role played by refugees in transnational activities could help to dispel some of the more idealistic notions of transnationalism from below as a people-led process, which take advantage of processes of globalization and ease of travel in the modern world" (2001, p. 66). Refugee movements resulting from conflicts are often fashioned by previous migration flows and correlated network structures that are re-mobilized during the humanitarian crisis. Therefore, tracing a genealogy of Palestinian refugees from Syria between their place of habitual residence and Lebanon can help to better understand current forced migration processes and their connections with other forms of social organization built over time in a specific region.

References

Abou Zaki, H. 2015. "The Syrian refugees in the camp of Shatila: legitimacy of conflict and solidarity between" new "and" old "refugees" *Confluence Mediterranée*, 92: 49-59

Al-Ali, N., R. Black & K. Koser. 2001. "Refugees and transnationalism: The experience of Bosnians and Eritreans in Europe", *Journal of Ethnic and Migration Studies*, 27:4: 615–634.

Bastaki, J. 2017. "The Legacy of the 1951 Refugee Convention and Palestinian Refugees: Multiple Displacements, Multiple Exclusions", *Berkeley Journal of Middle Eastern & Islamic Law*, 8 (1). Available at: http://scholarship.law.berkeley.edu/jmeil/vol8/iss1/1

Benezer, G. & Zetter, R. 2014. "Searching for directions: Conceptual and methodological challenging in researching refugee journeys", *Journal of Refugee Studies*, 28 (3): 297-318.

Black, R. 2001. "Fifty years of refugee studies: From theory to policy", *International Migration Review*, 35: 57–78.

Chaaban, J., H. Ghattas, R. Habib, S. Hanafi, N. Sahyoun, N. Salti, K. Seyfert, & N. Naamani. 2010. "Socio-Economic Survey of Palestinian Refugees in Lebanon", Report published by the American University of Beirut (AUB) and the United Nations Relief and Works Agency for Palestine Refugees in the Near East (UNRWA).

Doraï, K. 2015. "From Syria to southern Lebanon. Course of Palestinian refugees seeking asylum", *European Journal of International Migration*, 31 (3): 103-120.

Doraï, K. & J. Al Husseini. 2013. "The vulnerability of the Palestinian refugees in the light of the Syrian crisis," *Confluence Méditerranée*, 87: 95-108.

Erekat, N. 2014. "Palestinian Refugees and the Syrian Uprising: Filling the Protection Gap during Secondary Forced Displacement", *International Journal of Refugee Law*, 26 (4): 581–621.

Hein, J. 1993. "Refugees, Immigrants, and the State", *Annual Review of Sociology*, 19: 43-59.

Ma Mung, E. 1999. "The dispersion as resource", *Cultures & Conflict*], 33-34, http: // conflits.revues.org/225

Richmond, A. H. 1994. *Global Apartheid. Refugees, Racism, and the New World Order*, Toronto, New York, Oxford: Oxford University Press.

Shami, S. 1996. "Transnationalism and refugee studies: Rethinking forced migration and identity in the Middle East", *Journal of Refugee Studies*, 9 (1): 3–26.

Sfeir, J. 2017. "Le Liban, pays de refuge. Généalogie des réfugiés arméniens, palestiniens et syriens (1915-2015)", *Relations internationales*, 4 (172): 39-50.

Wahlbeck, Ö. 2002. "The concept of diaspora as an analytical tool in the study of refugee communities", *Journal of Ethnic and Migration Studies*, 28 (2): 221–238.

PART TWO

CHILDREN'S MOVEMENTS ACROSS BORDERS

A LEFT-BEHIND CHILD FROM EL ALTO

PROTECTION STRATEGIES AND REDEFINITION OF KINSHIP TIES FOR THE CHILDREN OF MIGRANT WOMEN IN BOLIVIA

Robin Cavagnoud

Daniel, a Left-Behind Child

Daniel is a 16-year-old teenager living in El Alto, Bolivia. He has no siblings and never met his father. For the past 10 years, his mother has lived in Buenos Aires, Argentina, where she moved to work in a sewing factory. After her departure, Daniel moved to his grandmother's home, where his aunt, uncle and cousins also live. Following the death of his grandmother, Daniel's maternal aunt became his guardian, responsible for caring for him and raising him. Daniel is a left-behind child. Like many other children in Bolivia, he did not travel with his parents, in this case his mother, when she decided to emigrate. She preferred to entrust this care to his grandmother, then his aunt, two female members of her own family. Most of the left-behind children in Bolivia are the children of migrant mothers who have moved mainly to Argentina and Spain, and these parents have often experienced marital breakdown. Their unique individual situation raises questions that are at the intersection of blended families, protection strategies, redefinition of kinship ties, and the journey to autonomy in adolescence.

Bolivia: A Country of Female Emigration

Bolivia is a country that has historically experienced significant migratory movements, both internally and abroad. Since the mid-19th century, the presence of Bolivians in Argentina has been attested by several censuses.[1] This trend has intensified since the 1950s, with a focus on employment, initially in the agricultural sector in the north of the country and then in trade and textiles in Buenos Aires.[2] Since the 2001 economic crisis in Argentina and the terrorist attacks in the United States, Europe, and Spain in particular, has emerged as the new destination of choice for Andean migrants, particularly Bolivians.[3] In recent years, the share of the Bolivian population residing outside the national borders has been estimated at between 25–30%.[4] At the start of the 21st century, this increased significantly due to the combined effect of the prolonged deterioration of the labor market in Bolivia

[1] INDEC, La migración internacional en la Argentina.

[2] Grimson, "Relatos de la diferencia y la igualdad"; Sassone, "Migraciones limítrofes en la Argentina."

[3] Baby-Collin, Cortes, and Miret, "Andean Migrants in Spain."

[4] Hinojosa, Migración transnacional y sus efectos en Bolivia, pp. 6-7.

and the political crises in the period before Evo Morales came to power in 2006. Moreover, statistical sources of data indicate that there is a feminization of these migratory movements; the share of women among the Bolivian population living outside the country was as high as 70% at the end of the 2010s, and a majority of them, 52%, emigrated without their children.[5] Both the ECLAC and the OECD note this progressive feminization of migration throughout Latin America and a common choice of migrant women not to return to their countries of origin.[6] With regard to Bolivia, it is likely that domestic and conjugal violence lead women to choose this life project.[7] The majority of these women are mothers[8] and leave the country without their spouse or children.[9] At the same time, the results of a survey on living conditions[10] indicate that 52% of Bolivian emigrants of both sexes who emigrated for economic reasons over the past decade left their children in their country of origin. This unique feature of international migration from Bolivia, which is characterized by a feminization of persons leaving and their tendency to leave their children behind in their country of origin, is due to two factors. First, the availability of an extended family network that is able to care for these children, and second, the mothers' preference not to expose their children to the risks inherent to migration (uncertainty as to how they will be received in the host country, living conditions, discrimination, etc.), in addition to the costs related to travel (airfare, visas, etc.). Furthermore, the migration networks that connect Bolivia to Spain (or Argentina) are clearly feminized and are based on relational or family ties, which tend to favor women's integration into a segmented labor market in the destination country, where there is high demand for labor in the service industry (childcare, personal services, housekeeping) or the textile industry (in the case of Buenos Aires).

Mothers' Migration, Turning Point, and Their Children's Life Journey

A mother's departure raises the question of the care and protection of their children, who remain behind in her country of origin. While maternal migration has been identified as a turning point in a child's life course,[11] other studies have focused on the role of grandparents in caring for children[12] or the "sacrifice" caused by the departure of parents beyond national borders without their children.[13] Based on the portrait of Daniel presented here, this

---

[5] Arroyo, La migración internacional, p. 37.

[6] ECLAC, Latin America and the Caribbean. OECD, International Migration Outlook.

[7] Salazar, Jimenez, and Wanderley. Migración, cuidado y sostenibilidad de la vida.

[8] Román, Mientras no estamos.

[9] This trend is confirmed by a survey conducted in 2008 in Cochabamba, which revealed that 55.1% of migrant women leave on their own (Bastia, "I am going, with or without you").

[10] Encuesta de Condiciones de Vida, quoted by Arroyo Jiménez, La migración internacional, p. 37.

[11] Guaygua et al, La familia transnacional.

[12] Bastia, "Women's migration and the crisis of care".

[13] Dreby, Divided by Borders.

chapter offers an analysis of the situation of left-behind children, particularly as regards the new configuration of family dynamics and norms following the mother's departure, the extended family's role in protection and education strategies, the redefinition of kinship structures, and these children's plans depending on their mother's marital and reproductive situation in the destination country.[14]

Daniel's case study is part of a study conducted in 2012 and 2013 in the city of El Alto among a population of 30 children and adolescents aged 6 to 18 years old, whose mother, father, or in some cases both parents, migrated abroad, mainly to Argentina, Brazil, Spain, and Italy.[15] For these three different contexts (departure of mother, father, or both) the sample consisted of 17, 5 and 8 cases, respectively. The children interviewed were encountered through the *Fé y Alegría* school system, which has a vast network of elementary and mid-high schools located mainly in working class neighborhoods (Yunguyo and Villa Tunari) and white middle class neighborhoods (Villa Adela, 16 de julio) of El Alto. This allows some socio-economic diversification our samples.[16] These secondary schools, like other public and private schools in the city, have a large population of students whose mothers live and work in a foreign country. Thanks to their cooperation, we were able to conduct our interviews at the schools themselves.[17]

Our empirical material consists of life stories that describe each child's life from birth to the present. What makes this approach unique is that it focuses on the stories of the migrant mothers' children in their own words, their evaluation of their family's dynamics, and their feelings about the key events that have marked their lives to date. From a methodological point of view, the decision to focus on the children's narratives reflects the difficulty of interviewing other, non-migrant, family members outside of the school environment. Despite the absence of triangulation, which is an undeniable limitation on our research, our approach is unique because it allows us to study the children's subjectivity in detail, as well as the factual elements

[14] Cavagnoud, "Migrations féminines et reconfigurations familiales." Cavagnoud, "El impacto de las migraciones internacionales de mujeres bolivianos." Cavagnoud & Bruslé, "Le matricentrage comme stratégie de protection des enfants".

[15] This survey was carried out as part of a post-doctoral research project focusing on the ruptures and reconfigured entourages of children in precarious situations in El Alto, in coordination with the *Institut français d'études andines* (IFEA).

[16] Unlike the Cochabamba region, international migration away from El Alto is a recent phenomenon, as this city had essentially been a host city for rural migrants since the 1960s. However, it appears that the increasing feminization of migration and women's work in the destination countries (as domestic workers, in textile factories) are drawing the two regions closer together. For both locations, Spain has become a highly popular destination since the 2000s. In the absence of large-scale statistical surveys of this phenomenon, it is difficult to assert the unique character of female migration from El Alto as compared to migration from Cochabamba or Santa Cruz.

[17] Psychologists and school administrators distributed sign-in sheets to each class to identify students for whom at least one parent had migrated. As a result of this self-reporting, the number of migrants may in fact be underreported, due to the stigma the children face after their mother's departure

related to their mother's migration and their family situation since her departure. Firstly, this approach allows us to identify maternal migration as a structuring event in the child's life that has modified their personal life course; and secondly, it enabls us to study *a posteriori* the family reconfigurations that followed this departure. The data from this survey were analyzed using the *Ageven* form. This biographical tool allows us to situate in relation to one another all of the the significant events in a person's life (child =*ego*)[18] that have contributed to their personal history up until the day of the survey. The unit *t* in this form is expressed in years from the *ego's* birth to the time of the survey. The significant events in the individual's life journey are plotted on the appropriate trajectory (family, migration, home economics, school) to demonstrate a change or the starting point of an extended situation. This tool offers a dynamic approach that is conducive to studying the consequences of maternal migration over a long period and the phases of recomposition that follow this structuring event in their lives.

Daniel's Life Journey: From his Mother's Departure to his Aunt's Care

Daniel is 16 years old and lives in El Alto, a working-glass city bordering La Paz, Bolivia's political capital, situated on the Altiplano. He has no siblings and never met his father, who abandoned him before his birth. For the past 10 years, Daniel's 42-year-old mother has lived in Buenos Aires, Argentina. She works in a textile factory six days a week, with a work contract and social benefits (health coverage and paid vacation). She chose to migrate out of a desire for social mobility faced with the unstable labor market in the working-class areas of Bolivian cities (low wages and irregular income, lack of social protection). Unlike many Bolivian migrants who leave their home country for Spain or Argentina, Daniel's mother had no contacts or family network in Buenos Aires. While she was able to take advantage of the large Bolivian population in Argentina, this was more helpful in terms of finding employment than in dealing with the practical aspects of her move. Since she arrived in Buenos Aires, she has never changed jobs in the textile sector.

After his mother's departure, Daniel lived at his maternal grandmother's home, where his aunt, uncle and cousins also resided. He stayed there for the next six years. It is unclear where exactly his grandfather resides, but it seems that he travels regularly to the department of Béni while keeping close ties with the family in El Alto. After he turned twelve, Daniel and his mother decided he would go to Argentina to live with his mother. She lived with her new husband, who was also of Bolivian origin and had his own sewing workshop. The couple had three children, Daniel's half-brothers and sisters, aged 3, 5 and 7 years old. One of the main goals of this migration was the hope that Daniel would receive a better education in Argentina. However,

[18] In sociodemographic studies, *ego* is the name that designates the individual whose life story is being studied.

after just six months in Buenos Aires, Daniel began to have problems. He fought with his stepfather and was having trouble adapting to the Argentinian school system (he was held back a year because of his poor grades in history). This prompted him to return to El Alto and move back into his grandmother's home. Since his stay in Buenos Aires, Daniel has not seen his younger brothers and sisters again and has had almost no contact with them.

A few months after his return to Bolivia in 2008, Daniel's grandmother died of diabetes. Following her death, he was taken in by his maternal aunt, who was then 30 years old, and he lived with her, his cousins, and his three uncles—his mother's younger brothers. Having grown up with them since his childhood, he sees them as brothers, not uncles, in a kind of alternative kinship and substitute brotherhood. Similarly, he sees his grandfather as being the central paternal figure in his life since childhood.

Every two months, Daniel receives 50 dollars from his mother. The money is managed by his aunt, who uses it to pay for his daily expenses (mainly food, clothes, and school supplies). However, this is hardly enough to cover the costs of his schooling and other needs in their entirety. Every morning before he goes to middle school, and again in the afternoon after school, Daniel helps his aunt at her mobile cosmetics stand at the *Feria de la 16 de Julio*, one of the biggest bulk markets in South America. He organizes the products on the stand and helps customers while his aunt takes care of her children at home. He receives no income from this activity, which he and his aunt see as a form of mutual aid and exchange of services within the family.

Daniel feels that his academic performance is not very good and wants to join the army after high school. He doesn't like to tell his classmates that his mother lives in another country. She has only come back to Bolivia twice in the last four years, and he talks to her on the phone about once a month, which to him does not feel like enough, given their emotional attachment.

Daniel is a child who was left behind. Like many other children in Bolivia, he did not travel with his parents, in this case his mother, when she decided to emigrate. She preferred to entrust this care to his grandmother, then his aunt. Most of the left-behind children we encountered during our survey in El Alto in 2012 and 2013 were children of mothers who had migrated almost exclusively to Argentina and Spain, and who had experienced a marital breakdown; sometimes, as in the case of Daniel, this occurred even before the child's birth. These separations lead the child's abandonment by the biological father and an increase in the mother's exposure to precarious labor market conditions. For these women, migration is seen as an option that provides a reasonable route to better living conditions for both themselves and their family members, migrants and non-migrants alike.

Care for Left-Behind Children by Female Members of the Maternal Line

Female emigration generates a range of new family and parental configurations for children who do not migrate with their parents. In most cases, the families' histories are not marked by a single migration of one of the parents, but rather by a series of international movements that often involve both parents, who use the migration networks created by other family members, neighbors, or close friends. This is not the strategy observed in the case of Daniel's mother, but it is often used by migrants to reduce the risk of failure during the setting-up and job-seeking phase in their host country, thus optimizing the benefits of migration from their very first months in the country.[19] The majority of the time, migration that follows this type of organization does not include the children, who remain in the country of origin with their non-migrating family members. This choice can also explained by the uncertainty of the situation in the destination country in the first weeks and months after arrival, and by the differences between the school systems, which can impact the children's education. Reduced travel costs, a fear of being arrested in countries where migrants enter without a visa, and a fear of racism and discrimination also influence the parents' decision, especially that of mothers, to make the journey alone.

According to the survey results, the migration of the father on his own does not lead to major changes in how the family is structured. In the five cases we observed of fathers migrating alone, we invariably noted the transition from a two-parent structure (nuclear family or extended) to an extended single-parent family structure, which is broadened to include grandparents, especially maternal grandmothers. In this case, the majority of fathers migrate to Brazil and Argentina to work in textile factories and send a large portion of their wages back to increase their family's budget in their country of origin. After the father leaves, the children stay with their mother, who often is assisted at home by her own mother. This relative stability of the family configuration in this case is a stark contrast with cases where both parents migrate (the mother and the *ego*'s father or stepfather), and, even more strikingly, when just the mother migrates. In these cases, the woman who migrates may entrust the care of her children to her spouse, who is not himself migrating, or to her eldest children. This is possible in the case of a woman who was in a stable conjugal relationship prior to her departure. In these circumstances, migration is often the result of an event that pushes the mother to leave in order to earn a better income and overcome the hardships her family is facing. This is what happened to Pedro, an 18-year-old teenager, whose father's illness led the mother to migrate to Argentina, where her eldest daughter was already living, to seek a better income to be able to afford her husband's medical care. Another frequent scenario is to repay a loan taken out from a bank to purchase land and build a house. In these examples,

[19] Arroyo, La migración internacional, p. 41.

the father cares for and educates his children while the elder siblings, especially if they are girls, look after the youngest children.

However, in the majority of instances of female migration, the fathers do not appear to be in any way responsible for their children, who instead live with members of their extended family, without either of their parents. These are situations where a woman's migration most profoundly affects the lives of her children who remain in Bolivia. These situations lead to a new family composition and structure, bearing the marks of the mother's absence, the distancing or even abandonment of the father, and the creation of forms of extra-parental protection. This event can be described as a "turning point" because it causes a profound change in the children's status and usual social and emotional reference points.

> My mother went to Argentina when I was little. I was 6 years old at the time. She went there for work because at that time, it was difficult for her to find a good, stable and well-paid job in Bolivia. Her departure changed everything in my life. She left and we didn't live together anymore. That changed our whole family and all of my habits. (Daniel)

Female migration and the family reconfigurations it entails represent a turning point, or even an instability, for children who are used to a certain order and established family routine. They also give rise to the creation of transnational families and new parental relationships within the extended family following the rupture tied to the mother's departure.[20] Mothers embark on their migration project once they have found an acceptable solution for the care and protection of their children in their country of origin. For many women, this search for an appropriate strategy relies on female members of their biological family, such as their own mother (*ego's* grandmother) or sister (*ego's* aunt). Elder sisters, if they are in their twenties and have a sufficient degree of independence through work, can also care for their younger siblings after the mother migrates. The central role of women in the reproduction of the domestic unit and the care of children is a defining feature in Latin America, particularly in Bolivia, where the distribution of responsibility is largely determined by gender relations.[21] As a result, in cases of female emigration, the care, protection and education of children overwhelmingly fall to the maternal aunt, grandmother or older sister of the *ego*.

> When my mother left for Argentina, I stayed here and lived with my grandparents, mostly with my grandmother. My aunt also lived with me. Since my grandmother passed away when I was 8, my aunt–my mother's sister–has been taking care of me. Now I've been living with her for many years. Our house is in Villa Adela, here in El Alto. It used to be my grandmother's house. I've always lived here with my mom's side of the family. (Daniel)

The mothers' choice to entrust their children to women of their own

---

[20] Coe et al., Everyday ruptures.

[21] Salazar, Jiménez, Wanderley. Migración, cuidado y sostenibilidad de la vida. Dreby, Divided by Borders.

lineage corresponds to the search for a stable and trustworthy family member who will be able to provide the best possible future for their children. This matricentric female implication also demonstrates the importance of the "intermediate" circle of the nuclear family, such as the grandmother and the maternal aunt (this level falls between the restricted circle of the parents and the more distant peripheral circle of extended family or family friends).[22] This involvement also is a response to the relatively high instability of family units (due to separation, divorce, paternal abandonment), and therefore allows mothers not to tie their children's fate to marital uncertainty. Finally, when the children reside with their aunt, sibling-type relationships arise between the *ego*, his siblings, and his first cousins at their place of residence.

Transnational Motherhood, the Care Economy and the Transformation of Kinship Ties

Women's reliance on extended family in their own lineage to care for their children demonstrates a sort of "transnational motherhood,"[23] because, despite the distance, these women continue to fulfill their role as mothers through the maternal figures in their own families, who are part of their first emotional circle. This delegation of their children provides a guarantee for their education and the social continuation of the families of migrant mothers. In this reorganized family structure, an extended and transnational motherhood therefore plays a decisive role in exercising control over children and their social relationships. It is an agreement between the mother and the family members who care for the children, which gives the migration project its objective.

> First my grandmother, and then my aunt, promised to take care of me. They agreed on that before my mother left for Argentina. Now she sends my aunt $50 every two months to pay for my needs, which used to be taken care of by my grandmother and grandfather. My aunt mostly uses the money for school fees. (Daniel)

The mother reaches an agreement with other female family members with regards to the care and education of the children who remain in the country of origin. As an expansion of motherhood here, kinship, the network of female family members and their partners (brothers-in-law), plays an essential role in a form of a system of exchange of goods and services, in particular through the sending of financial (remittances) and material (care packages, photos) support. These interactions reflect an "economy of care" that maintains an equilibrium and sustains all the members of the family.[24]

Through transnational motherhood and the associated economy of care, a majority of left-behind children and adolescents hold a job outside of school hours, which allows them to contribute to the household budget of

---

[22] It should be mentioned our study did not identify any cases of children staying with family friends.

[23] Hondagneu-Sotelo & Avila, "I'm here, but I'm there."

[24] Anderson & León, La incorporación del género.

the adults they live with. Like Daniel, they work as assistants or salespeople for the family business, or have jobs as masons or bus ticket collectors, and their income is partly used for the family's daily expenses. Thus in many cases, the delegation of motherhood implies a form of payment, which demonstrates that the child's care is in fact part of a domestic exchange system. Many children report looking after the health and well-being of their grandparents, especially their grandmother, if she is very old.

> My aunt sells shampoo and stuff like that. She's a shopkeeper and I help her on Thursday mornings and all day on Sundays. I take the products out of the boxes and display them for the customers. I go to class at nine o'clock, and after school I come back to work. It's like that on Thursdays, and on Sundays I work all day. I talk to the customers and sell them the products, especially when my aunt is away taking care of my cousins during the day. I like working and and it seems normal to me, because it's my job to help my aunt with the family's needs. (Daniel)

Moreover, the transfer of migrant mothers' children to other family members, when the fathers do not take care of them, contributes to the creation of a new form of motherhood in their daily lives, shifting from a biological form based on the mother/child relationship to a "domestic" or "practical" form, arising from the relationship between grandmothers and grandchildren, aunts and nephews, or older brothers and sisters and younger siblings. This implies a redefinition of filiation, insofar as the mother's physical (through not emotional) presence is erased and replaced with a relationship across generations that does not stem from direct descent but a chosen and voluntary kinship. In this regard, girls frequently remark that their grandmother or aunt with whom they live is "like a mother to me." It is not uncommon for them to refer to them as "mom" and their grandfathers as "dad." This assertion is evidence of the construction of a dual maternal figure: on the one hand, the biological mother who migrated to improve the family's social mobility; and on the other, the domestic mother responsible the child's new daily life.

> My grandmother who died was like my mother, actually. I saw her as a mother. It's the same for my grandfather, even through I see him less; he's like my father. (Daniel)

This transformation of kinship tie reflects a rebuilding of the family through new forms of care and other forms of obligation and mutual aid. Family structures are reconfigured following the mother's migration to provide a new form of stability for the left-behind children, thus softening the social and emotional cost of the mother's absence. Although this is not true for Daniel, it is common for mothers to exercise control over their children remotely by calling often. Some children also report having difficult relationships with their mother when she returns to El Alto after being away for several years. In this case, the "practical" motherhood has taken precedence in their daily life over biological motherhood.

From a Dual Mother Figure to the Child's Independence

When the family is reorganized due to maternal migration, the extended and transnational forms of motherhood, embodied mainly by grandmothers and aunts, play a vital emotional and educational role, in addition to exercising control over children and their social relationships. This new form of kinship, which combines a "biological" part based on the uterine mother/child relationship and a "domestic" or "practical" part based on the relationship between grandmothers and grandchildren or aunts and nephews, changes over time according to the marital and reproductive situation of the mother in the destination country. Mothers who migrate alone to Spain or Argentina have very different fates, to say the least. While most of them remain single throughout their stay in the destination country, others, on the contrary, form intimate relationships, which usually result in the birth of one or two children, half-siblings of the children who were left behind in El Alto, as in Daniel's case.

Two categories of left-behind children emerge from the data in our study. First, there are the children whose life course is closely tied to the decisions and family organization due to maternal migration. They have mothers who do not enter into a new intimate relationship in their destination country. These mothers tend to send remittances that are significantly higher than average, covering both their children's needs and the repayment of a bank loan for the purchase of land and a house for their future return to Bolivia. These mothers maintain strong and regular ties to their children through the daily use of social media and online communication methods, such as Skype. They also send packages with toys and clothing for their children on a regular basis. These children demonstrate satisfactory academic results and a high level of involvement in their middle schools.

Daniel fits into second category of left-behind children, those whose mothers have formed a new intimate relationship in their destination country. Whether or not these children find their place in this new family is unpredictable and no longer based on a daily emotional bond. These children tend to perform less well in school than other students and have more job-oriented plans for the future when they finish school. Moreover, these children frequently report an emotional detachment from their biological parents, not just from their father, with whom some have had no contact since birth, but also from their mother, who is now part of a new family formed with her spouse and children from this new relationship. This estrangement from their biological parents is compensated by a stronger emotional bond with their grandparents and uncles, whom they see as their "parents," in a reconfigured form of kinship that stems from the mother's migration and new relationship in the destination country.

> My maternal grandparents' children, meaning my uncles, I actually see as my brothers. Since we lived together for a long time, we grew up together in the same house and they're young like me, they're more like my brothers than my uncles.

> They're my mother's younger brothers, so there isn't a big age difference. They're in their twenties and we're really close. (Daniel)

There are, however, nuances within this category of left-behind children, depending on the number and age of their siblings in the home country, as elder children play a more protective role with their younger siblings. At the same time, some of them wish to take advantage of better access to quality higher education where there mother lives, and are are motivated to leave Bolivia to join her.

More generally, these teenagers acknowledge feeling abandoned by their mothers. They are also more independent with regards to their daily lives. Often they have after-school jobs outside their families, and their plans for the future involve leaving the family after they finish their secondary education.

> My mother is coming to Bolivia for a few days in December for the holidays, but I won't see her much because she's not staying for long and she has to go to Oruro for my stepfather's sister's graduation party. My mother comes back to Bolivia once every two or three years but we don't see each other much. In Argentina, she has a house and everything she needs. Her life is there, and mine is here. We probably talk on the phone once a month at most. I miss her a little bit but not that much... Since I'm a teenager now, I have to be responsible for my own life and plan for the future by getting a job that lets me pay for everything I need. That's why I want to be a soldier and make a decent living. (Daniel)

This autonomy increases with age and leads to their independence from the family after secondary school, during their transition to young adulthood, when most left-behind children either choose to work rather than continue their studies, or migrate themselves to pursue higher education. In the example we have chosen, Daniel hopes to finish school to join the military and quickly find a job that will allow him to be independent from his mother in Argentina and his family in El Alto.

Conclusion

Daniel's case illustrates the fact that many women who decide to migrate to a foreign country in order to improve their families' socio-economic situation delegate the care of their children to female members of their own lineage (grandmothers or maternal aunts). The role of men is much less present. Although a separation or divorce before the mothers' migration may offer a partial explanation for this decision, it would seem that the importance of women for the care and protection of children in a male-dominated society is also at play in migrant women's decision to entrust women from their own families with the upbringing of their children. On the other hand, their decision to migrate to a foreign country may be rooted in more personal motives, such as the hope of finding fulfillment in a new marriage in the destination country, liberating themselves from their family's control in their home country, or the potential for finding a new, more stable and more lucrative career.

In addition to exploring the question of matricentrism and the role of the extended family in caring for left-behind children, the survey results allow us to study the life course and plans of these children in relation to their mother's migratory experience in the destination country, on a spectrum ranging from temporary migration for employment and a lasting, or even definitive, move, with a new marital relationship and the birth of children. Although left-behind children in the second category, like Daniel, tend to claim their independence from their family in late adolescence, some of them plan to migrate themselves to join their mother and take advantage of her presence in the destination country to enter a university system with a higher standing, either in Spain or Argentina, both of which offer a better education than Bolivia. Their life plans are less dependent on the choices of their mother and extended family. Nevertheless, these children have internalized a form of migration culture, which for some of them leads to a desire to migrate to seek social mobility by pursuing higher education outside Bolivia. In order to confirm this trend and ascertain whether these plans were fulfileld, it would be necessary to continue to observe these young people as they continue their journey beyond their temporary, circumstantial and constructed status of the left-behind child.

References

Arroyo, M. 2009. La migración internacional: una opción frente a la pobreza. Impacto socioeconómico de las remesas en el área metropolitana de La Paz. La Paz: PIEB..

Baby-Collin, V., G. Cortes, & N. Miret. 2009. "Les migrants andins en Espagne. Inscription spatiale et repérage de filières". Mélanges Casa de Velázquez 39 (1): 115-45.

Bastia, T. 2009. "Women's migration and the crisis of care: grandmothers caring for grand-children in urban Bolivia". Gender and development 17 (3): 389-401.

Bastia, T. 2012. "I am going, with or without you": autonomy in Bolivian transnational migrations". Gender, place and culture: a journal of feminist geography 20 (2): 160-77.

Cavagnoud, R. 2016. "Migrations féminines et reconfigurations familiales autour des enfants left behind en Bolivie". Amérique Latine Histoire et Mémoire. Les Cahiers ALHIM, 31.

Cavagnoud, R. 2014. "El impacto de las migraciones internacionales de mujeres bolivianas en el trayecto de vida de sus hijos no migrantes: el caso de El Alto". In M. E. Cosío Zavala & V. Rozée (eds.), Género en movimiento: familias y migraciones. México: El Colegio de México: 139-158.

Cavagnoud, R. & T. Buslé. 2013. "Le matricentrage comme stratégie de protection des enfants: le cas des migrations internationales de femmes boliviennes". Autrepart 66: 115-32.

CEPAL. 2006. América latina y el Caribe: migración internacional, derechos humanos y desarrollo. Santiago de Chile: CEPAL.

Coe, C., R. R. Reynolds, D. A. Boehm, J. M. Hess, & Heather Rae-Espinoza. 2011. Everyday ruptures. Children, youth, and migration in global perspectives. Nashville: Tennessee, Vanderbilt University Press.

Dreby, J.. 2010. Divided by Borders. Mexican Migrants and Their Children. Berkeley:

University of California Press.
Hinojosa, A. 2009. Migración transnacional y sus efectos en Bolivia. La Paz: PIEB.
Hondagneu-Sotelo, P. & E. Ávila. 1997. "'I'm here, but I'm there': the meanings of Latina transnational motherhood". Gender and Society 11 (5): 548-71.
INDEC. 1997. La migración internacional en la Argentina: sus características e impacto. Buenos Aires: Estudios, INDEC.
Guaygua, G. (coord.) 2010. La familia transnacional. Cambios en las relaciones sociales y familiares de migrantes de El Alto y La Paz a España. La Paz: PIEB.
Grimson, A. 1997. "Relatos de la diferencia y la igualdad: los bolivianos en Buenos Aires". Nueva Sociedad 147: 96-107.
Román, O. 2009. Mientras no estamos: migración de mujeres-madres de Cochabamba a España. Cochabamba: UMSS, CESU.
Salazar, C., E. Jiménez & F. Wanderley. 2010. Migración, cuidado y sostenibilidad de la vida. La Paz: CIDES-UMSA.

JOURNEY TO THE ORDINARY "INTEGRATION" OF AN UNDOCUMENTED MOROCCAN MIGRANT IN FRANCE

Mustapha El Miri

In answer to the question: "How would you describe your experience, since you left Morocco, stowed away in the hold of a fishing boat, and all the way to your present situation in France?" Réda replies, without hesitation:[1]

> It's been quite normal. I'm like everyone else. I have a family, children, a house, a job. Everything's OK [...] It's true, I've been lucky, sometimes it's been hard, but the result has been positive and I'm happy that things are all right. The only thing I'd say about my life is that you mustn't be afraid to work, and then after that things run smoothly [...] My life is quite ordinary, I feel OK [...] I think this is what most people want: just to have an ordinary life.

If we can understand Réda's view of his experience—as something normal and focused on the finished result rather than how it happened—it is interesting to note that it is based on it being an ordinary life story, when it is in fact extraordinary. Though today, Réda has a typical lifestyle for his generation and current social class—lower-middle class—his life experience is characterized both by a rapid social upward mobility and a series of unstable and insecure social statuses.

Réda was left out of the family reunification by his father to make repatriation easier administratively for the rest of the family and was entrusted to the care of someone close to the family.[2] He was separated from his mother, father, brothers, and sisters for several years when they settled in France, at the end of the 1980s, and Réda then sought to join them, using his own means and without their help, which was slow in coming. After several costly and unsuccessful clandestine journeys to Spain, he finally managed to cross the border and found a job through a network of Moroccan immigrants from the same Berber community as himself.[3] He worked without authorization in Spain for a long period of time as an agricultural worker and was finally given a residence permit. After acquiring legal resident status, he made regular visits as a tourist (sometimes clandestinely) to his family in the south of France. His regular visits to the Bouches-du-Rhône region led to him forging links with other members of the Moroccan community in France and contracting an "arranged" marriage with the daughter of a naturalized

[1] We have used a pseudonym to keep our study anonymous.

[2] Family reunification is strictly limited by the level of resources and the minimum surface area available in accommodation in comparison to the number of family members. These provisions have been continually restricted by legislation in France (the law of November 26, 2003, of July 24, 2006 and of November 20, 2007).

[3] The Berbers, although a majority in the population, constitute a non-Arab minority in Morocco. Their language and customs began to be officially recognized in the 1990s.

immigrant.[4] After his marriage, he was given resident status and could begin the ordinary process of economic and social integration in France.

Réda's experience of migration did not follow a straight line, and required him to cross different types of borders and boundaries:

- Geographic: Before traveling to Spain as an undocumented migrant, he first had to leave Morocco. This first step conditioned the others, since the success of migration depends on the network of people-smugglers chosen. The second border to cross was in Spain, and the issue was not only to enter but to stay there. The status of an undocumented migrant makes the confrontation with the border and the necessity of crossing it unnoticed each day part of immigrants' daily lives (Stephan Le Courant, 2010).

- Social: Once he had crossed the geographic borders, there still remained the social, social-cultural and socio-racial boundaries (Park, 1928, 1950; Fassin, 2010; Mbembé, 2016). The change from being a citizen, to an undocumented migrant, to an employee with a steady job and resident status, from being an agricultural worker in southern Spain to a temporary worker in the south of France, from being a laborer on a building site to the foreman of a major public works company, from being a foreigner to a French citizen, all called for continual social readjustments. It required him to adopt the codes and norms that each status involves without breaking with the previous ones. Integration works here not as the adoption of the mainstream culture, but as the capacity to link up with several social classes, across several socio-racial boundaries: to cross the social boundaries on a daily basis through family, professional and social-life networks, to unconsciously organize communications between different social environments and different cultures, and to become the bearer "of multiple elective identities" (Judt Tony, 2004).

Réda's situation is representative of the experience of a number of migrants we met all through our investigations (El Miri, 2011, 2014). He illustrates the ordinary and invisible adaptation (Favell, 2001) of legal and illegal migrants to a multitude of sometimes contradictory norms. He also shows how one can get around administrative and social constraints by mobilizing resources:

- Collective: the experience of migration of Moroccan pioneers, who are the sources of information and road maps for those who leave later; the community networks (Massey 1990), providing sites of passage and transit; the ties of family and friendship that are a source of reciprocal solidarity regarding information, logistics and funding; the network of employers of authorized and unauthorized migrants result in a kind of map being created and passed on through the principle of co-optation.

- Individual: the determination to carry out the migratory project, despite the dangers and obstacles; the initial reduction in wage and income ambitions by joining a "low-cost" labor force; the increase in work capacity; adopting forms of communication in line with all the local norms; the obligation to respect a form of social transparency and discretion in public areas.

[4] Arranged marriages are organized by families who agree to their children's union. In many cases, an intermediary (a member of the family, a member of the community or the neighborhood) arranges the union.

The Meeting (Methodology and Justification)

The case of Réda as presented in this article is based on materials collected during an ethnographic study into migration, which was carried out in Morocco, southern Spain, and the south of France. We made several visits (over 12 months in all) to Morocco and southern Spain, as well as meeting several people in the south of France (in the towns of Berre, Marseille, Avignon, and in the Vaucluse region). During this study, we met almost 200 migrants (most of them Moroccans, plus 30 migrants from sub-Saharan Africa traveling through Morocco) in their workplaces, at their homes and in public places (bars, shops, weddings, baptisms, religious events). What makes our research stand out is that we followed the journeys of some 50 migrants over all these years and tracked the changes in their migratory status, their jobs, marital status, and way of life.

Speaking Arabic and/or French, we conducted formal and informal, individual and group interviews; with participant observation fieldwork on migrants, but also on some of their family members who had stayed in Morocco. We also looked at interactions with the local populations in the regions where migrants had settled.

At the beginning of the study, I met Réda at the wedding of an agricultural worker in the south of France. At that time, he was an agricultural worker in Spain and had come to see his family in France. At each of these visits, he attended as many events as possible that were organized by the Moroccan community (weddings, baptisms, engagement parties) to broaden his network of contacts. These ceremonies were meeting places and social-community footholds for migrants who lacked security (regarding their stay in Europe). Individuals with different statuses mixed here: seasonal workers, residents, undocumented migrants, naturalized citizens, and second-generation children. Hence, they represented particularly advantageous occasions for making contact with different migrants and promoting a dialogue between the researcher and research subjects, which were nonetheless obtained at the price of sustained efforts outside of this context. My presence at this wedding, along with the goal of maintaining a network of contacts, was aimed to make contact with migrants whose experience had begun in "illegality." This was how I met Réda during the wedding through a contact we both knew. Although my identity as a researcher and the themes of my study were explained to Réda, our relationship grew afterwards due to generational and cultural proximity (since we come from the same country).

> You want to understand what a hard time we had [...] you've never experienced that yourself, have you? Here, you could talk to anyone and you'd hear life stories like that (people who have had a hard time).

From our very first conversation, Réda associated the idea of hardship with the past, and didn't link it to his economic and social situation—unlike (Dubet, 1987) in reference to youth from immigrant families in poorer areas—but to his status as an undocumented migrant. For me, Réda's experience was a chance to study the lives and processes of undocumented migrants' integration into urban lifestyles in European society.

Presented as undesirable elements in political discourse or as disaffiliated (Castel, 1995) by some humanitarian associations in Europe, undocumented migrants in fact form professional and social groupings. But this silent social membership goes hand in hand with low visibility in the public space, to the point where changes in status and ordinary integration, often including upward mobility, are obscured. To grasp how this requirement for low public visibility and silent social insertion develops in the experience of migrants, I became interested in undocumented immigrants. A project like this can only be conducted over a relatively long time frame and requires individual follow-up on migrants for as long as possible. The challenge is to grasp the change in status, the capacities to cross the various borders (geographic and social) demonstrated by undocumented or insecure migrants all throughout their migratory experience.

I have followed Réda from our first meeting until today. In addition to the information about his past and his first attempts to cross the Moroccan and Spanish borders, I have witnessed his social insertion as it took place. The process was discussed during regular meetings where the formal interviews in the beginning were replaced by ethnographic field notes. Réda's case is only representative of certain male and generally young migrants. Nonetheless, the study of the procedures of how resources were mobilized to get around issues and the confrontation with the hardships involved in multifaceted integration (we have in mind all the forms of integration occurring during the migrants' experiences) can teach us about the capacity for linking the multiple identities of migrants (authorized or not) and prompt us to take issue with the idea of integration or assimilation in their generally accepted sense.

Context

Réda's migration took place in a sociopolitical and economic context marked by messages that are contradictory for migrants. In the main destination countries for migrants, the political message conveyed by public policy, the different laws and the governments, is characterized by limiting immigration figures and tightening residence policies (Wihtol de Wenden, 2013; Tassin, 2014), as is shown in the recent agreement about refugees signed by the European Union and Turkey. The electoral debate is often marked by a focus on the theme of immigration, and hostility to it is shown by xenophobic political parties, but also, more and more frequently, by the "traditional" parties. This openly proclaimed message of political inhospitality is counteracted by a message transmitted by the migratory networks for economic integration, at the margins of the agricultural, tourism, building and care sectors (Lénardo & Imdorf, 2012; Chauvin, 2009), and in subcontracting and temporary work. The context of economic globalization and outsourcing of part of European industry towards the countries in the South that are a source of migrants reinforces the idea among candidates for migration that there is an opening in the European job market. The migratory routes often follow the routes to work that are open to legal and undocumented migrants. The reasons to leave, as for Réda, are often backed by the certainty of formal or informal economic integration. The action of European leaders to limit the number of migrants crossing borders is undermined by the fact that national borders take second place to the borders of the job market, which extend beyond national entities. Migration is part of this context of tension between the political aims anchored in local and national debates and the economic aims guided by issues of internationalization. Immigration, which was seen in the 1960s as a source of unskilled labor that would cost national economies very little, is today experienced as an indicator of globalization, or even as the destabilization of national harmony (both economic and sociocultural). The migrant has gone from being the social representative of a subordinate (at work and in social life) to having the status of an unfair competitor (in work, welfare payments, or even lifestyles). This is shown by the restriction of access to social protection measures implemented in some countries in Europe, and the debate that has been launched about these questions in others (Antecol & Bedard, 2006). These changes and this new tension concerning the migratory question have redirected the debate about immigration, shifting it from economic themes and the needs of the employment market to social themes based on the changes in lifestyles, and on conflicting norms and values.

In these circumstances, Réda needed to combine participation in community networks that have strong visibility in Europe with individual invisibility. Setting out "illegally" from Morocco, Réda represented the unwanted economic and social figure in Europe. This pressure would have an impact all through his journey on the price of crossing the borders, but also on his working conditions and his relations with other members of the community that had settled in Spain and France. But this vulnerability produced in him, as it does in other migrants in the same situation, a form of activation of social practices, prompting him to break free of fragility as quickly as possible. Réda's crossing of the borders (both geographic and social) appears in this context as a permanent readjustment between his aspiration to access the urban way of life in European countries and the stages and obstacles that need to be overcome to reach it.

Life Story

Réda was born in Morocco near Khemisset, in the Rabat-Salé-Kénitra region. He was the second of six children, but was considered the eldest because his elder sister, who is six years older than him, married when she was 18 and left home. His father left Morocco in the 1970s and worked as an agricultural worker in market gardens in the south France. All through his childhood and teenage years, Réda was in indirect contact with France, through:

- Regular remittances from his father, representing a proof of the promise of a change in lifestyle provided by wage work in Europe.

> My father used to send my mother a postal order at the end of each month. Since the rest of our family knew this, my uncles and aunts generally paid us a visit at that time of the month and asked my mother to lend them some money.

- His father's annual return for the holidays with the things he brought back from France.

> I remember that as soon as my father got back, we opened his suitcases to see what he'd brought us. Generally, he used to bring toys, clothes, food, like chocolate, coffee and sweets, perfume, shaving cream, soap and other stuff. You could find this sort of thing in Morocco, too, but what he brought back had a special taste. It came from France, we looked at the packaging as much as the products inside. There were pictures that represented Europe, and that was the most important thing for us. I remember that I had a cap with "Marseille" on it. My friends always wanted to borrow it so they'd look French.

Long before they left for France, Réda and his family were socialized into the material way of life of the French working classes through these exchanges with the father and the idea of upward mobility that is widespread today. Although they lived in a village in Morocco, they were gradually seen as urbanized in the eyes of the other villagers.

> My father renovated and upgraded our house. At that time, we were the first ones in the neighborhood to have running water, a fridge, a color TV and even air-conditioning. Later on, the neighbors who had money did the same [...] Then my mother wanted a washing machine, because she'd heard about that [...] Everyone wanted something more modern.

This socialization and upward social mobility in the family led them to want to leave for France in the 1980s. Réda's mother put pressure on his father so that they could all join him in France. This request was part of a process of competition with other migrant families, who began to leave for France from the 1980s. Modern home appliances were no longer enough to stand out socially and leaving for France came to be a new form of social distinction (El Miri, 2011).

> My mother nagged my father each time he came back. She made a long list of all the families who'd gone to live in France. For her, the problem was what the other villagers would say: your husband doesn't care about you, he won't manage to get you to France. That was the kind of stupid thing you heard at the time. But it worked: what finally prompted my father to act was when his cousin moved his family to France. He didn't want to seem inferior to his cousin.

"Abandoned"

The day the family had long been waiting for arrived in 1984: the process of family reunification had been launched by his father, and the family started to prepare for the idea of finally going to live in France. But Réda, who had just turned 18, was told a few months before the departure that he would not be going with them. His parents explained to him that, according to the family reunification process, it would be complicated for him to join them, due to his age. Moreover, his father only earned minimum wage, which meant he could not prove he could take care of five children, including the rent for a big enough home for all of them, as required by law.[5] The family decided to organize the departure in two stages: the first stage with the mother, the two younger brothers and the two younger sisters; and then a second stage with Réda. But his father tied this decision to "abandon" Réda to traditional local cultural codes[6] by asking Réda, the eldest son, to look after the house and the family's plot of land.

> My father invited my sister, her husband, his brother, and his sister-in-law to dinner to explain why they were going. There he told everyone that they'd decided that I would be staying behind to look after the house and take care of the family's affairs and he asked my sister to help me. But the truth is, it was his decision [...] It wasn't easy to pretend I was happy, because I would have liked to go with them [...] but in the old way of thinking in Morocco, you can't say: "No, I don't want to," when your father tells you, "Now you're the man of the house, everything depends on you." The only thing I found reassuring was that I knew that my turn would come to go with them, and all the rest was just old folks' talk.

The cultural aspect of the traditions invoked by the father had no persuasive effect on Réda, but accentuated a feeling of "abandonment," which the distance in their relations increased throughout the period of separation. Just after the family left for France, Réda's mother would call him twice a week, but the contact between them weakened over time and was limited to a monthly phone call and irregular remittances to help Réda pay for the upkeep of the house in Morocco. The promise that he would join his family also faded to the point that it was no longer mentioned by his parents. His family's first return to Morocco for the holidays was a major event in Réda's life.

> One year later, my family came home for the holidays. My two brothers and sisters spoke French fluently. They'd changed, and it was strange, I felt like I was meeting them for the first time. It was as if this was a new family that I didn't belong to anymore. That was when I realized I would have to get by on my own if I wanted to go to France, too [...] As he was leaving, my father said: see you next year! That

[5] The decree of November 10, 1977 restricted family immigration. Admission to the country through family reunification was suspended for three years, except for family members who did not request access to the job market. This decree was canceled by a decision of the French Council of State on December 8, 1978 after an appeal made by the GISTI (*Groupe d'information et de soutien aux travailleurs immigrés*), the CFDT and CGT trade unions. The Council of State's decision restated the principle of the right to family reunification as resulting from the general principles of law. See the decree of December 4, 1984 and the memorandum of January 4, 1985 relating to the application of the procedure of permission given to members of immigrants' families to enter France.

[6] These codes are maintained by the legislation on inheritance, which grants a larger share to boys than to girls, and places them in real terms as responsible for the inheritance as a whole.

meant that his ideas had changed, too. My mother still said she was going to arrange for me to come, but she couldn't really do much /

Learning to Cross Borders

Two years after his family left, Réda set off for Europe in turn. His married sister, who lived in the same village in Morocco as him, helped him to pay the people-smugglers (1,500 euros) for a first attempt to reach Spain. Réda made contact with the people-smugglers' network through colleagues and asked Moroccan migrants living in Spain about the prospects of finding work in the industrial agriculture sector. Réda's aim was to work in Spain and to move to France later.

> I remember the evening I crossed over. We were all on the beach at about one in the morning. There were about 20 of us. I was afraid, but I was looking forward to getting across and I was so excited that I forgot for a while that I couldn't swim. I only remembered when I was on the boat and it started to pitch about. I remember the silence; no one spoke during the crossing, not a word, until the guy (the people-smuggler) suddenly shouted out: "Go on! Jump, it's only 200 meters; if you don't jump, you'll have to go back to Morocco with me." So, I jumped with the others and we found ourselves in Spain in the darkness on the beach.

After this first crossing, Réda spent about two months in Spain and found work on a farm in Murcia. He was introduced to the supervisor by a Moroccan migrant from the same region as Réda. But two months after this promising beginning, he was deported after the police stopped him after he had run a red light.

> We were coming back from work. Usually I went straight home, but this time I wanted to go and have a drink with a colleague. We turned into the town's main road and at the red light my friend braked at the last minute. There was a policeman standing there. He came over and at once I knew that it was all over. We made the mistake of going from work right through downtown without even getting changed. It was as if I'd put a sign on the car, saying: "We don't have a residence permit."

For Réda, as for migrants with the same status, crossing the border was part of daily life. Any visit to the town, all his dealings with the authorities, any conflict at work or outside could lead to him being deported. Migrants generally learn the "map" of these borders all through their stay (Stephan Le Courant, 2015) and through the experience of other migrants. Acquiring this information on the ground, the conflicts, interactions that need to be avoided and the least risky routes in the area,all this is gained by experience and/or passed on by a "tutor" (family member, friend).

Back in Morocco, Réda, immediately started planning to leave again, but was now wiser from his experience, which he saw as a partial failure. He could not again call on his sister, who had already helped him make the first trip. Réda had to pay for the journey himself and borrowed 1,000 euros from friends for the new attempt. But this was not enough for him to pay the more trustworthy people-smugglers.

> The problem was that you needed at least 2,000 euros to be sure to get across. For less than that, you ended up with the Senegalese. The people I knew who set off with them turned back after less than 600 meters, because the boat was filling up with water.

In his search for a way to set off again, Réda moved to the departure towns and looked for a job working with fishermen in Al Hoceima (a coastal town in northern Morocco). After a few months in the area, he met the owner of a small fishing business who agreed to help him cross the Mediterranean for 1,000 euros. In addition to the professional people-smugglers working in these areas, there were individuals working on an occasional basis who saw the activity as a source of extra income.

Réda set off in the hold of the fishing boat and was put ashore on the Spanish coast in the middle of the night. This time, he took care to prepare his trip and organized his arrival before setting out. He had a shared apartment and was able to return to the same farm where his work had been appreciated.

Finding Roots in the Community to Gain Freedom as an Individual

Back in Spain, Réda had a single objective: to get a residence permit and free himself of the daily dependence on the border:

> I didn't want to make the same mistake as the first time, when I wanted to live (have fun) before I had a secure home. I had to pay back my sister for the first trip and my friends for the second. I tried to stay in one place for work and we'd meet up in each other's homes for the first six months [...] to relax and have fun.

During this first year, Réda's life revolved around work, where he spent over ten hours a day. This meant he could repay his debts and save money, since his leisure activities were non-existent. He spent the first phase of this stabilization period among the community of Moroccan agricultural workers. The network of sociability he forged helped him find a rented apartment on his own, extra jobs when he had a day off from his main employer, people to open a bank account on his behalf, and other services requiring official proof of identity. Membership in the community was also required by employers as a guarantee of stability. Employers were reassured by the fact that mixing people with different statuses (residents, seasonal workers and undocumented migrants) did not give rise to conflict. The racialization of work, an inheritance from the 19th century, which attributes physiological, mental and behavioral characteristics to natives of the former colonies (Dornel, 1995) continues to be seen in recruitment and labor management practices used by employers.

Stereotypes about the "disciplined Moroccan agricultural worker" are adopted by the undocumented migrants themselves to give them access to some sectors of the labor market:

> One day my boss came to see me and said: "Réda, you're not in good shape right

now. You're not doing as many crates [of melons]. You think about girls too much, you watch too much TV, or you go out drinking. It's as if you're not a Moroccan anymore or something. Look at Hamed, he's been the same since he arrived. Get back to work, don't let the young people around here influence you [the Spanish natives]. They're lazy, they just think about going out... That's when I understood I had to be careful not to let some things show [...], for example, not to speak Spanish too well and to watch how I dressed. You had to fit the image of a Moroccan from the countryside if you wanted to be left in peace and pretend you still didn't understand anything. For them, a real Moroccan worked like a dog without understanding anything.

This way of presenting oneself adopted by Réda corresponds to the reification of the unauthorized Moroccan migrant by the employers. It is a kind of inversion of the stigma that can be found here, with the aim of attaining a kind of invisibility at work.

In fact, anchoring oneself in the community helps people to access a form of individual freedom from certain constraints and to take a first step towards adapting to the way of life in Spain. For the first five years after arriving in Spain, Réda stayed in contact with his family in France. He visited his parents two or three times, taking the risk of an identity check. But the experience he had acquired helped him understand the codes governing visibility in public spaces. Although employers thought a form of rural and Moroccan identity should be displayed, the opposite was required in the social world outside of work, especially in urban areas. The goal was not to attract the attention of the police, and for the rest, adopting the attitude of urban populations that (Simmel, 1984) called "reserve" was a way to blend in with the crowds.

Resident Status in Spain

After five years as an undocumented migrant in Spain, Réda was living a rural way of life at work and an urban lifestyle in his free time. He had an apartment, a car, and substantial savings, and began to take steps to acquire legal status from the Spanish authorities. To his surprise, his request was accepted, and he was given a residence permit:

I remember the day I got the answer: a friend brought it to me because I'd given his address to the authorities. I thought he was mistaken and I couldn't believe it. I sent my colleague on my behalf and they told him that I'd have to come myself to pick up the papers [...] It took me a while to understand. At first I was still being careful in the street about the police, even when I had my permit.

Thanks to this new status, Réda could buy a small apartment in an urban district of Murcia with the money he had saved over the first five years, when he focused mainly on work. In just a few months, he went from being an undocumented migrant to a legal resident and property owner. After his situation became legal, Réda changed jobs and went to work in the building sector as a worker. Going from a rural to an urban environment helped him forge new forms of sociability based on intergenerational and interpersonal relations that were no longer limited to the Moroccan community. Among his friends were Sub-Saharan Africans and young Spaniards, as well as his existing friends. His work in the building sector brought him into contact with other social classes, too, and he did undeclared work for private individuals from the local middle classes, as well as acting as a go-between for other unauthorized migrants in search of work, including his cousin.

Official status also meant Réda could visit his parents more often. His trips were more and more frequent and led him to develop new social networks with the Moroccan community in the south of France. He even played a supportive role for his family by giving his parents money and renewed his close ties with them, and especially with his mother.

Moving to France

Réda's mother asked him to come, as often as he could, to the ceremonies (weddings, baptisms and even funerals) she was invited to. The aim was to have him meet young women living in the south of France and help him find a suitable partner for marriage. The first goal of Réda's migratory process was to move to France: first, to join his family and then to acquire the French resident status, which is much more highly valued in Morocco (El Miri, 2011). This dual motivation prompted him to agree to a marriage in France. Marriage would also help him acquire stability, without having to return to the undocumented status he had experienced in Spain.

Through a "matchmaker," he met a young French woman of Moroccan origin who was following a similar process through the same network. While traditional arranged marriages are rejected by the daughters of migrants (Lltaief W., 2007), the development of arranged meetings through websites and other methods has helped to revive such rituals, turning them into new ways of forming couples in urban societies. Calling on the services of a matchmaker is no longer seen as the same as a traditional arranged marriage. The young woman with whom Réda made contact was a civil servant and was taking part in the process on her own initiative through a network of friends. After several meetings, they decided to live together and then to get married to give their relationship official status. The future couple did not take up a request made by Réda's parents to be married according to the customs of their home country. Réda took care of the entire process and asked the matchmaker to organize the wedding ceremony, which established Réda as a resident in France, in the town where his fiancée lived. The use Réda made of a community network in the migratory process ended up reinforcing his individual autonomy and his detachment from the cultural norms of his parents' generation.

After settling in France, Réda applied to temp agencies and found a job just after his wedding. His rapid recruitment as a temporary building worker was linked to his experience in the sector but was mainly due to his status as a newly arrived immigrant, which he chose to highlight. Réda made use of the racialized form of recruitment he had come across in the agricultural sector in Spain, where migrants who are thought to be culturally non-integrated are preferred.

> When I arrived, the secretary asked me how long I'd been in France and if I had a residence permit. That was the first question she asked, so I saw what she was looking for. I told her I'd just arrived and that I understood French, but I wasn't fluent [...] She said it didn't matter. Two days later she called me back with a job.

Réda's two brothers, who had arrived in France as children, are unemployed and are seldom contacted by temporary work agencies. This ethnicization of work, attributing to new arrivals a form of natural docility and endurance, produces two kinds of discrimination: one that is "positive," resulting in the acceleration of occupational integration of the new arrivals, even though it is racialized; and one that is negative (Tucci et al., 2013), legitimizing views about the refusal to work and to integrate among young people born or having grown up in the country. This dual process can be seen in Réda's family, with the two brothers who grew up in France who are unemployed and very seldom contacted by temporary work agencies, like most of the young people living in the area.[7]

Réda worked with the temporary agency for two years without interruption. Work on building sites lasting a few days was soon replaced by jobs continuing for several months. He was then "poached" by a public works company, where he worked for over six months, to the regret of the temp agency.

A few years after joining the Mallet company, he was promoted to foreman. The fact he spoke Spanish, Arabic, and French fluently helped in this promotion, since he was asked to manage workers on temporary assignment from Spain and migrants from the Maghreb:

> My boss offered me the job. I didn't have the most seniority, but he noticed I spoke Spanish with the other workers and Moroccan. He asked me where I'd learned the language, and I told him I'd worked in Spain. So, after that, he put all the foreign workers who'd just arrived in my team.

This new, unexpected status for Réda helped him to imagine buying a house with his wife and moving away from the working-class neighborhood where they were living. The family has three sons, and Réda and his wife attach great importance to their education (Kao & Thompson, 2003), while signing them up for a wide range of activities (music, judo, private lessons) that are mainly attended by children from middle-class families. Their planned move was part of this strategy in pursuit of academic excellence for the children and a way to distance themselves from stigmatized areas and schools (G. Felouzis, Perroton Joëlle, 2009). Réda justifies this attitude about the effect of the neighborhood by referring to the experience of his parents

[7] The unemployment rate of young people under age 25 in this area, inhabited mainly by families of Moroccan migrants, is 25%.

and brothers, while his wife speaks to the positive experiences of her parents and brothers, as well as her colleagues at work. They both describe their departure from the neighborhood where they were living as a necessity for their children's future, but also as a desire to escape from a restrictive collective space (that is both communitarian and working class).

The educational aspirations they have for their children produced a cultural distance from the working-class population, and also from the community. Réda now lives in a single-family home with a garden in a middle-class housing development with his wife and three children. Réda's way of life is at the intersection of different social and ethno-racial groups. These groups are formally constituted by the contacts the couple maintains with Moroccan migrants, with Réda's parents, his wife's friends, through his children and the parents of their friends, his co-workers, his former and current neighbors, as well as the members of his family in Morocco (his sister, cousins, uncles and aunts). It has become a *cultural "border crossing"* with an identity linked more to an abilityto share references (social, cultural and ethno-racial) than to a sense of belonging.

Theoretical Discussion

Despite his silent social integration, Réda represents the epitome of the imaginary figure of otherness, as a migrant and unauthorized resident. Although thousands of migrants have the same experience of invisible social mobility as he had, they represent a political and social issue in debates, since they are the most visible signs of the ethno-racial tensions running through host societies for migrants. Thus, this integration is silent since it is masked by a tempestuous debate about migrants from former colonies in France and in Europe. The debate is based more on the representations and constructions of the figure of the migrant as a problem than the reality of their integration.

Through the case of Réda's migrant experience, we want to initiate a debate about the social and sociological issues around the theme of integration-assimilation,[8] the ethnicization of migrants as a new form of the construction of the *"inner border"* (Fassin, 2010).

From the official decree in 1974 about working migration in France (Sylvain Laurens, 2008, 2009) to the emergence of Islamist terrorism in the 1980s in France and worldwide since the attacks on September 11, 2001, the debate about immigration has focused on integration, which is said to have

[8] This notion has been at the center of political discourse in France since the 1980s, after the social movements of youth from an "immigrant background": the "March of the *Beurs*" (second-generation North African citizens), demanding real equality, and the riots in the suburbs that often resulted from incidents with the police. But this term is also a category employed in the social sciences in France to question discrimination, inequality or the tensions linked to migrants and their children. In many cases, the term is linked to the idea of the assimilation of migrants into French society and involves the French republican ideology in constructing indicators for assimilation.

"broken down," on migrants and their descendants in "the second generation" that are already settled in Europe.

This idea of "integration," which in the French context is tied to assimilation, has constantly varied in terms of definition and indicators in political discourse, from being an issue of rights to an issue of duties in the 1990s. Today it includes socioeconomic, cultural, moral, political, and religious dimensions. It is not enough to have a job and pay taxes to belong to the category of integrated individuals or to the national community. One must also display a determination and proof of this integration,[9] with the contours varying according to the sociopolitical context and the centrality of the theme of immigration in local, national, and European political issues. This political debate is itself amplified by the return of differentiating theories mediated by the theme of the "clash of civilizations," advocating the non-compatibility of certain cultures, and particularly "Islamic" and "Western" culture, by building them up as two epitomes of otherness (Logier, 2015).

In this context, integration appears more as a multiplication of social and socio-racial borders (Barth, 1969)—an inner border, as Fassin called it (Fassin, 2010)—which is reduced or expanded according to the current dominant debate (Portes, 1995).

This notion is very often linked, in its political and scientific use, to a unilateral relationship between the host society and migrants. It contains the idea that there a homogenous central core (Gordon, 1964) in the host society that constitutes not only the reference and the goal of all migratory experience (Park & Burgess, 1921), but also an instrument by which to measure and assess the integration (or otherwise) of foreigners. The other idea contained in this term is linked to "phenotypical and cultural characteristics" (Portes, 1995) that are naturalized as markers in sociopolitical discourse and categorized by some research in the social sciences.

Thus, the integration of migrants in host countries is often understood and expected in terms of the creation of a distance from the supposed culture of origin or even by making a complete break with it. The visible preservation by some migrants of what is considered to be part of their original culture is widely seen as a form of archaism, as a problem or a refusal to integrate. For example, some hybrid religious or cultural practices that touch on the multiple identities of migrants are seen as suspect and criticized in terms of traditionalism (marriage, ceremonies, diet, clothing, certain forms of social behavior among young people, etc.); community solidarity is seen in terms of withdrawal, and some religious practices are interpreted as an affirmation of

[9] The level of determination and proof has been institutionalized in most European countries through public measures whose aim is to track foreigners' determination to "integrate." For example, mastering the host country's language was not something required from workers who arrived in Europe during the 1960s and 1970s. These requirements have been extended to migrants who are already living here and to their children who choose to become citizens of the host country, through setting up institutional ceremonies, like the naturalization ceremonies for new citizens in the United States.

identity, or even a rejection of "modernity." These tensions make migrants the markers of a confrontation between "traditional" culture (in the country of origin) and "modern" culture (in the host country), which is implied as "Western."

Yet Réda's experience helps us distinguish a certain cultural fluidity, consisting of passages from one identity to another, according to the environment and his interactions. In his experience, cultural practices are more part of the negotiation of social and ethno-racial boundaries rather than a logic of identity.

Moreover, it is important to note that the debate about integrating migrants in Europe has little impact on their aspirations to move there. Réda, like most of the migrants we met during our research, showed no concern in the face of the increasingly open hostility to migrants in European societies. This distancing from the political debate that is focused on the problems of integration results from their feeling that they do not correspond to the xenophobic or racist portrayals made of them in the sociopolitical debates of the moment. This distance is reinforced since the migrants are registered in spaces for producing convergences of identity, as represented by:

- Urban areas, non-national ways of life, where the socio-ethnic barriers are more part of residential experience than a sense of belonging linked to cultural identity.
- Globalized employment markets and wage work, where access to the equality of (professional) status appears more probable and simpler than the space of symbolic identities constructed by national political discourse.

Thus, the notion of "integration" is more linked to an attempted social construction, delimitation, and reinforcement of socio-ethnic boundaries (Barth, 1969), in reaction to their blurring, by groups that see themselves as the representatives of the central core of the host society. For them, the most recently arrived migrants, and in particular the undocumented ones, become the materialization of the idea of the real existence of boundaries. In this sense, the notions of integration or assimilation are indeed an indicator and a by-product of the processes of transformation of the ethnic boundaries at work due to globalization.

The concept of *boundary blurring*, developed by Alba and Nee in their study of the transformations of the mechanisms of ethnic boundaries (Alba & Nee, 2003), seems to us the most pertinent way to understand the migratory process in the context of globalization.

In this respect, the resurgence of the category of ethnicity in its different forms (religion, cultural practices, identities, phenotypes) in debates in Europe is more the expression of the overflow of mechanisms of socio-racial distinctions that are part of the processes of single-identity construction of affiliations than their strengthening. As Alba and Nee point out, blurring boundaries is a process of constructing convergences between groups resulting from "contacts with equal status, as symbolized by intermarriage," but above all through work and changes in residence. This notion helps us envisage the study of migrations as an indicator and a field for empirical expression of the tensions involved in these transformations.

Réda's experience contributes as much to illustrating the process of "boundary blurring" as the individual experience of a migrant. His case helps us highlight the central role of employment in the process of constructing convergences and in going beyond the traditional boundaries of ethnicity. The combination of migration/work mainly studied through the prism of socioeconomic conditions must be expanded to the study of work as the place where identity boundaries are redrawn.

References

Alba R. & Nee V. 2003. *Remaking the American Mainstream. Assimilation and Contemporary Immigration*, Cambridge, Massachusetts and London: Harvard University Press.

Antecol H. & Bedard K. 2006. "Unhealthy Assimilation: Why Do Immigrants Converge to American Health Status Levels?" *Demography*, 43 (2): 337-360.

Barth F. 1969. Ethnic Groups and Boundaries: the Social Organization of Culture Differences, Bergen: Universitetsforlaget.

Boltanski L. & È. Chiapello. 1999. *Le Nouvel esprit du capitalisme*, Paris, Éditions Gallimard.

Castel R. 1995. Les métamorphoses de la question sociale, Paris, Fayard.

Chauvin S. 2009. "En attendant les papiers. L'affiliation bridée des migrants irréguliers aux États-Unis", *Politix* 3 (87): 47-69.

Dornel L. 1995. "Les usages du racialiasime. Le cas de la main d'œuvre en France pendant la première guerre mondiale". *Genèses*, 20: 48-72.

Dubet, F. 1987. *La Galère: jeunes en survie*. Paris: Fayard.

EL Miri Mustapha. 2014. "Border Makers: Clandestine migration from Morocco", In J. Gertel and S. R. Sippel (eds.) *Seasonal workers in Mediterranen agriculture. The Social costs of eating fresh*, London: Routledge.

EL Miri Mustapha. 2011. "Quand les migrants se choisissent: qualification sociale et sélection des postulants à la migration au Maroc", *European Journal of Sociology*, 52 (2): 209-235.

Didier F. (dir.). 2010. *Les nouvelles frontières de la société française*, Paris: La Découverte.

Favell A. 2001. Philosophies of Integration: Immigration and the Idea of Citizenship in France and Britain, London: MacMillan.

Felouzis G. & J. Perroton. 2009. "Grandir entre pairs à l'école. Ségrégation ethnique et reproduction sociale dans le système éducatif français", *Actes de la recherche en sciences sociales*, 180: 92-100.

Gordon M. 1964. Assimilation in American Live. The Role of Race, Religion and National Origins, New York: Oxford University Press.

Judt, T. 2004. "Israël: l'alternative". *Le Débat*, 128: 26-32.

Kao G. & Thompson J. S. 2003. "Racial and Ethnic Stratification in Educational Achievement and Attainment", *Annual Review of Sociology*, 29: 417-442.

Laurens, S. 2008. "1974 et la fermeture des frontières. Analyse critique d'une décision érigée en turning-point", *Politix*, 82: 69-94.

Laurens, Sylvain. 2009. Une politisation feutrée, les hauts fonctionnaires et l'immmigration en France, Paris: Belin, 2009.

Le Courant, S. 2010. "L'intériorisation de la frontière sous menace d'expulsion. Le quotidien des étrangers en situation irrégulière", In D. Fassin (éd.), *Les nouvelles frontières de la société française. Enquête sur l'altérité nationale*, Paris: La Découverte: 455-476.

Le Courant, S. 2015. "Le poids de la menace l'évaluation quotidienne du risque d'expulsion par les étrangers en situation irrégulière", *Ethnologie française*, XLV (1): 123-133.

Lendaro A. & Ch. Imdorf. 2012. "The use of ethnicity in recruiting domestic labour. A case study on French placement agencies in the care sector" *Employee Relations* 34 (6): 613-627.

Logier, R. 2015. Le complexe de Suez le vrai déclin français (et du continent Européen), Paris: Le Bord de l'Eau.

Ltaief W. 2007. "Jalons du mariage mixte dans l'immigration: entre la loi, la foi et la trace identitaire", In S. Benjamin & E. Temmine (ed.) *Immigrances, l'immigration en France au XXe siècle*, Paris: Haccette.

Massey D. 1990 "Social structure, household strategies, and the cumulative causation of migration", *Population Index*, 56 (1): 3-26.

Mbembé, A. 2016. *Politiques de l'inimitié*, Paris: Éditions La Découverte.

Park R. E. 1928. "Human Migration and the Marginal Man", *The American Journal of Sociology*, 33 (6): 881-893.

Park, R. E. 1950. *Race and Culture*, New York: Free Press of Glencoe.

Park R. E. & Burgess E. W. 1921. *Introduction to the Science of Sociology*, Chicago: University of Chicago Press.

Portes, A. 1995. "Economic Sociology and the Sociology of Immigration: a Conceptual Overview". In A. Portes (ed.) *The Economic Sociology of Immigration: Essays on Networks, Ethnicity and Entrepreneurship*, New York: Russell Sage Foundation: 1-41.

Sennett, R. 2000. *Le Travail sans qualités*, Paris: Éditions Albin Michel.

Simmel, G. 1984. "Métropoles et mentalité", In Y. Grafmeyer & I. Joseph (dir), *L'École de Chicago. Naissance de l'écologie urbaine*, Paris: Éditions Aubier: 61-77

Tassin L. 2014. "Accueillir les indésirables. Les habitants de Lampedusa à l'épreuve de l'enfermement des étrangers", *Genèses*, 96 :110-131.

Tucci I., A. Jossin, C, Keller, O. Groh-Samberg. 2013. "L'entrée sur le marché du travail des descendants d'immigrés: une analyse comparée France-Allemagne", *Revue française de sociologie* 54 (3) :567-596.

Wihtol de Wenden, C. 2013. La question migratoire au XXIe siècle. Migrants, réfugiés et relations internationales. Paris: Les Presses de Sciences Po.

CHILDREN CIRCULATING BETWEEN THE UNITED STATES AND MEXICO

Víctor Zúñiga and Betsabé Román-González

Based on multi-site, long-term, ongoing research into the migratory trajectories of international migrant children living in Mexico, this chapter will describe and analyze the stories of three children who arrived from the United States to the state of Morelos, Mexico in 2012. Beto was born in Morelos, Mexico, while Flor and Lulu were born in the United States (Oregon and Arkansas, respectively). Beto moved to the United States when he was 2 years old. Flor was 10 and Lulu was 12 when they moved to Mexico. Beto and Lulu still live in Mexico, while Flor returned to Oregon two years ago.

Beto crossed the Mexico/United States border accompanied by a couple of U.S. citizens who declared at the border checkpoint that he was their son. He does not remember the event, but his mother told us that it was simply to trick the U.S. officials when entering San Diego (California) from Tijuana (Mexico). After a successful crossing, Beto met his parents in Santa Anna, California and lived there as an undocumented child for nine years. In 2012, when he was 12, an event disrupted the course of his life. His mother reported a robbery, of which she was the victim. One of the thieves went to jail. One week later, a member of a Santa Ana gang visited Beto's father and mother and told them he knew who Beto was and where he went to school. As a result of these events, the three members of the family left the United States immediately, because Beto's life was in danger.

Lulu, on the other hand, arrived in Tlaltizapán, Morelos when she was 12. We met her at the school she was attending. The first thing her teacher told us was: "She does not know Spanish; she just got here" (in fact, Lulu spoke Spanish but, as expected, was not able to read or write it). Lulu, an American because of her birthplace, returned to Mexico because her parents had attempted several times to legalize her residency in the United States without success. Lulu had experience with deportation: an uncle, her mother's brother, had been deported several weeks earlier. In 2012, the fear of deportation caused the entire family to move from San Diego back to Tlaltizapán: Lulu, her three sisters, her father, and her mother. Her family packed up their belongings and rented a trailer to travel all the way to Tlaltizapán.

Lastly, Flor comes from a divided family. Her father lives in Oregon, while her mother decided to return to Jiutepec in 2012, when Flor was 10. This was her first contact with Mexico and the rural town where her mother's family resided. She started 4th grade in the local school and suffered the consequences of the linguistic and social ruptures. Flor's mother had decided to return to Jiutepec for several related reasons: she had divorced Flor's father; she knew that some of her relatives in Mexico were using her land and house and had tried to sell them without her permission; she realized that her life in Oregon did not allow her to be close to her daughters, and she was worried because her oldest daughter (Flor's sister) had dropped out of high school, had gotten pregnant and was spending time with the gang her boyfriend was in. Once in Mexico, Flor was unable to find her place in her school and the neighborhood. Moreover, she missed her father and the lifestyle she had left behind in Portland, Oregon. During our third visit to her family's house, we learned that Flor had returned to Oregon to live with her father and attend her former school. However, she called her mother in Jiutepec daily. Sometimes it seemed like Flor wanted to come to Mexico, once again.

The Context of Child Mobility

These three children are not extraordinary boys and girls. They are completely normal. They are just a few of the more than half a million minors (Zúñiga & Giorguli, 2019) who recently moved from the United States to Mexico. Some of them truly are returnees because they were born in Mexico. Others are not, because they were born in the United States. Thus, when they arrived in Mexico it was not a return; they had come to their parents' homeland for the first time. However, all of them are international migrants because they moved from one country to another. In fact, they are circulating, particularly those who have dual citizenship. They are what we have referred to elsewhere as "American-Mexican children" (Zúñiga & Hamann, 2013). Moreover, because of their transnational education (partly in U.S. schools, partly in Mexican ones), they are becoming bicultural, with proficient bilingualism. These children mark one of the emergent changing migratory patterns between Mexico and the United States.

In 2004, we conducted a survey of a representative sample of students attending schools (1st–9th grades) in the state of Nuevo León, Mexico. Among the total students surveyed (n = 14,473) we found: 2.3 % of them had previously lived in the United States; 1 in 100 was born in the United States; 4.6 % of those students lived in Mexico while their father was living and working in the United States. At that time, the Great Recession (2007–2009) had not yet had negatively impacted the lives and jobs of workers in the United States. We conducted the survey again in 2010 on a representative sample of students matriculated in the school system of the state of Jalisco, Mexico. This time, we surveyed 11,479 students (1st–9th grades). We found that 4.2 % of them had previously resided in the United States and had moved from that country to Mexico (twice the percentage we found in 2004). 2.5 in 100 were born in the United Sates (more than the double what we had observed in Nuevo León), and 5.3 % of those children and youngsters lived separated from their fathers because they continued to reside in the United States (slightly more than the proportion in 2004).

These figures show an emergent flow of immigrants with two singular traits: (a) they move from the United States to Mexico, in an inversion of the historic trend; and (b) they are children and adolescents (i.e., they are international migrants while still undergoing socialization). Given their age, international migration very often includes school transitions. For example, for some children who were born in Mexico, they moved from Mexican schools to the U.S. school system, and later moved from U.S. schools to Mexican ones. During their migratory journeys, they frequently live separated from their father or mother. They know very well what belonging to an internationally dispersed family is like (Zúñiga, 2015).

Why are they moving from the United States to Mexico? In chronological order, there was first the Great Migration from Mexico to the United States (Hernández-León & Zúñiga, 2016). This Great Migration occurred over two and a half decades ago, when millions of Mexicans regularized their residency in the United States (Massey, Durand and Malone, 2002), and participated in the expansion of the U.S. economy in the late 1990s and early 2000s, and reunited with family members who had remained in Mexico. "Great is not a metaphor"; in fact, the number of Mexicans living in the United States grew from 0.8 million in 1970 to 12.5 million in 2007, all of them Mexicans born in Mexico (González Barrera & López, 2013; Zong & Batalova, 2016). The Great Migration turned into a Great Expulsion (Hernández-León & Zúñiga, 2016) from 2005–2008. The reasons for the expulsion are well documented by Golash-Boza (2015), Hagan, Eschbach, and Rodríguez (2008), and Bhatt and Roberts (2012): militarization of the border, policy of interior enforcement, hundreds of state-level bills and local ordinances designed to criminalize immigrants, both documented and undocumented (Varsanyi, 2010), anti-immigrant public sentiment, permanent fear of being deported or separated from family members (Dreby, 2015), as well as the catastrophic consequences of the Great Recession (Leal & Rodriguez, 2016) on jobs, savings, and the financial stability of immigrants.

Certainly, immigrant families were victims and were often publicly presented as scapegoats by politicians and mass media (Fluery-Steiner & Longazel, 2010). However, they were (and are) more than just victims. Adult migrants and their families created strategies to protect themselves from State policies against them. One defensive strategy is to return to Mexico to reunite with family members. Family reunification in Mexico allows them to prepare and imagine new forms of circulation, especially for those who are U.S. citizens (children and adolescents). In any case, the aggressive measures taken against immigrants in the United States, the economic circumstances, the criminalization of migrants, and the new immigrant's responses explain why almost 1 million Mexicans "returned" to Mexico between 2005 and 2010, and among them, 25 % were children and adolescents (Giorguli & Gutiérrez,

2011).

Lulu, Beto, and Flor are children of the Great Expulsion. Lulu might circulate in the future. Flor is already circulating and Beto, despite his bilingualism and biculturalism, will have to overcome legal obstacles if he plans to circulate between both countries. For all three, their parents cannot legally return to the United States.

Methodology

Before we introduce an overview of the methodological approach in this research project, it is important to understand that our methodological perspective is centered upon the premise that children communicate and form relationships with others around them, and give meaning to their environments, just like adults do (Gaitán et al., 2007). This premise is sustained by three main principles: (a) children are social actors and actresses; (b) descriptions and analyses of the school, family, and social experiences of children are incomplete if the narrative does not come from the child's perspective, and; (c) the experience of child migration has its own singularity, due to the fact that age is a determining factor in how migration is experienced. Therefore, the life stories that are presented in this chapter were written from the children's point of view and portray their migratory and educational trajectories in their transit between the United States and Mexico.

In order to write life stories, we needed a methodological approach that would allow us to follow the migrant children and their families for a long period of time (Román-González, 2017). Therefore, we designed a mixed-method longitudinal and multi-site study with different ethno-sociological tools to gather information over a four-year period. Fieldwork was done inductively; in other words, there were no pre-determined answers, nor categories; the information, categories, and topics were organized throughout the dialogue with the young migrants and their families. As a result, we went into the project without our own prejudices and focused on the children's narratives about their trajectories. In the following paragraphs, we briefly describe the five different stages in this research. Each of them served a different purpose and had a different time frame.

Phase 1: Morelos database. There were two main objectives for this phase. The first consisted in finding schools with the most migrant children enrolled to get in touch with principals and teachers and talk to them about the research project. Secondly, the database allowed us to find which schools enrolled children who were underage, in elementary and secondary schooling, and who had just arrived in the state of Morelos.

Phase 2: Research project design. After finding schools with a sufficient number of young migrants, we designed a rough draft of the project and presented it to the Public Education Department in Morelos (*Secretaría de Educación Pública de Morelos*, SEP). After they agreed, they provided us with the permits to do research in Morelos' schools and to speak to young migrants during school hours.

Phase 3: Selection of young migrants. The first step towards selecting the migrant children for this study was to send 1,395 questionnaires to the entire population of two elementary schools and two secondary schools. We needed to use a different strategy for elementary school students; the questionnaire had to be read to the students, and their teachers helped us to monitor them during the survey. From the total of students at the four schools, only 49 had had previous school experience in the United States and were able to answer the question: "Why did you return/move to Mexico?" Of the 49 young migrants, only 10 were selected to begin the longitudinal study. They had the following characteristics: (a) they had arrived in Morelos in 2010 or later; (b) they had been enrolled in an American school for at least two years; (c) they were enrolled, at the time, in either third to sixth grade of elementary school or first year of secondary school; (d) they were residing in Cuernavaca or in a nearby municipality; (e) they still remembered and could describe their school and migratory trajectories in the United States; and, finally, (f) they were willing to meet us again. The ten children in this study are listed in Table 1; pseudonyms were used to protect their identities.

Table 1. List of selected children with their place of departure in the United States and place of arrival in Mexico

Name	Country of birth	Age at arrival in Morelos	Place of departure from the United States	Place of arrival in Mexico
Astrid	United States	10	Porterville, CA	Jiutepec
Luis	United States	14	Porterville, CA	Jiutepec
Salvador	United States	13	Porterville, CA	Jiutepec
Flor	United States	11	Portland, OR	Jiutepec
Enrique	United States	13	Chicago, IL	Jiutepec
Marco	Mexico	8	Chicago, IL	Cuernavaca
Lulú	United States	13	Los Angeles, CA	Tlaltizapán
Sofía	United States	15	Los Angeles, CA	Tlaltizapán
Elena	United States	9	Los Angeles, CA	Tlaltizapán
Beto	Mexico	15	Santa Ana, CA	Temixco

Phase 4: Trust-building throughout the study. This phase can be divided into three parts: building trust with school officials, trust with parents, and trust with children. At schools, we started by interviewing principals and teachers on how migrant children were reacting to the new environment, and whether these children faced problems with teachers and classmates. Before we moved to interviews in the home, during our first conversation with the young migrants, we asked them if we could have their parents' phone numbers. Contacting parents and getting them to talk to us was particularly difficult. Some parents did not answer our calls. Some answered the phone but did not agree to meet with us, and others canceled meetings at the last moment, claiming that they were working and did not have time for a short

meeting. Once the parents who agreed to talk to us got to know us, it made building trust with the children easier. At first, the girls and boys were more comfortable talking to researchers who were their same gender; however, after more visits, they were willing to share their stories with any of us.

Phase 5: Life stories. We chose life stories over other methodologies because we wanted to have a complete and comprehensive vision of the trajectories of young migrants, a vision of time, and a vision of the children interacting in different contexts (Torstenson-Ed, 2007). Even though we gave priority to the children's narratives, it was necessary to have a variety of testimonies from parents and family members, teachers, classmates, neighbors, and other people that the children interacted with. Furthermore, it is important to underline that we reconstructed the stories from the children's narratives to give them uniformity. Once the stories were written, it was very helpful to use Valdés' (1996) innovative ethnographic methodology where she divides families in her study depending on their experience and familiarity with the United States. In this study, the families were divided according to the migratory trajectory of the ten young migrants. As a result, there were three different categories: (a) families with young Mexican-born migrants residing in Mexico, (b) families with young U.S.-born migrants residing in Mexico, and (c) families with young U.S.-born migrants who returned to the United States.

Children's Stories and Trajectories

Beto: The "Californian" Who Did Not Know He Was not American

Before Beto and his parents moved back to Mexico, they were doing well in the United States. Daniel, his father, had a stable job that he had held down for over 10 years. Andrea, Beto's mother, was starting a cooking business for weddings, *quinceañeras,* and other events. Beto was doing well in middle school and getting ready to enter high school. Beto is a teenager who enjoys listening to music in English, watching movies, playing basketball, and drawing. All his hip-hop, rap, and techno music is downloaded on the cell phone that he brought back from the United States. He also has pictures and videos that he shares with us when we visit him. He likes downloading scary pictures of clowns and dragons from the Internet so that he can draw them in a notebook that he keeps under his bed. He has cable TV with channels in English and he likes watching shows like *The Big Bang Theory*, *Friends*, *South Park*, MTV, and other music channels. Beto's activities in Mexico seem to reflect those of a child who had lived in the United States. Boys in Ahuatenco, where he lives now, enjoy playing soccer outside in the main street. Girls are not seen very often, but when they are outside, they stand or sit on the sidewalk to talk in groups. Unlike Beto, most children in Ahuatenco do not have cable TV with channels in English, and there is no internet service in town. The traditional music in the town is *ranchera*, *corridos,* or *banda.* Also, cell phones are an accessory that only adults have, and that they specifically use for phone calls or texting. Moreover, there are no kids who speak English, and only a few adults, like Beto's parents, speak some English because they lived in the United States. Things are very different from what Beto was used to; for this reason, he spends most of his time by himself, in his room, with headphones stuffed in his ears. He does not like to go outside to play with other boys. He says he does not like to get dirty playing soccer in the street, and that he needs to practice English all the time so that he does not forget. He prefers to do it by himself.

Contrary to how Beto behaves in Mexico, he was a very independent child in the United States. He would go to stores near his house by himself; he visited his friends at their houses and most days he would walk to school with his friends. Also, his parents would ask for his help if they needed to translate bills or report cards from school. He would sometimes translate for his mom at stores, but had little patience and would tell Andrea to learn English instead. Now that he is Mexico, he prefers to stay quiet and let his parents do things for him. When he is at the store, he tells his parents what he wants to eat or drink and waits for them outside. When his mom goes to the *mercado*, he prefers to stay home to watch movies. He says:

> It's boring to go with my mom. I prefer to stay and just tell her what I want to take to school for lunch or to eat at home. I don't like going out. I like my room and my TV.

One of the reasons he was told they were visiting Mexico was that his grandmother was suffering from diabetes and needed help.

> My parents said we were visiting grandma, but then they started packing everything. I didn't want to come and now I'm here. I don't like it; I wanna go back.

A few weeks after they arrived in Mexico, summer break was almost over and Beto was eager to go back to his school in Santa Ana, California to see his friends and play video games and basketball and go to the lake near his school. When his parents explained that they had come to stay, and that they could not go back because they had no legal papers to do so, he tried to convince them to go back, or to let him go by himself.

> I felt really bad and started crying. I didn't say goodbye to my friends. There were so many things I had planned with them, and here I was not being able to go back home. I stopped talking to my parents for a few days, I stopped talking to everybody. I didn't want to leave- my room. It was unfair.

Education in Mexico

School in Mexico was quite difficult for Beto at first. Unlike schools in the States, where Beto felt free to ask his teachers questions and participate in class, in Cuentepec, where he first lived in Mexico, he felt lost. It was more difficult for him to speak to his teacher here, and he had to learn new school rules.

> I didn't know how to talk to teachers, not like in Spanish, but like if I needed something, like to go the restroom for example, in the States they only give you like three passes for the whole semester and here I didn't know if I had to ask or just go or what, it was so confusing… and then, I didn't know about grades. Over there they use letters like A for excellent and F for fail, here, they use numbers. I didn't know if I was doing good or bad, I had to ask my parents. I always have to ask my parents about things 'cause they know stuff. I'm new here, I sometimes don't know what to do.

All these circumstances caused Beto to interact poorly with his peers at school, and his grades dropped because he lacked reading and writing skills in Spanish. Also, in the small town he did not have anyone to share his love for video games, movies, and anime in English with. Beto became a very quiet, shy and lonely *compare* (stranger in Náhuatl). He became frustrated whenever he was in class: "I can't talk in Spanish that much, and then my classmates speak Náhuatl all the time when the teacher is outside. I don't know what they're saying; I really miss my friends." Despite the teacher's efforts to include Beto in the classroom, he usually felt lonely and excluded by his classmates.

Two years after our first meeting with Beto, we observed that he had become a more active participant in family decisions: he influenced his parents' decision to move from Cuentepec to Ahuatenco, Morelos; he selected the school he wanted to attend, and now spends more time with his friends after school. It was very surprising for us that for the first time in two years of visits, Beto spoke to us, with so much enthusiasm, in Spanish. He was now in his third semester of *preparatoria*—high school—and he told us how much he loved his new school. He was more outspoken and mature and no longer talked about the United States, but his plans were still the same when we teased him and asked him if he had a girlfriend: "no, no, no… I have to finish high school first and then go to college…"

Settling in and Plans for the Future

Beto's parents had never explained what "*no tener papeles*" meant (not to have legal permission to live in the United States) until the moment he wanted to go back home to California. In Beto's mind, he will someday return to the United States. He now knows he needs certain documents to do so and is constantly asking about the possibility of either studying or working in the United States. He is always asking: "How can I go back to the States? What do I need? Is it hard to get [a visa]?" At first, he was very confident about his plans to go back to the United States; he now knows that, in order to go back, he must do it the right way. He also knows that he needs to remember the language in order to succeed in the United States, as he once told us: "I don't want to forget [the language] for when I go back. So, can we please speak English whenever you come?"

Beto still does not know the "real" reason why he and his family moved back to Mexico in such a hurry. After a few home visits and late-night talks with his parents, they opened up to us and told us that they were running away from a gang member who threatened to kill Beto if they did not leave after Andrea, Beto's mother, had turned him in to the police.

Beto experienced an abrupt international migration. In his eyes, everything was taken away from him—friends, school, and house—without a valid reason. Clearly, his parents' decision to return did not take Beto's opinion into consideration. Like many children and teenagers, Beto had to abide by the decisions his parents made on his behalf. At the same time, their return was essentially the only way to protect Beto's well-being. Instead of simply illustrating children's subordination, we argue that this story in fact demonstrates children's importance in the migratory decision-making process (Orellana et al,. 2001; Ní Laoire et al., 2010).

Lulú: "I Know I Have That [U.S.] Nationality, But to Tell You the Truth I Feel More Mexican Than Anyone Here"

Lulú's story showed us that being in Mexico, after having been born, raised, and educated in the United States, can be hard, sad, disappointing, and every other "negative" adjective imaginable, but at the same time it can be quite the opposite if the family is together and if their goals are aligned for success, no matter the circumstances. Lulú is the girl who taught us the most about American-Mexican children living in Mexico (Zúñiga & Hamann ,2013).

Lulú was the first girl we interviewed in Morelos. During the implementation of the survey instrument at her school, a teacher pointed at Lulú and said "she does not know Spanish, she just got here." When we asked her to come to the principal's office and asked if she wanted to complete the survey, Lulú replied: "I can't read in Spanish, or in English, because of my problem, but if you read me the questions I can answer." She later told us that she had been diagnosed with dyslexia in the United States, a condition that made it hard for her to read or write in English too.

Lulú was born in Arkansas, but lived in San Diego most of her life, and had arrived in Morelos two months before our visit to the school. After Lulú's uncle's arrest and deportation a few weeks before, Lulú, her three sisters, and her parents had jointly decided that it was time to move to Mexico.

> My parents told us they wanted to talk to us; we sat down in the living room and they asked us what we thought about moving to Mexico. They also explained how much they worried about one of them being deported and how that would make it difficult to be together, all six of us. They told us that things [in Mexico] would not be as good as they were there [in the United States], that we would have to work hard for the things we wanted and that we needed to stick together. We didn't mind that, we wanted to be with our parents, and that's why we didn't take

long to pack our things; that same week we were leaving California and moving to Mexico.

The family rented a truck and Ernesto, Lulú's father, drove with all their belongings to Morelos, while Paloma, her mother, brought Lulú and her sisters in a van and stopped at the beach on the way. Traveling separately from her father was not difficult. Lulú, her mother and sisters were used to traveling without him because he was always working double shifts. As their parents had warned the girls, things in Mexico were not easy. Lulú remembered how uncles, aunts and cousins did not welcome them with open arms, which made it difficult to adjust to the new place. Her cousins did not want to play with them. According to Lulú, "they called us '*fresas*'[1] because we spoke English, but we are not, we just talk different."

At first, the family did not have a place to stay; however, before they left the United States, Paloma and Ernesto got in touch with a relative, the girls' aunt, to rent them a house. They even sent her the payment for an entire year in advance. Nonetheless, Lulú explained, "Whenever it rained everything got wet, so we had to start looking for a new house; also, the house was scary. We heard things at night and my little sister was always crying."

When they found a new house, Lulú's aunt did not want to return any of the money they had paid, even though they had lived in the house only for one month. Despite the bad experiences with school and finding a house, and contrary to what adult-centered studies say about how children "might" feel when they move to a new country, victimizing them, Lulú and her sisters explained that their experience was quite the opposite (James, Jenks and Prout, 1998). According to Lulú, "[They] like being here [in Mexico] because we get to spend more time with our dad. We barely saw him when we were in the United States; he was always working."

An important component of Lulú's family migration to Mexico has thus been transitioning to new family dynamics: in California, the girls spent their free time with their cousins, their grandmother, and their mother because her father worked both day and night shifts. In Morelos, things are different; as Lulú indicates, some things are better, and others "are not that bad." She and her sisters are happy that their father works 6–8 hours a day, and that he stays home on the weekends. They enjoy the time they spend with him after school and during his free time; he has taught them about hunting and fishing, and he also helps them with homework and does chores at home. Lulú told us that she would not exchange having her dad at home for any of the comforts they used to have in the United States. Lulú and her sisters are aware that it has been hard for their parents to find a proper house for the six of them, to find jobs to pay for their expenses and to develop a strong network of family and friends to help them transition into the new community; nonetheless, the

[1] "*Fresa*" is a Mexican-Spanish slang word referring to people who generally belong to the upper social classes and who are perceived as snobs.

girls and their parents' discourse remains the same: "We are here as a family, that is the most important thing for us" (interview with Paloma in 2014). Lulú's family has moved to six different houses, in three different towns in Morelos, in the four years they have been in Mexico. They have been enrolled in four different schools. We know that their trajectories are not over yet; nonetheless, they have managed to fit in as if they were born in Morelos, and we believe Lulú when she tells us: "I feel more Mexican than anyone here."

Living in Mexico: Fall Down Two Times, Get up Three

Lulú has her own routine, her own way of getting around in Morelos, and her own way of making friends. Lulú surprises us every time we visit her family. On our first encounter with her at the *secundaria* (7th–9th grades) she cried and told us how "frustrated" she was about being in Mexico and in a new school. She did not know why the teachers treated her the way they did: "They think I'm from here, but I'm not, they don't know. They ask me to work the same as everyone else, but I can't, I don't get it." She was very upset about the teachers in Mexico, how they were not patient with her. However, she was very thankful that she was with her family, especially now that her dad was spending more time with her and her sisters. She was also happy that her new classmates in the Morelos' school were nicer with her than the ones in the United States: "here they help me, they lend me their books. In the English class, they ask me for help, that makes me feel good because I can help."

With each visit, Lulú replaced English with more and more Spanish, until the moment where she only spoke Spanish during our visits. Lulú's transition from the American school to the Mexican one was a bit difficult. Her problem, in her perspective, was that she had "dyslexia"; therefore, she had trouble reading in English and later in Spanish. She recalled having a special computer that helped her to read better. She would also be taken from her regular classes twice during the day to go work with a Special Education teacher on her reading and spelling. She told us she liked American teachers better: "[be] 'cause every time I felt bad, I felt like frustrated or something they would let me out and here I don't feel that way."

In Mexico, however, she did not feel the same about the teachers. She recalled her Biology teacher who was not patient with her. The teacher's main method of teaching was dictation; Lulú could not keep up with the lesson and the teacher would make fun of her and embarrass her in front of the class for not completing her assignments: "The teacher started yelling at me because I am *mexicana* and I'm supposed to read and write Spanish. Then she said to me that I was stupid and it was disrespectful to say I don't know [*sic*] write in Spanish."

In United States, teachers know that they cannot say things like this to students; instead, they try to support the students. "That is why I said to my father I felt bad in that school. Then I used to say to my teachers they had not the right to tell me stupid [*sic*]." After that, her classmates started talking to Lulú even more: "They know I'm different, they said to me: 'You are our hero, we cannot say anything to the teacher.'"

Nonetheless, Lulú also recognized other teachers that would help her through her transition, such as her History and English teachers. Both teachers would lend her their books when they dictated to the class, so that she could copy and not lag behind the others. In addition, the English teacher would ask her to help him with the pronunciation of words, with spelling, and by helping her classmates with their assignments after she was finished. Unfortunately, just when Lulú was getting used to the school, the family had to move to another town and the girls had to enroll in a new school. The new school's principal took Sofía's and Lulú's situation very seriously and helped them to transition from one school to the next one. Although the principal helped them, Lulú started having problems with her new teacher. After two months of being at the new school, Lulú told her parents that she no longer wanted to attend school: "I really felt bad being in the school. I only had one teacher and she didn't want to help me. But I know how a teacher must be: That was the reason I asked my parents to leave the school and they agreed."

Paloma and Ernesto had watched Lulú's transition from school to school and felt bad for her. They allowed her to stay at home, but Paloma told her that if she was not going to study anymore, she needed to learn how to work. Lulú took her mother's words very seriously and began to learn and help her do chores while Paloma cooked food and sold it during recess at the school. In addition, Lulú had to help clean the bedrooms and bathroom, and at night, when her father came home from work, she would read out loud to him in Spanish. Lulú did not mind; in her free time she started practicing drawing and making jewelry for her and her sisters. She also enjoyed learning about gardening and fishing.

Being out of school allowed Lulú to interact more with people from the town. In 2015, on our last visit during that year, before she turned fifteen, she had cut her hair short and dressed like the locals, and she even stopped speaking in English. She started using Spanish slang, words that they used in her new home and that we did not recognize; she had to explain some of the meanings for us. For her fifteenth birthday, in September 2016, Lulú invited the whole town to her party and told her parents that she did not want anything fancy. She wanted her party to take place at the town's *cancha de basket* near the Catholic chapel. She also requested that the theme of her party be Mexican, green, white and red, just like the Mexican flag. The food had to be Mexican too, so her mother and her aunts made *antojitos* for dinner, *tacos dorados,* and *pozole, agua de jamaica y de horchata*. Ernesto made sure there were all kinds of music and drinks. Lulú, with a big smile on her face, thanked us for being with her on her special day.

After two years of not attending school, Lulú gave us the good news that she had decided to go back and finish her last year of *secundaria* in a *telesecundaria*. We do not know what the next step in her trajectory will be. Nonetheless, she is aware that her American citizenship can provide her a way out in case she needs it, though that would be her last option. She and her sisters speak English at home; they still watch movies in English, the ones that they brought from California and some new ones that their grandmother sends them for their birthdays or on holidays.

Flor: Between Parents and Countries

Flor's story is not as complete as the other stories. However, it is an interesting story because it describes the life of a U.S.-born child who came to Mexico for the first time and did not stay. Flor was born in Portland, Oregon. When she turned 10, her mom took her to Mexico for the first time; a year later, Flor went back to Portland to live with her father. Her father was working in the United States at the time and he was in the process of filing for U.S. residency; returning to Portland and going back to school was no trouble for Flor. Although we tried to portray Flor's story from her own perspective and in her own voice, it has been more difficult to get in touch with her now that she is living with her father. We only spoke to Flor twice in person before she left for the United States: once at her school and another time at her home. The rest of the story has been pieced together through follow-up with her mother and sisters in Morelos, and text messages with Flor; recently, she accepted our friend request on Facebook and we were able to discuss her school and her future plans.

Unlike the other stories, Flor's might sound as if it were an unsuccessful story in Mexico. However, as we listened to her and her mother discuss the reasons why they came to Mexico in the first place, it was clear that Flor did succeed in her main objective: to become more aware of her Mexican background and culture, and to learn life-long lessons about family, friends, and school. When we asked Flor what she had learned in Mexico, she said: "I learned that my mom and my sister will be always with me and even if we don't have things we wanted to have, little by little we are going to be better."

Flor's father left Juany, Flor's mother, when Flor was two years old. Juany's first months as a single mother and worker were very hard. Flor's father never sent her money, nor would he pay for childcare. With two children to care for and housing bills to pay, Juany had to ask for another shift at work. Juany started working full time when Flor turned 6. After 8 years of separation from David, Flor's father, Juany decided that it was time for him to either start paying for a babysitter or to take care of Flor after school. He did not want to pay for a babysitter, so he agreed to pick her up from school and take care of her.

Flor grew very close to her father because he was not as hard on her as her mother was. Flor started to become stubborn with her mother, and one time she even pushed back when Juany was trying to discipline her. Juany started noticing that Flor wanted to spend more time with her father than with her, even on her days off work. Juany realized she had left Flor alone for too long and she wanted to win back her love and trust. Flor was in second grade when Juany decided to move to Mexico. Juany thought it was the only way for her to win back her daughter's trust and love. She thought that the trip would not only help her bond with her daughters, but that they would learn about their culture, family, life sacrifices, and work.

Flor told us that she was happy to spend time with her mother while traveling back to Mexico. Instead of traveling by plane, they decided to take a minivan packed full of their belongings. They stopped at Disneyland and later went to visit their relatives at the beach in Baja California. Flor told us: "When we arrived, there were bugs everywhere and dust on the floor, because there was no floor, and we had to carry water in a bucket to use the bathroom or to take a shower. It was nothing like our home over there."

As a result, Flor would call herself and mother "poor" in Mexico because they did not have all the commodities they had back in Oregon. However, she enjoyed being in Mexico because she was with her mother, her sister, and her little nephew; they even had a dog. Although she missed her father and friends from school in the United States, she once told her mother: "Mommy, I like to be here with you, even if we don't have a nice bathroom." This made Juany very happy. It was evident to Flor that their family bonds were getting stronger and the relationship with her mother was beginning to heal.

School Issues: Smart but not Integrated

Flor was enrolled in the third grade of *primaria* (elementary school) when they first moved to Mexico. Her first language was English, so at first it was hard to communicate with her teachers and peers. However, she is a very bright girl and learned how to read in Spanish by herself. Writing was not a problem, since she loved writing in English too. Whenever Flor felt like she could not do any better at school, she would call her father crying and would tell him she wanted to go back with him. When we met her, she was very quiet and shy. She told us she missed her school:

> Over there it's very different, over there the school has a ceiling and air conditioner [...] My teachers used to give us prizes if we did our homework correctly, like stickers and candy. Over here we don't get any of that. I loved going to the library and reading, here, there is no library.

Returning to the United States: Keeping Family Bonds in the Distance

While Flor was in Mexico, her father always stayed in touch with her, and they would talk to each other 3 times a day through Tango. He also sent Juany money to buy Flor all that she needed. Nonetheless, only 4 months had gone by when we learned that Flor had gone back to Oregon to live with her father. According to Juany, Flor could not get used to the school and the neighborhood in Morelos. Even though Flor's experience in Mexico was not what her mother had expected, she was aware that being born in the United States gave her the opportunity to move between the two countries. She developed different strategies to keep in touch with her father in the United States and now with her mother and her sisters and nephews in Mexico. In the United States, she enrolled in 4th grade in a new school without any problems. The last time we spoke with her by phone, she said, "I'm doing good over here, but I miss my mom, my sister and my nephew… School is good, I am getting B's, like *ochenta* in México [80 in a scale of 100 for grades]."

Flor uses smartphone applications and social media to communicate with her mother and sisters. She is involved in the constant negotiations between her divorced parents and recognizes the significance of her participation in family dynamics. On the one hand, she manages to talk to both of her parents, even though they do not get along very well; on the other hand, Flor strengthens her family bonds by planning visits to Morelos and asking for *consejos* [advice] from her mother and sisters in Mexico. Flor was supposed to visit Morelos after her first year back in Oregon; however, her father did not want her to travel and did not buy her a plane ticket. Flor was very sad that she would not be able to visit her mother; however, she is now fully dependent on her father and Juany, her mother, does not have the means to pay for a plane ticket.

Discussion

Children like Lulú and Beto are missing from the contemporary literature on international migration. Their conspicuous absence is due, first, to the fact that they do not live in the traditional immigrant receiving countries (like the United States), and, second, because they are children, not adult workers (they are not economically relevant, yet). When Lulú and Beto lived in the United States, they were classified as members of the Second Generation (Lulú) or 1.5 generation (Beto). However, now they are minors residing in Mexico. Which category could describe them now?

Second Generation children (Portes, 1996) are sons or daughters of international migrants (Lulú and Flor). They are not immigrants; they are children born in the countries of destination of their parents. It is worthwhile to point out that they are the children of migrants, not migrants themselves (not foreign children, but citizens of the country where they were born). As citizens, international migration scholars in traditional receiving countries have paid special attention to these children because they demonstrate how the integration process into the host society is progressing. As such, research on Second Generation children focuses on the language spoken by the children belonging to this group, their success or failure in school, the national loyalty they are developing (host society versus the parents' homeland), the job opportunities they find in labor markets, and the intergenerational social mobility they achieve (or don't). The key question in this literature is to understand whether children of migrants, born in the country of destination, are experiencing a process of integration or not. To do so, scholars use a single country as the unquestioned frame of analysis; as FitzGerald (2012) noted:

> Adopting the destination, usually the majority population of a single country, as the unquestioned frame largely predetermines the conclusions about an immigrant group's level of wellbeing. Faring well or faring poorly are relative concepts, and defining the comparison groups will determine the conclusions about immigrants' trajectories and whether the alarm bells ring warning of downward assimilation, balkanization, and ghettoization. (p. 1733)

In contrast, 1.5-generation children (Rumbaut, 2004; Harklau, Losey, and Siegal, 2009; Rojas-García, 2013) are, like their parents, immigrants. They moved from their country of origin (Mexico) and arrived in the country of destination (United States). Instead of considering them members of the First Generation (of immigrants), even though they are, scholars have suggested that they be classified as the "1.5 generation," because they moved when they were minors. Their age during migration is a relevant and perdurable fact because the type of integration and assimilation experienced is clearly different whether immigrants are adults or children. Arriving in a new country during childhood includes the experience of being educated in a new school system, learning the national language as native speaker, and internalizing the symbols, values, and principles of the host culture during the socialization process. Scholars of international migration in traditional receiving countries have debated the future of children who are members of 1.5 generation (Gonzales, 2011; Gonzales & Chavez, 2012; Hirai & Sandoval, 2016). Legal issues are crucial for the fates of members of the 1.5 generation, especially if they entered the country of destination without authorization. Before coming of age, undocumented children are protected from the risk of deportation. Once they come of age, they must learn what illegality is and how to manage this legal status. In conclusion, scholars' concerns about children in the 1.5 generation focus on legal conditions and contexts that constrain their current lives and may produce undesirable consequences in the future.

Lulú was born in the United States and since 2012, she, like hundreds of thousands of other children, has resided in Mexico. As a result of her migration, she is not member of the Second Generation; once in Mexico, Lulú was no longer part of the Second Generation. The label "Second Generation" is coherent with cohorts of generations of migrants arriving to the country of destination (i.e., the United States). By contrast, Lulú would be more appropriately labeled "First Generation," because she migrated to Mexico for the first time in her life. However, it is hard to classify her as First

Generation migrant, because Lulú's parents are not migrants in Mexico, and, most importantly, Lulú is also a Mexican citizen (because her parents are Mexican). From one perspective, Lulu is an American girl who left the United States and went to live to Mexico. From the other, she is a Mexican girl who was born in the United States and spent the first twelve years of her life in that country. Is she Mexican like the other children she met in her school and neighborhood? No, she is not. In contrast with her peers, she is bilingual, bicultural, and binational. So, the label "Mexican," even though she is in fact a citizen, does not adequately encapsulate her migratory experience and her singular ontology.

Beto is a return migrant. He left his country of origin when he was two years old, and "returned" nine years after. At the very least, we know that in Mexico, the 1.5 generation category does not capture the nuance of his situation, because it was developed for a particular context of reception, that of the United States. The most salient condition of Beto's life that drastically changed when he arrived in Mexico is his legal status. Even though Beto was socialized in the United States, educated in U.S. schools, and speaks English like a native speaker, he is "legal" in Mexico. He is experiencing what it's like to be a foreign resident in his own country of origin.

Flor's case is more complicated. To begin with, she was member of the Second Generation in Oregon. Her status changed when she moved to Morelos, Mexico. When she decided to return to the United States to live with her father, she became a member of the Second Generation again. Though once in the United States, she is actually a returnee, because she was born in the United States. Flor's experience demonstrates the kind of circulation between Mexico and the United States which is (or will be) a by-product of the Great Migration (1986–2005) and the Great Expulsion (2006–present). These children are not just a new generation of Americans, they are also a new generation of Mexicans. They are creating (and will create) new forms of migration between both countries. Even children like Beto, who do not have dual citizenship, will likely participate in these forms of migration as adults, having developed their biculturalism and bilingualism.

References

Bhatt, W. & B. R. Roberts. 2012."'Forbidden Return': Return Migration in the Age of Restriction". *Journal of Immigrant & Refugee Studies*, 10 (2):162–183.

Dreby, J. 2015. Everyday illegal, when policies undermine immigrant families. Oakland: University of California Press.

FitzGerald, David. 2012. "A Comparativist Manifesto for International Migration Studies." *Ethnic and Racial Studies* 35 (10): 1725-1740.

Fluery-Steiner, B. & J. Longazel. 2010. "Neoliberalism, Community Development, and Anti-Immigrant Backlash in Hazelton, Pennsylvania." In M. W. Varsanyi (ed.) *Taking Local Control: Immigration Policy Activism in U.S. Cities and States*. Stanford: Stanford University Press: 157-172.

Gaitán, L., M. Díaz, R. Sandoval, R. Unda, S. Granda & D. Llanos. 2007. Los niños como actores en los procesos migratorios. Implicaciones para los proyectos de Cooperación. Estudio realizado en el marco de la IV Convocatoria de Proyectos de Cooperación al Desarrollo de la Universidad Complutense de Madrid.

Giorguli, S. & E. Gutiérrez. 2011. "Niños y jóvenes en el contexto de la migración internacional entre México y Estados Unidos." *Coyuntura Demográfica, SOMEDE* 1: 21-25.

Golash-Boza, T. 2015. Deported. Immigrant Policing, Disposable Labor and Global Capitalism. New York: New York University Press.

Gonzales, R. G. 2011. "Learning to be illegal: undocumented youth and shifting legal contexts in the transition to adulthood." *American Sociological Review* 76 (4): 602-619.

Gonzales, R. G. & L. R. Chavez. 2012. "'Awakening to a nightmare' abjectivity and illegality in the lives of undocumented 1.5-generation Latino immigrants in the United States". *Current Anthropology* 53 (3): 255-281.

González-Barrera, A. & M. H. López. 2013. *A Demographic Portrait of Mexican-Origin Hispanics in the United States.* Pew Research Center. Hispanic Trends. http://www.pewhispanic.org/2013/05/01/a-demographic-portrait-of-mexican-origin-hispanics-in-the-united-states/

Hagan, J., K. Eschbach & N. Rodríguez. 2008. "U.S. Deportation Policy, Family Separation, and Circular Migration." *International Migration Review* 42 (1): 64-88.

Harklau, L., K. M. Losey & M. Siegal (eds). 2009. Generation 1.5 meets college composition: issues in the teaching of writing to U.S.-educated learned of ESL. New Jersey: Lawrence Erlbaum Associates.

Hernández-León, Rubén & Víctor Zúñiga. 2016. "Introduction to the Special Issue: Contemporary Return Migration from the United States to Mexico – Focus on Children, Youth, Schools and Families". *Mexican Studies/Estudios Mexicanos*, 32 (2): 171-198.

Hirai, Shinji and Rebeca Sandoval. 2016. "El itinerario subjetivo como herramienta de análisis: las experiencias de los jóvenes de la generación 1.5 que retornan a México". *Mexican Studies/Estudios Mexicanos*, 32 (2): 276-301.

James, A., C. Jenks & A. Prout. 1998. *Theorising Childhood.* Cambridge: Polity Press.

Leal, D. & N. Rodríguez (eds.). 2016. Migration in an Era of Restriction and Recession, Sending and Receiving Nations in a Changing Global Environment. Switzerland: Springer.

Massey, D. S., J. Durand & N. J. Malone. 2002. *Beyond Smoke and Mirrors, Mexican Immigration in an Era of Economic Integration.* New York: Russell Sage Foundation.

Ní Laoire, C., F. Carpena-Méndez, N. Tyrrell & A. White, A. 2010.. Introduction: Childhood and migration—mobilites, homes and belongings. *Childhood.* 17 (2): 155-162.

Portes, A. (ed.). 1996, *The New Second Generation.* New York: Russell Sage Foundation.

Rojas-García, G. 2013. "Transitioning from school to work as a Mexican 1.5er: upward mobility glass-ceiling, assimilation among college students in California." *The Annals of the American Academy of Political and Social Science* 648 (1): 87-101.

Román González, B. 2017. *"Pa' cuando me regrese, can we speak in English?": trayectorias de menores migrantes que llegan a México.* Ph. D. dissertation in social sciences. Monterrey: Tecnológico de Monterrey, Campus Monterrey.

Rumbaut, R. G. 2004. "Ages, life stages, and generational cohorts: decomposing the immigrant first and second generations in the United States." *International Migration Review* 38 (3): 1160-1205.

Torstenson-Ed, T. 2007. Children's Life Paths through Preschool and School. *Childhood.* 14 (1): 47-66.

Orellana, M., B. Thorne, A. Chee & E. Lam. 2001. "Transnational childhoods: the participation of children in processes of family migration". *Social Problems*, 48 (4), 572-591.

Valdés, G. 1996. Con Respeto. Bridging the Distances Between Culturally Diverse Families and Schools. New York: Teachers College Press.

Varsanyi, M. (ed.). 2010. Taking Local Control: Immigration Policy Activism in U.S. Cities and States. Stanford: Stanford University Press.

Zong, J. & J. Batalova. 2016. *Mexican Immigrants in the United States.* Migration Information Source. http://www.migrationpolicy.org/article/mexican-immigrants-united-states

Zúñiga, V. 2015. "Niños y adolescentes separados de sus familias por la migración internacional: el caso de cuatro estados de México." *Estudios Sociológicos de El Colegio de México* XXXIII (97): 145-168.

Zúñiga, V. and E. T. Hamann. 2013. "Understanding American-Mexican Children." In B. Jensen and A. Sawyer (eds.) *Regarding Educación: Mexican-American Schooling.*. New York: Teachers College Press, Columbia University: 172-188

Zúñiga, V. and S. E. Giorguli Saucedo. 2019. *Niñas y niños en la migración de Estados Unidos a México: la generación 0.5.* Mexico: El Colegio de México.

PART THREE

FROM ADVENTURE TO WAITING: EMANCIPATION OF RESTRICTED TRAJECTORIES

LIFE WHILE WAITING: EXPERIENCING THE ASYLUM APPLICATION IN FRANCE

Carolina Kobelinsky

It is half past ten. Edona and Gazmadh Bashe[1] finish their coffee and sit around the small round table, next to the bed that was already made. Gazmadh goes downstairs to the first floor where the social workers' offices are to look for his mail. He then goes to the ground floor, at the entrance of the reception center for asylum-seekers (CADA), where smokers sometimes gather. He meets Omar, a neighbor from his hallway, and a "Russian from the fourth floor" whose name he doesn't know. They talk about the weather, go out to smoke, have two cigarettes. They say hello to those who come in, to those who go out. Edona, on the other hand, goes to wash the cups in the shared kitchen. I go with her. There is already a lady there preparing lunch. Back in the room, Edona turns on the television, mutes it, takes out a small French dictionary and a paperback she borrowed from the municipal library. She systematically looks up the definitions of all the words she doesn't know, asks me them "to make sure," and then writes them down on a blue notepad. Gazmadh comes back. Edona asks him if there was any mail. "No" he replies. He turns the sound on the TV back on and stretches out on the bed. Edona continues to read. I leave. [...]

At 12:20, I knock at their door again. Edona is still reading and Gazmadh has gone down to smoke. She suggests that we make lunch, so we take onions, tomatoes, rice, and some spices and go to the common kitchen where three other people are working at the same task. We go back to the room, where Gazmadh has returned. We set the table and eat while discussing entertainment activities organized by the CADA, and the Albanian football league. Gazmadh makes some coffee and we eat tangerines. He goes down to smoke and we sit in front of the television. Edona flips through all the channels and stops on an American TV series dubbed into French. When the show is over, Edona goes to do the dishes in the kitchen while I make some tea. Edona comes back with Anna, Omar's wife, who sits down with us. They have been at the CADA for three months and are staying in the room next door. She shares the bad news that her husband received about his family who stayed in Palestine [...] She leaves. I go out with her [...]

Around four in the afternoon, I come back. Edona and Gazmadh are sitting around the small round table. "What are you doing?" "Nothing, as usual," answers Edona. I offer them some figs that a Somalian resident has just given me, and we talk. Gazmadh goes downstairs to smoke a cigarette, then comes back up. "The watch does not move forward," he says staring at her. It is only five fifty. (field notes, CADA, 12/10/04)

This day in October 2004 is similar to many others. Not much happens: there are no milestones, no particular activities. Nevertheless, this ethnographic vignette depicts an essential aspect of the asylum application process as experienced by Edona and Gazmadh Bashe: the waiting and, more

[1] To preserve my interlocutors´ anonymity and to keep their comments confidential, names and dates have been modified.

particularly, the experience of a motionless temporality.

In the following pages, I will explore Edona and Gazmadh Bashe's waiting experience during their asylum process and their life in a CADA situated in the Parisian suburbs where I met them in April 2004. The chapter draws on four interviews carried out with Edona, and numerous informal conversations with both spouses that took place during afternoons in the shelter, dinners at my home, or outings to the library located at the George Pompidou Center in Paris, which Gazmadh particularly liked. Instead of building the analysis around Edona and Gazmadh Bashe's life story, I suggest taking a cross-sectional look at their path and focusing on their waiting process and experiences bounded by a precise time and space, but which extend beyond the CADA and the asylum process. Moreover, waiting is a recurrent theme in migrants' trajectories, each time in a different form and intensity, involving a singular relationship to both time and space.

The Bashes see the pending decision concerning their refugee status and their life in the shelter as the possibility to breathe again after a period of wandering; later, as the boredom and inactivity of their daily lives settle in, they also see it as an obstacle to the realization of their projects. They pursue individual activities, outside of the CADA, to fight inactivity and push back against the imposed temporality. This multiple experience of waiting—sometimes perceived as an advantage, sometimes as a hardship—is shared by most of the asylum-seekers I met during my ethnographical study, carried out over 26 months from 2003 to 2008, in CADA shelters around Paris. Two brief detours are required before exploring Edona and Gazmadh Bashe's practices and experiences, one concerning what causes this waiting time—the bureaucracy of asylum—and another concerning the place where it spreads: the reception center. Regarding the process, the person who requests asylum must to demonstrate that the reasons that led them to come in France are in compliance with those stipulated by the 1951 Geneva Convention, which defines a refugee as a person who:

> Owing to well-founded fear of being persecuted for reasons of race, religion, nationality, membership of a particular social group or political opinion, is outside the country of his nationality and is unable or, owing to such fear, is unwilling to avail himself of the protection of that country; or who, not having a nationality and being outside the country of his former habitual residence as a result of such events, is unable or, owing to such fear, is unable to return to it.[2]

After submitting a request to the administrative office, the person is given a renewable residence permit valid until the end of the procedure. The request is examined by the French Office for the Protection of Refugees and

---

[2] At the time Edona and Gazmadh Bashe petitioned for asylum, law no. 2003-1176 of December 10, 2003 set down the Geneva Convention's conditions for application and the granting of protection as conventional asylum, or of what is now called "subsidiary protection." This is granted to individuals who face inhuman or degrading treatment or punishment in their country of origin, regardless of the cause of persecution. Much weaker than refugee status, subsidiary protection is subject to an annual review from authorities of the French Office for the Protection of Refugees and Stateless Persons.

Stateless Persons, which most of the time summons the applicant for an interview before giving its decision. If the request is rejected—which happens in most cases—it is possible to appeal the decision to what was called at the time of this study the "Refugee Appeals Board".[3] This institution is in charge of studying the case and of summoning the applicant to a public hearing in front of three judges before they make their final decision. In the event that the initial rejection is upheld, the person may not renew their residence permit again and is, from that very moment, considered an illegal immigrant, who may be removed from the French territory at any time. There are few possibilities to turn the situation in the applicant's favor. If a legal issue is identified, which is not frequent, it is possible to use a lawyer to appeal the decision to the Council of State and to the Court of Cassation. During the review period, no residence permit is given to the asylum seeker, and a decision to remove the asylum seeker from French territory may able to be enforced. If the decision is overturned, the appeal is sent back to the Refugee Appeals Board to be heard again. It is also possible to ask for the case to be reopened by the administrative court, but this requires the applicant to produce new elements in order to provide evidence to substantiate their fears if they are forced to return to their country of origin. In this case, the Office delivers a certificate of re-examination and the Prefecture must extend the residence permit. The case starts again along the path towards the Office, then possibly towards the court of appeal.

Funded by the French government, the CADAs are managed on a day-to-day basis by NGOs or companies that employ social workers, educators, and lawyers, to take care of the social and legal needs of the asylum seekers, who are housed there for the entire duration of asylum process. The housing provided by the CADAs is split between individual apartments, located outside the CADA administration building, or "collective," in shelter-type buildings. I conducted my field research in collective structures, which are more numerous than those offering a scattered accommodation. These structures were created in 1991, two months after the effective application of a circular effectively forbidding asylum-seekers from working.

CADAs are ambiguous institutions. They offer a specific form of hospitality that combines assistance, control, and confinement. Professionals provide legal advice to understand the application, increasing asylum-seekers' chances to obtain the refugee status or, at least, subsidiary protection.[4] They also take care of the necessary steps to get access to universal health care[5]

[3] Since 2009, the Refugee Appeals Board became the French Court of Asylum (*Cour nationale du droit d'asile*).

[4] This was highlighted in a report written by the General Inspectorate of Finance, Social Affairs and Administration in April 2013. It reinforces the findings of a statistical study conducted in almost sixty CADAs by the NGO *France terre d'asile* at the time of my fieldwork. The study revealed that the average rate of the recognition of a form of protection was above 70% in the CADA vs. 16% at the national level (FTDA, 2005, p. 6). The filtering done at the time of candidates' selection for the allocation of spaces in CADAs (because there are not enough spaces for all the applicants) can also constitute an explanation for these results.

[5] A social security benefit allowing access to health insurance to any individual who has regularly resided

and school for the residents' children. They sometimes also provide support to people who share their sufferings. On the other hand, the social workers monitor the asylum-seekers' movements. Even if they may freely leave the shelter, the internal rules of these institutions, which newcomers are required to sign, require that any absence of more than a day must be reported to the CADA team, and absences lasting multiple days must be approved by the management. The asylum-seekers' mail is monitored, as it transits through the social workers' office. A photocopy of all official letters is kept, whether they involve questions related to the asylum procedure, the renewal of their temporary residence permit, health coverage, or fines for transport fraud. In certain shelters, the team organizes regular room "visits" to verify the current condition of the building and ensure a good atmosphere between neighbors, but to also monitor the cleanliness, housekeeping, and the residents' habits. In other shelters, inspections are replaced by meetings with a social worker who acts as the "hall advisor," who ensures, as is explained to me, that there is a "good relationship and respect for the premises." Besides, a more or less formal form of control is exercised on a daily basis. Comments expressed by social workers in a joking manner, such as "Ah, sir, I'm pleased to see you, I had almost forgotten what you looked like!" point to the residents' absence during social activities, or their lack of involvement the meetings organized by the CADA. Other comments also informally expressed in a playful tone point out late arrivals to collect the mail or the tokens allowing residents to do their laundry. They remind the people staying in the shelters that they are being watched and their attitudes are monitored. A more formal type of control is exercised regarding visitors, who, in certain institutions, must be declared at the entrance of the building or to social workers.

CADAs are not spaces of imprisonment like detention centers, waiting areas at airports, or prisons. They can, however be considered structures of confinement which participate (with the aforementioned spaces) in a system of containment for migrants that has been developed over several decades in France and elsewhere in the European Union (Kobelinsky, 2010; Kobelinsky & Makaremi, 2009).

Time as a Resource

In May 2003, Edona and Gazmadh Bashe decided to leave their hometown, Korçë, in southern Albania. "The violence had gotten out of hand." They were afraid. Edona's injury motivated their departure. Not knowing what to do, they first left for Tirana, the country's capital. Next, they spent a few weeks with some relatives in a remote village in the north, "to think and try to see more clearly," as Gazmadh explained during a conversation years later. They went "almost everywhere in Albania" before being able to come up with the 5,000 dollars requested by the people-smuggler who helped them reach France. Hidden in a truck with about ten

in France for more than three months and who is not yet covered by the social security regime.

other people, they crossed Montenegro and the border with Bosnia–Herzegovina; then, still hidden in the back of the truck, they took a boat to the port of Bari. Once in Italy, they continued their journey for a few more hours before taking another vehicle that drove them to Charenton-le-Pont, in France. They arrived in December, and they especially recall the cold and the nights spent in the Parisian subway. One day, Edona called out to a young woman in the street and spoke to her in English. After a long conversation, the woman told them to call 115 to find a place to sleep. [6] After three days of fruitless attempts, they were allowed to stay at a hotel for a few nights. They told me that they were then able to stay at a hospital for two months, sleeping in a "small bed." They requested asylum in January 2004 and arrived at the CADA three months later, eleven months after leaving Korçë. [7]

A social worker introduced me to Edona Bashe three days after their arrival at the shelter. She told me she felt "light." Since she arrived there, she had been sleeping better, she felt "peaceful." She had difficulty speaking French, so we spoke in English and Italian. A few months later, we met to talk in her room. She spoke French well enough to carry on a conversation; she had learned on her own. She could not attend the class offered by the CADA because she had to go to the hospital often. She had had surgery recently and was soon to have two others.

> When we went to Thérèse's office [their social worker] the first time, I told her that I needed to see a doctor for my face. She made calls, it was very good. I went to the hospital and everything is good, Gazmadh came with me every time. I feel better. (interview with Edona Bashe, shelter, 10/14/2004)

Edona's long, dark hair always covered the left-hand side of her face. She tried to hide a deformed eye, a swollen cheek, and an impressive reddish scar, which was the reason that had caused her to leave Korçë, she told me one day. She felt better since the first surgery and the regular treatments helped her a lot; she was relieved to be able to take care of her health. Their arrival at the CADA gave Edona and Gazmadh the means to physically and psychologically recover from what they had suffered along their journey. They "were happy and relieved" to have a place where they could sleep and have some money to meet their needs.[8] They had a small room that Edona carefully decorated. They shared the kitchen and the bathroom with other asylum-seeking families from Russia, Angola, Palestine, Cameroon, and Sri

[6] National emergency phone number at the district level, for homeless people.

[7] At that time, the Republic of Albania was not yet on the list of so-called "safe" countries, established by the administrative board of the French Office for the Protection of Refugees and Stateless Persons. A country is considered "safe" if, by law, it "ensures respect for the principles of freedom, democracy and the rule of law, as well as human rights and fundamental freedoms." In December 2013, Albania was added to the list and its citizens may no longer seek asylum. They could, however, request that their application be fast-tracked for evaluation within 15 days of submission. In June 2014, Albania joined the European Union.

[8] This is a living allowance paid by the CADA. The amount varies according to the services provided by the shelter and the number of family members. Edona and Gazmadh received 267 euros per month.

Lanka.

> We are happy to be here. Of course it is not our home, but we are not in hotels anymore, or at the hospital. I do not know how long it is going to take but we have been here for several months. That is really good [...] We are lighter, relieved. We have learned all about our papers, CMU [universal healthcare coverage], meetings, asylum. Thérèse and all the advisors help us understand how all of this works. (interview with Edona Bashe, shelter, 10/25/04)

The "lightness" and "relief" that Edona mentions—terms also used by other interviewees—can only be understood in terms of their journey of forced circulation. From the day they left their home in Albania until their arrival at the shelter, their singular journey found many parallels with the trajectories of escape and wandering of all the people I met. The CADA gave Edona and Gazmadh Bashe the feeling that they were safe. In the beginning, the shelter provides a temporary form of stability for newly arrived migrants. As they have time ahead of them, this period is often perceived as the opportunity to learn the ins and outs of French bureaucracy, as Edona explained. The "know-how" of the social workers is highly appreciated, as it covers a whole set of topics often underestimated by newcomers to France: social benefits, access to health care professionals, the construction of the narrative of asylum that is fundamental for the residents, and, for many asylum seekers, language learning. While Gazmadh admitted to having more difficulty with French, Edona, on the other hand, spent at least two hours a day going grammar exercises with a borrowed book or reading and studying the words she did not understand, as the vignette at the beginning of this chapter illustrates. She also watched TV to improve her understanding.

> We bought the TV cheap and it is very practical because I listen and I learn French. I have improved a lot since we got the TV. I also listen to the radio. It also helps me but it is more for the music!" (conversation with Edona Bashe, shelter, 10/25/04)

Five months after their arrival at the CADA, they were scheduled for an interview at the French Office for the Protection of Refugees and Stateless Persons. Their application for asylum was rejected a few months later. Apart from the disappointment, they urgently needed to appeal the decision before the Refugee Appeals Board within thirty days after receiving the notification of their rejection. During this time, their social worker provided them with "great moral and legal support," in Gazmadh's words. She saw them three times a week in her office to talk and prepare their appeal. They decided to follow her advice and hired a lawyer to try to put the odds on their side. They spoke to him by telephone. Once the appeal was submitted, a new waiting stage began. Their social worker immediately warned them that they would not get a summons before 10 months to one year.

Time as a Constraint

Edona and Gazmadh met in the social services' Office for Youth in the city of Korçë, where she worked as a receptionist and he was Section Chief of the governing party. She was 18 years old and he was 23. A short time later, they got married. This was two years before leaving Albania. At that time, they "worked a lot," but they also "went out a lot": meetings with friends, parents, Gazmadh exercising. She did embroidery, like her mother did. Their life "was filled with activities," Edona said, evoking her past, in contrast with her monotonous daily life in the shelter.

> Since I have been here, I have the impression that there are thirty hours in a day, and yet I sleep a lot! [Laughs] Well, we do not have much to do [...] I do not go out a lot; I do not like going out, people look at me all the time. My husband goes out to walk a little, but I do not do anything here. There is nothing to do. We get up late; we go to bed around midnight. We watch TV. We get up, I do the cleaning, and I cook. We speak, we fight, we watch TV, or we listen to the radio. Chéri FM is very good. I go to the hospital or I stay here to read in French. They lent me some books. I do nothing. We have too much time here. We walk round and round, we are bored. (interview with Edona Bashe, shelter, 10/19/04)

The Bashes spent their time between their room and the hospital, where Gazmadh would takee Edona for outpatient care twice a week.[9] Sometimes, Gazmadh also took brief strolls through the neighborhood or stood in front of the entrance to the building, just long enough to smoke two or three cigarettes. The daily life of people I met in the CADA was structured by the impression of "doing nothing" and "turning in circles." The boredom Edona spoke about describes a weariness caused by the dullness of the days with no particular interest, which keep repeating themselves. This experience of a redundant temporality, of a time that is difficult to fill, recalls the figure of the vagabond described by Bauman (1999), who lives *in the space*, a heavy space, resistant, untouchable, which encloses time and shields it from the control of these people. At the CADA, this space is, most of the time, made up of the domestic environment. Watching TV, listening to the radio, doing the cleaning, sleeping, reading, talking with the neighbors, seem to be the only available activities. They are perceived as ways to "spend" time and as the symptoms of the time that does not move. Many interviewees expressed how they felt like their days had "thirty hours," as described by Edona, or as suggested by Gazmadh in the opening vignette, saying that "the watch does not move forward." This "time-reifying" language (Gell, 1992) underlines the speaker's impression that he is suspended in an uncertain situation. As Elias mentions (1996 [1984]), time is often given certain properties of the processes' evolutionary aspects. Speaking about a watch that does not move forward is first of all reporting on a stagnant situation that is seen as the polar opposite—at least, as Edona and Gazmadh and many other interviewees often expressed—of life in their country, before asylum, before the CADA, before the waiting began.

From time to time, Edona and Gazmadh almost reluctantly participated

[9] Edona sometimes mentioned her husband's patience and support, "anyone else would have divorced with a wife like this," she told me once, pointing her injured face.

in activities organized by the CADA entertainment team: visiting a museum, making cakes during a cooking class, going to the botanical gardens. Gazmadh found these "outings" childish, "we are not children!" he would often repeat. The reason they participated was, above all, to fill their "empty" time. One afternoon, seated around the small table in their room, Gazmadh told me about the feeling of "getting stuck:"

> We are here all the time. We don't know what to do. The days last forever, and they are always the same. We have too much time so far [...] When are we going to have a normal life? We are stuck, we cannot do anything. I smoke downstairs and that's all. We are locked up here. We are sometimes treated like children. (conversation with Edona and Gazmadh, shelter, 11/2/04)

The feeling of being "trapped" was shared by most of the interviewees I met in the CADA. It implies both a confinement in time (a present where one "does nothing") and in space: a partially closed institution where one's movements and visits are controlled, activities and daily routines are monitored, where they sometimes feel they are treated like children, which leads to a loss of their agency and autonomy for the benefit of the institution. The feeling of being treated like a child sometimes motivated Gazmadh to convince his wife not to participate in CADA activities. Many interviewees used the semantics of a prison to report their feeling of being "like in prison," "as prisoners," "behind bars".

Gazmadh's impression of being "trapped" perfectly captures the temporality of waiting and the spatial confinement: they are trapped in (and because of) the waiting, just like they are trapped in the shelter (because of the containment it induces). The previous quote also reports the feeling of being in a situation that is considered abnormal. The hope to have a "normal life" was often evoked by Edona and Gazmadh.

> We would like to have a house, or an apartment would also be good. Finish the treatment and be healthy. Stop with all this, have papers, find a job, for both of us. Have stability, be busy, work like everybody, a normal life. And then have children. (conversation with Edona Bashe, cafeteria of the Pompidou Center, 1/27/05)

The normalization that Edona dreams of depends on their material autonomy, the stability of a permanent legal status, and the control of time. In other words, the temporality of waiting also includes the hope of its ending, of a "new life" with all that they do not have in their present life in the CADA.

Adjusting to Time

Ten months after her arrival at the shelter, Edona accepted an unexpected opportunity and began to work under the table as housekeeper. A young Russian woman living with her children on the same floor as the Bashes told her that she worked as a housekeeper several times a week for a "French couple" she met through the mother of one of her son's classmates. As she needed to take care of her children, she could not work the extra hours she was offered, and told Edona she could introduce her to an "old French couple." She encouraged her to accept the job, telling her that it would allow her "think of something else."

> I do not like to do that, but, well, at least I would be doing something. I do not want to stay in the room in front of TV anymore, sleeping. It is not good for me, for my head. I do not like to clean the house; I prefer to cook and iron clothes. But it's good, it has kept me busy for one month now, I go there three times a week, they are kind. I do not do it for money. Yes, money is good for later, to rent an apartment, but I do not do it for that. I have to do something and, for the moment, I can only do the cleaning, so I do it." (interview with Edona Bashe, shelter, 2/23/05)

In spite of what is experienced by Edona as a social downgrading, the most important thing for her is not so much the salary she earns, but the impression of being useful and busy. One month earlier, Gazmadh had found an undeclared job as a replacement on a construction site in a neighboring town. He had worked for three weeks and it had made him "feel a lot better." After this first experience, he found a dishwashing job in a Paris bar where he worked for four months. He was later hired as a construction worker.

Like refugees living in humanitarian government camps, the asylum seekers I met often expressed feelings of powerlessness and uselessness, linked to their professional inactivity (Agier, 2008, p. 207). Having a job allowed Gazmadh and Edona to feel "active" and to avoid dealing with time any longer. The money they earned was undoubtedly one motive to take on jobs they would never have imagined doing in Albania. Feeling "less dependent" was also an important motivation, perhaps even more important, according to my interviewees. For Edona and Gazmadh, working was a way "to do something" while waiting. Other asylum seekers also fit into the underground economy—making their waiting time less boring—through the implementation of informal economic exchanges inside the shelter, such as hairdressing salons and sewing workshops set up secretly in their rooms, or selling cigarettes or perfume in the kitchens. Finally, for other asylum seekers, it was volunteer work or political activism that fulfilled the same function. Although different, all these activities contribute to feeling "less assisted" and to regaining a positive self-image. They create obligations, allowing individuals to enter a temporality guided by specific constraints, creating a new pattern for their days and a semblance of "normality." Finally, these experiences open up the possibility of meeting people outside the CADA, and existing in another way that is unrelated to their request for asylum, allowing them to be something other than an asylum-seeker whose only activity is waiting. These activities can thus be understood as tactics—in the sense of being small daily practices that take advantage of opportunities that appear in the moment (de Certeau, 1980)—that allow them to bypass the heavy effects of waiting by injecting a new element into their present.

> Getting out of the shelter for a moment, of all this: it makes me feel good. To see

> other people, to take the bus to go to work, these things. I know we are not supposed to do it, but, we don't hurt anybody, and it is not theft. We really have no choice; it is just not to go completely crazy!" (conversation with Edona and Gazmadh, my apartment, 3/29/05)

Gazmadh was aware that his activity was illegal. In theory, within the context of the European directive laying down the minimal standards for the reception of asylum-seekers,[10] candidates for refugee status can request a temporary working permit before the Departmental Division of Labor, Employment and Professional training, if the French Office for the Protection of Refugees and Stateless Persons has not ruled on their request after one year, or if they are waiting to be summoned before the Court of Appeal. In this case, asylum-seekers are subject to the common legal rules applicable to immigrant workers for the delivery of a temporary working permit. As access to the job market is reserved as a priority for French people, asylum-seekers may be authorized to work only if, in the sector of activity and the geographical zone concerned, the number of applications is not greater than the offer. Obtaining this permit is highly unusual and, in most of the French departments, the administration systematically refuses asylum-seekers the right to work, no matter what the employment situation is (CNCDH, 2006a p. 147). This practical prohibition on employment creates a "field for illegal practices" (Foucault, 1975a p. 285). Neither Edona nor Gazmadh requested an authorization to work. I have never met an asylum-seeker in the CADA who did. Thus, concretely, in spite of the directive, the asylum-seekers' reality did not change; they participated in the economic market in an informal way.

While recognizing that his activity was illegal, Gazmadh discarded the idea of being a thief or a person who "hurt" others. He justified his actions by saying that he did not want "to go completely crazy," that he wanted to take care of himself.

On April 15, 2005, Edona and Gazmadh did not go to work. They were summoned to the Refugee Appeals Board "to defend their application for asylum." They were accompanied by a CADA social worker. Their lawyer was not there when they arrived. They unsuccessfully tried to contact him at his office and on his mobile phone. They had spoken to him for one hour just three days earlier, had paid him the 850 euros he had requested, and were told that "everything was ready." Ultimately, the hearing was postponed due to the lawyer's absence. The next day, they would learn that he had been sick.

> I believed that we were going to finish with that, that we were going to wait 21 days and then it was going to be over.[11] Frankly, I was a little afraid this morning. I did not know how it would go, but that… How long are we going to wait to be summoned again? We're still stuck with all this. (conversation with Edona and

[10] Decree of August 23, 2005 (no. 2005-1051).

[11] Following the hearing at the French Court of Asylum (previously the Refugee Appeals Board), there is a clear ending to the waiting time, as the decision is posted in the lobby of the Courthouse exactly three weeks after the hearing.

Gazmadh Bashe, at a coffee shop near the Refugee Appeals Board, 4/20/05)

If working had helped them to pass the time as they waited, the postponement of the hearing had reminded them that they were still waiting on a decision and, therefore, "stuck waiting."

Rethinking Time

Sometimes concealed, occasionally almost tangible, waiting time is a part of life for the men and women who seek asylum in France. It is also the fate of "vagabonds" (Bauman, 1999), "players" in globalization (Bayart, 2004), "poor people" (Auyero, 2011), and "clandestines" (Laacher, 2007). Waiting, however, shapes every person's time in a different manner. In migrants' journeys, waiting can be people lining up in front of a consulate to get a visa, as waiting for a people-smuggler or for better weather conditions to cross the border. Each waiting period has its unwritten but well-established codes, its rhythms and spaces.

Edona and Gazmadh Bashe's practices and perceptions demonstrate various ways to experience and understand this imposed temporality, which is divided into three main sequences:

- The temporal space between the submission of the asylum application and the decision appears first as an opportunity, as it provides a time of respite in the CADA and the possibility of reconstructing oneself after a trajectory of circulation and wandering.

- The waiting time is experienced as a constraint that is manifested through a retreat, a sense of emptiness that is compounded by a feeling of uncertainty related to the outcome of the application and one's future projects. In this stressful period, it is often also inevitable to reflect on the suffering of past violence that led to the decision to go into exile.

- The waiting time is bypassed by participating in activities outside the shelter—in this particular case, working—which create new temporal frames, new networking, new spaces.

These sequences must not be understood as a uniform and linear chronology. They are, on the one hand, marked by the phases of the asylum procedure and, on the other hand, there may be comings and goings between the temporal stages, thus moving from a period where waiting is taken over by other temporal constraints, to another one where it returns and is translated by the confinement in the shelter. It is in these moments of boredom that the double dependence, both institutional and economic, faced by candidates for refugee status is felt most deeply, as it is established by the effective ban on employment. Sometimes waiting may not only be due to the asylum request, but is also due to the waiting for news from parents with whom contact had been lost, waiting for a political change in the country of origin, or waiting on the hope of a "new life." To wait and to hope were then both articulated in the same temporality.[12]

In Edona and Gazmadh Bashe's experience, waiting was at once a break in their trajectory, which they perceive as being put on hold, and a continuity, as they sometimes experienced a stretching temporality that seemed permanent.

If the waiting experiences of poor people subjected to the Ministry of Social Development' decisions in Argentina "persuade the destitute of the need to be patient, thus conveying the implicit state request to be compliant clients" (Auyero, 2011, p. 6), thus associating the waiting with a disciplinary aspect (see Schwartz, 1975, p. 189), those of the asylum-seekers encountered in reception centers in France instead combine waiting and confinement. The normalized waiting is here aggravated by the particular living conditions in the CADA—assistance and control, support and vigilance, protection and childish treatment—where people whose only shared experience is asylum seeking live. This alienation through time is more an effect of the bureaucratic process than a political objective, but it certainly is a way to test the administration. Waiting "durably changes, that is to say, during all the time that the expectative lasts, the behavior of the person being, as we say, suspended to the awaited decision" (Bourdieu, 1997, p. 270).

The public hospitality offered in the CADA entails a close relationship between time, space, and the exercise of power. As with most of the interviewees I met during my fieldwork, Edona and Gazmadh Bashe experienced a contraction of space and an expansion of time. The waiting of asylum seekers can be understood both as a form of government and as a daily (social and relational) activity that involves many practices. Contrary to what seems to be suggested by often-used expressions such as "it is an empty time" or "it is a complete void," waiting is not in fact absence. Rather, it is populated by a multitude of everyday activities that contribute to filling it.

It is through these activities, from the most ordinary and trivial to the more inventive, that the possibility of finding freedom (at least partially) from the imposed temporality is likely to emerge. In other terms, it is in this ability to find ways of coping with the waiting process that the possibility of agency lies. It is a question of the possibility of (once again, at least partially) choosing, deciding, in a present characterized by uncertainty and doubt.

***

Edona and Gazmadh Bashe waited a year for their next summons before the Refugee Appeals Board. Anxiety filled the three weeks that followed the hearing. Their waiting ended when they received the outcome of their appeal.

---

[12] The Spanish language is here very explicit, because *esperar* means both to wait and to hope. This double meaning can be found in the etymology of the French word *attendre,* which comes from the Latin *tendere,* meaning "lay our spirit toward." The focus here is on the dimension of hope and the expectative held by waiting. This dimension can be found in the dictionary of the Académie Française, 1762 edition, where the verb *to hope* appears within the meanings of waiting.

It was denied. They were given four weeks to leave the CADA. The last time I heard from them, two years later, they were still in France, without papers, sharing an apartment with two other couples near Lyon. She cleaned private homes, and he worked on a construction site. They were expecting a baby.

References

Agier, M.. 2008. Gérer les indésirables. Des camps de réfugiés au gouvernement humanitaire. Paris: Flammarion.

Auyero, J.. 2011. "Patients of the State. An Ethographic Account of Poor People's Waiting." Latin American Research Review 46 (1): 5- 29.

Bauman, Z.. 1999. Le coût humain de la mondialisation. Paris: Hachette.

Bayart, J.-F. 2004. Le gouvernement du monde. Une critique politique de la globalisation. Paris: Fayard.

Bourdieu, P. 1997. Méditations pascaliennes. Paris: Le Seuil.

Certeau de, M. 1980. L'invention du quotidien, 1: Manières de faire. Paris: Gallimard.

CNCDH. 2006. Les conditions d'exercice du droit d'asile en France. Rapport de la Commission nationale consultative des droits de l'homme. Paris.

Elias, N. 1996 [1984]. Du temps. Paris: Fayard.

Foucault, M. 1975. Surveiller et punir. Paris: Gallimard.

FTDA. 2005. "Asile: sortir de l'arbitraire et de l'injustice." Proasile 12: 5-11.

Gell, A. 1992. The anthropology of time. Cultural constructions of temporal maps and images. Oxford: Berg Publishers.

Inspection générale des finances, Inspection générale des affaires sociales et Inspection générale de l'administration. 2013. Rapport sur l'hébergement et la prise en charge financière des demandeurs d'asile établi par l'inspection générale des finances, l'inspection générale des affaires sociales et l'inspection générale de l'administration..

Kobelinsky, C. 2010. L'accueil des demandeurs d'asile. Une ethnographie de l'attente. Paris: Editions du Cygne.

Kobelinsky, C. & Ch. Makaremi (eds.) 2009. Enfermés dehors. Enquêtes sur le confinement des étrangers. Bellecombe-en-Bauges: Editions du Croquant.

Laacher, S. 2007. Le peuple des clandestins. Paris: Calmann-Lévy.

Schwartz, B,. 1975. Queuing and waiting. Studies in the social organization of access and delay. Chicago & London: University of Chicago Press.

A FAMILY RESEMBLANCE: MIGRATION, WORK AND LOYALTY

Frédéric Décosse[1]

Ayoub and Malika Amrani are husband and wife, former farm workers who, for many years, came to France on OMI contracts to do seasonal work for a farmer in the Bouches-du-Rhône area. In the early 1970s, the young woman's father and uncle, *fellahs*[2] from the Moroccan Prerif who had emigrated to the city, found a contract in the city of Grans, on the Crau plain, and gradually "sponsored" the next generation of migrants. In 1990, when Malika was recruited to join them, there were about ten family members already working on the farm. Though she was formally employed as a farm worker, she actually worked as a "servant" for the farmer and his family. Against the advice of her employer, who wanted nothing to distract her from her work, she got married and held a big wedding in Fez, to which her employer was invited. Ayoub, her husband, was recruited to work in the orchards. As a newlywed, Malika had more and more trouble accepting the abuse and bullying her parents had endured until then. She became increasingly opposed to her employer. 2000 marked a breaking point, when Ayoub fell from an apple tree and was seriously injured. His pelvis was fractured. Their employer was reluctant to report it as a work-related accident. The couple stood up to him, and the following year, none of the family's contracts were renewed. It was a form of retaliation. It was a collective punishment, as if to remind the migrants that they were bound to their employer by the same duty of loyalty. This incident would have lasting consequences on Malika's relationship with her family, who accused her of being selfish. In the meantime, Malika became a prominent figure in the movement to defend seasonal migrants' rights, almost in spite of herself. Her story was the subject of several articles in the media and was taken up by the *Collectif de défense des travailleurs agricoles saisonniers* (Collective for the Defense of Seasonal Agricultural Workers) (CODETRAS).

I met Malika in 2003, when I was starting my research on seasonal immigration from Morocco in Provençal agriculture (Décosse 2004; Décosse 2011). Although she was one of the first employees under contract with the OMI (Office of International Migration) that I interviewed, her story gave me a biased view of my topic from the outset, in the sense that she represented an "anomaly" within the corpus of interviews I was gathering. Her singular status is due, above all, to the fact that she is a woman, a woman

[1] Frédéric Décosse, CNRS Researcher, Aix-Marseille University, CNRS, LEST UMR 7317, 13626, Aix-en-Provence, France.

[2] *Fellahs*: Small farmers.

who is *a priori* condemned to exist drowned in the ocean of an exclusively male working class population. Her statistical invisibility is further compounded in the field by a relative physical invisibility, tied to the fact that, unlike her close relatives who worked in the orchards, Malika worked in the closed and private world of the employer's home. Although the OMI's temporary migration program was designed to bring in contingents of single men from Morocco and Tunisia each year to work in the fields—an "imported," "locally relocated" workforce (Terray, 1999), which allows Provençal fruit and vegetable growers to produce at low cost and export their goods throughout the French and European market—Malika was misappropriated by her employer, who in fact employed her illegally as a domestic worker. Here I would like to draw particular attention to the illegal nature of this arrangement, both to better lay the groundwork for the legal developments that are to follow, and also because it was the source of the paternalistic relationship between Malika and her employer. For now, let us return to what makes her an outlier among the cohort of OMI workers: her gender and her activity. The former defines the latter, since the catch-all term "domestic worker" belies a host of different roles (housekeeper, cook, nanny) whose common feature is their gender.

With Malika, the owner revived the ancient tradition of the *fille de ferme* (farm girl), a classic trope of the French countryside that was kept alive through immigration until the Second World War (Hubscher, 2005) and who faced harsh conditions that were well illustrated in Maupassant's short story. The young woman's work day typically began in the early morning (7 a.m.) and ended around 9 p.m., with an average of 13–14 hours of work per day; and yet at best, her pay stub would indicate 50 to 60 hours worked per week. In the summer, Malika's hours would be extended without her consent. This requirement of near-constant availability/flexibility was a reflection of the fact that in reality, she worked *au sifflet*.[3] Her tasks were diverse, since she was the *nounou*[4] for her employer's two children, the cook and the housekeeper all at the same time. In addition to the housekeeping (including cleaning, dishes, laundry and ironing, watering the plants, etc.) of the employer's large home, which has four bathrooms, a swimming pool and many outbuildings, she had to prepare meals, make traditional Moroccan bread every day, and watch and play with the children that she took to and from school. At first, Malika lived on site and was available 24 hours a day. She has almost no time off, as having Sundays off was exceptional until 1994. That was when her situation changed, as she decided to get married despite her employer's disapproval. After that, she would only work every third weekend.

Malika Hassani was born in 1959 in Douar Bouchmakh, a small Arabic-speaking Berber village in the foothills of the Rif, northeast of Fez *(qabilat Meziate, jbala* country, Taounate province). Or at least, this is the date that is

---

[3] Working *au sifflet* (on the whistle) means being on call and subject to the "whims of the job."

[4]. *Nounou* means nanny.

recorded on her birth certificate, which was registered some twenty years later at the Moroccan office of vital records. These records were not well kept in the Moroccan countryside at the time of her birth, so her father had to rectify the oversight with the administration before she could obtain a passport and leave to work in France. Malika was the second (daughter) of nine siblings in a family of small farmers who earned their living mainly from mixed farming (wheat cultivation, arboriculture and sheep farming), using community labor *(touiza)* when necessary. The family was unable to support themselves with their land, so her father had to farm further south, near the Idriss 1er dam, before obtaining an employment contract in 1977 that allowed him to travel to France for seasonal work. His elder brother Amin had been working with the same farmer in Grans, the "sponsor", for three years; I will return to this point in a moment. For now, let us discuss the five daughters' marriages: the eldest daughter married a *fellah* from Taounate. The three youngest daughters (Latifa, Malika, and Amal) married craftsmen (mechanic, autobody mechanic, etc.) from the working class district of Bab Sidi Boujida where the family settled in the 1980s. The fifth, sister, who has since lived in the new part of Fez, made a ("good") match with an "emigrant from France."[5] This brief overview of the young women's movements illustrates how the Hassani family was gradually moving away from their country origins to become more anchored in the urban territory and its sociability, and, furthermore, in international migration projects and networks. While Latifa went to work in Libya with her husband, Malika was asked to join the men in her family in France: her father, her uncle, her brother Mokhtar, and several cousins.

1990. The employer, who traveled to Fez almost every year on vacation to recruit the workforce he needed, offered her a position. Malika was 30 years old at the time and had been working for seven or eight years as a medical assistant for a Haitian ophthalmologist at a clinic in Fez. It was her first paid working experience. She was in charge of cleaning, greeting patient,s managing the waiting room, and translating conversations between the doctor (French-speaking) and the patients (Arabic-speaking) during their appointments. She received a salary equivalent to just under 75 euros per month, plus substantial tips.

She owed this professional situation above all to her mastery of French, which she had learned from the family that her maternal grandmother had entrusted her to at the age of four or five, a well-to-do family of Spanish Pied-Noir farmers who employed one of her cousins: the Perez family. This was a relatively common social reproduction/promotion strategy used in Moroccan working-class families. Malika's father explained that her placement with them was due to the fact that he had only daughters (three), whereas (according to tradition) he would need sons to take care of him in his old age. Without venturing too deeply into the murky waters of

[5] Interview with Malika Amrani, unrecorded (notes), about 60 minutes. Conducted in her home on 07/10/2015.

psychoanalytical interpretation, one might imagine that this singular experience could explain Malika's constant distancing from paternal figures throughout her life, her frustration with the traditional value system that these figures would attempt to impose on her. Her childhood, which she readily describes as "very happy," was spent far from her parents, in the new section of Fez (Dar Dbibegh), in the home of this rich European family who treated her as their own daughter and who saw no problme in hiring a French teacher to give her private lessons. She says: "probably because [I] didn't have a birth certificate," Malika did not attend elementary school, which would permanently hinder her progress in reading and writing. However, she entered a girls' school, a public institution left over from the French colonial period that was exclusively oriented towards "housekeeping." There, Malika learned to cook, sew, embroider, knit; in short, "to keep house" (Herman, 2008, p. 271). This education was also an opportunity for her to immerse herself in an Arabic-speaking world and to speak her mother tongue, which her separation from her family had caused her to forget. But above all, it was an opportunity to escape from the confines of her adoptive parents' home and their constant supervision, to make friends and, more generally, with all the worldliness of an eleven-year-old, to discover the world. For example, she would go to the movies, where she watched French films. The young girl thus grew up in the urban universe of the 1960s and 1970s, with one foot in the exclusive world of the rich European colonists and the other in the world of the poor Moroccan masses of the imperial city. In fact, her lifestyle irrevocably distanced her from her peasant family, from her origins in rural society and the conservative and patriarchal traditions that dominated at the time. In Fez, "the city air makes you free" (Weber, 2014, p.74), a freedom that was certainly relative for Malika, whose host family forbade her to hang out with boys, for example, but which was based on a certain anonymity and the fragmenting of society, which Lefebvre calls "individualization in socialization" (1968, p.154).

At the age of fifteen or sixteen, Malika was suddenly forced to leave this world, as her status as a pampered only daughter was threatened within her host family, and she no longer felt comfortable there. But let us take a step back for a moment. Malika was initially taken in by a group of siblings, two middle-aged men and their sister, who were all unmarried and childless. Malika was the center of their attention for ten years. When the sister and one of the brothers died, she stayed on with Michel, who was soon joined by a second sister and her daughter. The arrival of the second young girl's in the home upset the order of things. This second teenager, a French girl recently arrived from metropolitan France and the biological daughter of the now enlarged circle of siblings, gradually replaced Malika, pointing out her otherness and thus her illegitimacy within the household: "She would always say, 'She's Moroccan! You'll see. When she grows up, she'll get married and then she won't have time for you any more!'"[6] This jealousy, this hardening of hearts, as the primacy of blood relations over elective filiation was suddenly asserted, and what is appropriate to call, for lack of a better term, a form of "white" privilege, shattered Malika's confidence in this formative intimacy that had been built up over the years with the Perez family. Was it a prideful (over)reaction on the part of the rebellious teenage girl? It was probably more a matter of necessity than virtue. Sensing that she was no longer welcome there, she left, returning to the village and her biological parents. Michel came to get her, and for a time she returned to live in Fez, but the emotional attachment was broken, as her faith in the unconditional filial bond had been lost. The young woman returned once again to Douar Bouchmakh, where she found herself confronted with a world that was no longer hers, and that she could no longer stand.

I have very little information about the stage of her life after her return to the village. We pick up her trajectory a few years later (in 1982–1983), when she found a job in Fez. She went with her mother to an ophthalmologist's appointment. During the appointment, she offered her services as an interpreter to the doctor, who recruited her on the spot. Malika saw this as an opportunity to move to Fez and gain her independence. Indeed: "[...] the female wage earner constitutes a breach in the hegemony of men which cannot be openly contested, since it is of sacred origin [...] a silent defeat in the act, not in the word of patriarchal domination" (Mernissi, 1981, p. 36). Now that she was over twenty, she was seen as being of marriageable age, but she did not want to marry, to her father's great displeasure.[7] Though Malika understood that she would not be able to postpone this social norm forever, she also knew that the fact that she had a job—and could possibly contribute to the family's income, even if it was already "tied" to the salary that her father earned eight months of the year in France—was a means to justify her delay in complying with it. The banishment that was consubstantial with her single status could be avoided for a time on condition that she be economically useful and, in addition, that she assume the social role that went with it: that of the breadwinner. This strategy must be situated within the context of the struggle "from below" against the system of patriarchal oppression, of all these "behaviors (individual or weakly supportive) of preservation, nibbling, cunning; in short, [of] a whole underground work of creating a domestic counter-power that is always fragile, of an economic rebalancing that is always threatened, at the heart of a fundamentally unequal system" (Virolle-Souibès, 1986, p. 194).

At first, Malika lived in a small studio in Fez that she rented from her father's uncle. At the time, her father had gone to France for the season. He

[6] Interview with Malika Amrani, recorded, approx. 120 minutes. Conducted at her home by Emmanuelle Hellio, on 10/06/2015.

[7] In 1982, the average age for first marriages in Morocco was 21 in rural areas and 24 in urban areas (General Census of Population and Housing, 1982)

was outraged upon his return, when he discovered that his daughter was living alone, as he saw it as a disgrace to the family, something only done by women of easy virtue. Working women were never far removed from the stigma of prostitution in the sense that: "As she violates the cleavage of the social field and transgresses the sexual limits of the division of labor by infiltrating the public economic sphere, she can therefore only sell what she manages in the domestic sphere, in privacy, that is to say: sex" (Mernissi ,1981, p. 10). Pressured by her father, Malika left her studio and took refuge in an apartment above the clinic where she worked. She lived there on and off until her departure for France in 1990. She only lived there intermittently because, due to the dispute over the studio, her parents decided to move to Fez, and Malika split her time between the clinic and her parents' apartment when her father was not there or during times when their relationship improved. Was this the main reason for their departure from Dura Buchmakh? Nothing is less certain, as her brother Amin, who had been recruited three years earlier by the same employer, had done the same not long before. As for many farm workers in the Rif region (Bossard, 1979; Lazaar, 1987), the father's participation in international emigration ultimately led to the family's rural exodus. This is not symbolically neutral for this *fellah* from the Province of Taounate, because Fez was above all the metropolis of the commercial bourgeoisie, where the wholesalers who bought the local farmers' products at extremely low prices lived. Thus, the family's move to Fez must be seen as the consequence of the destructive effects of the relative proletarianization of the head of the family (seasonal participation in the wage-labor force) on subsistence agriculture and the domestic mode of production that had prevailed until then, even if their ties with the land were not completely severed. Their land was in fact converted to indirect tenure *(nzala)* and was now exploited by the clan members who remained in the village. Their ties to the land were no longer of an economic nature (in the sense that the family unit no was no longer sustaining itself by working the land) and became mainly symbolic, in the sense that land ownership now served only to maintain an affective and identity-bound relationship with the clan and the family's territory of origin. For Malika, on the other hand, the city was a space of freedom where her desire to live her life as a young woman, far from suspicion, far from being subject to what people would say and from being forced into marriage, could blossom. She went to cafés with friends and went away on weekend trips to visit this country she did not know well. In 1989, her brother Mokhtar also signed a seasonal contract with the same farmer. When the farmer offered Malika the same opportunity the following year, she saw it as a chance to increase her salary—from 75 euros (+ tips) to 655 euros, which was the net monthly minimum wage at the time—and also, more generally, to broaden her horizons, and in particular to escape the social control that was suffocating her and to "trap" her by forcing her to get married. Her first foray into migration was therefore as much for material reasons as from a desire to see the world, a desire for "adventure."

Very soon, Malika was faced with a reality that in no way matched her expectations, as well as the dominant narrative propagated by her family and friends; that is to say the myth that attempted to give meaning and dignity to a migration and an employment relationship that was essentially characterized by dependence, constraint, and economic overexploitation. "This collective ignorance of the objective truth about emigration [...] is maintained by the whole group" (Sayad, 1999: p. 51). It is certainly addressed first of all to the society of origin, seeking to repair the "original sin" of departure and absence. However, the other function of this "collective lie" is to conceal the real, illegal operation of a seasonal migration system where recruiters co-opt workers on a family (or village) basis and where the renewal of employment contracts is entirely at the employer's discretion. In this system, whose unwritten law is "if you talk, you stay in Morocco the following year," the entire workers' collective constructs and propagates a golden legend in which the employer is necessarily a "good boss." However, despite her hopes, the home of the employer and his clan was the only horizon for Malika's life and work, and the only time she went out was to pick up the children from school. Although she worked an average of 13 to 14 hours a day (including weekends), her salary was capped at less than 500 euros a month, i.e., about 30% less than the amount on her pay slip and the check that her employer would cash for her (and the other 150 OMI workers) at the Crédit Agricole de Salon-de-Provence, pocketing the change. Sometimes she was only paid in installments and the arrears would build up over two or three months. In addition, the employer withheld 150 euros from her last five months' salary, a withholding which, according to him, was meant to cover the fees for bringing over workers (medical examinations, transport, etc.) that the OMI supposedly charged to him, even though Malika purchased her own plane ticket and the cost of the OMI tax was not even one one-tenth of the amount the employer withheld. This completely illegal and yet widespread practice of outsourcing the cost of access to the French labor market to foreigners was not limited to the reimbursement of introduction costs: seasonal workers actually paid a very steep price (750 euros per year) for the privilege of returning to the farm the following year. These repeated deductions, as well as unpaid leave and overtime, reveal a system of overexploitation of the migrant labor force which, in addition to the the strict extraction of surplus value from paid labor (framed by positive law and the bourgeois morality of the capitalist), is equivalent to by plunder. This relationship of overexploitation is, however, embedded in personal relationships with strong paternalistic connotations, a classic means of managing the OMI migrant labor force which, in Malika's case, is reinforced by the intimacy that she shares with the employer's clan due to her role: she raises the children and takes care of the grandmother, but also and above all she is the one who witnesses, in spite of herself, the family's daily life, its intrigues and disputes. After the boss's divorce from a former employee in the packaging department, who left with another employee,[8] Malika found herself under the authority of her employer's mother, the wife of the former boss, the "big boss," the one who recruited the previous generation workers including Malika's father and uncles. Indeed, as Lautier points out: "in the relationship of domesticity, as with many care activities, it is one woman who exploits, humiliates and imprisons another, even if this is the result of the prior naturalization of the sexual division of roles" (2010, p. 24). This conflictual relationship between the women gradually made her job untenable and would eventually lead to a rupture with significant consequences for the entire Hassani/Amrani family.

If we attempt to retrace the history of this rupture, the analysis must factor in the biographical (Malika's trajectory), structural (functioning of the OMI system) and contextual (work-related accident) aspects. After having postponed the fateful hour of marriage for a "long time," Malika finally met Ayoub, a friend of her brother, during the winter of 1992 in Fez. Their respective families were initially opposed to their union, as was her employer. Malika's father resented the fact that he did not choose her suitor and objected to a marriage in which his daughter would leave her husband in Morocco to work in France for most of the year. For their part, Ayoub's family saw Malika above all as an older, independent woman (although these shortcomings were offset by her earning power in France), while her employer feared, as we have seen, that she would become less available to him. The couple did not have many options, which forced Malika to bide her time for more than a year, to play her hand patiently and discreetly to get rid of these various obstacles one by one. Knowing that her employer and her family were bonded to her by ties of intimacy (due to her status as the children's *nounou*, in particular) and interest (she was aware that they were happy with her services and that they would find it difficult to find a replacement for her who would be so readily available and be so poorly paid), she attempted to reconcile her professional life and her marital ambitions by offering to recruit Ayoub, which her employer ended up accepting. It should be mentioned that these negotiations were held in secret, behind the family's back, as Malika feared their reaction, and she wanted to present them with a done deal. The young woman knew that is was a "gamble," double or nothing, as the employer had threatened to retaliate against her family if she insisted on getting married. This was obviously unthinkable for her relatives, given the risks of collective expulsion (and even as Malika had recently joined the OMI system), so the young woman decided to keep quiet. However, the employer had one strict condition that aimed to guarantee her future availability: the couple must not have children. Is there any way that the violence of the social relationship of domination, created by the internationalization of reproductive work, can be more clearly expressed?

[8] Interview with Malika Amrani, recorded, approx. 120 minutes. Conducted at her home by Emmanuelle Hellio, on 10/06/2015.

With the marriage project, behind the work force–merchandise that the employer habitually used as he pleased, Malika's personhood (her irreducible support) and her desire to start a family would potentially rise to the surface again. The tension between productive and reproductive logic is not simply a symbolic dispute over the "right to have rights" (Arendt, 1982, p. 599). What is at stake here is the effective private appropriation of Malika's time and its reduction to the "work of social reproduction" (Moujoud & Falquet, 2010, p. 170) of the employer, a logic of exclusivity in contradiction with the young couple's own reproductive desires and agenda. The employer's imperative is not only imposed through the employer's force of persuasion (i.e., through blackmail of Malika's extended family's employment), but also through the actual system of migration control, since the annual medical exam that women underwent at the OMI office in Casablanca systematically included a pregnancy test.[9] For Malika, the unusual feminization of seasonal migration generated a specific form of "migratory utilitarianism," understood as the propensity of the State and employers to "regulate the migratory question through the expected interest (or disadvantage) of the foreigners they bring or allow to come, mainly in terms of the labor force provided" (Morice, 2004, p. 2). The system used to "channel of the flow" of seasonal migration combines a generic and sexually undifferentiated control of one's mobility on the labor market (assignment to a work sector and then to an employer) and in one's migratory practice (superimposition of residence and work rights, confinement in a perpetual movement of circulation) with a singular and gendered bio-political logic of the restriction of one's reproductive activity (prevention through lack of birthright citizenship and guarantee of one's availability for work).[10]

Malika's decision to marry highlights the existence of room for manoeuvre both in this very vertical employment relationship and within her family. In opposition to an orientalist and feminist vision which could lead the lazy analyst to view marriage only as a source of alienation and submission to the patriarchy, here one must understand that getting married, on the contrary, gave the young woman a lever of autonomy with regard to her employer and the family group. Ayoub's recruitment quickly calmed the objections of both families, since, on the one hand, it allowed them to combine professional activity and married life, but also, and perhaps above all, because on the other hand, it consolidated the clan's position on the farm and thus secured (or even increased) their migratory income. Compliance with the norm loosened the grip of their suspicion and social control. Malika acquired the status of a married woman which, although this did not totally remove her from the family's oversight, created an intimate space for the couple. Tradition and good morals served as authoritative arguments that

[9] Interview with Malika Amrani, recorded, approx. 120 minutes. Conducted at her home by Emmanuelle Hellio, on 10/06/2015.

[10] This type of arrangement was described and theorized by Hellio based on the case of female Moroccan agricultural workers recruited through *contratos en origen* in Huelva, Spain (2014).

allowed them to successfully assert their right to occupy a small apartment together, far from the workers' collective housing, but also, above all, away from the employers' house.[11] With Ayoub at her side, Malika felt stronger and showed less willingness to work weekends. She finally earned the right to work just one weekend a month. However, she was still on call at night, which regularly forced the couple to sleep at the employer's house in order to watch the children and/or their maternal grandmother. This example shows to what extent the demand for availability/flexibility was a constraint on Malika's free time and family time, which created frustration that led to more frequent conflicts with the employer's family, and ultimately to the termination of the employment relationship. However, this did not take place until 6 years after her marriage. Rather than going into the why and how of the termination, it seems appropriate at this point to change perspective and instead, try to understand what made the employment relationship last so long.

This detour is essential in order to understand exploitation from the perspective of those who suffer it; that is, to enter the black box of domination and understand its psychological underpinnings (Morice, 1996). To do this, one must to consider the dual bonds of loyalty and interest that tie Malika to her employer under the OMI system: the staff and the family. As we have seen, the individual/collective relationship is very strong in rural Morocco (even if Malika's personal trajectory tends to place her on the margins of this world and its social and moral norms), but it is above all the system of family recruitment that ties Malika's destiny to her family's. The OMI system is based on the recruitment of seasonal workers by name, which is carried out in practice by co-opting workers based on their sponsor(s)' family ties. When Malika was recruited, a dozen of her relatives already worked on the farm, and although the employer had personally chosen her, she was only hired because of the ties that already existed between the farmer and the previous generation: her uncles and her father in particular, who was given the role of a guarantor. Understandably, a system like this creates cross-dependencies, so that each family member's duty of loyalty (Jounin, 2006) to the employer is both individual and collective. The employer reminded Malika of this when she shared her desire to marry and have children: disobeying would have consequences for her entire family and would jeopardize all of their migration income. On a more personal level, for a time, Malika was able to find a certain number of compensations that allowed her to withstand the hardship of this form of "restricted salary" (Moulier-Boutang, 1998). Although it was not the only factor, the economic aspect

[11] Officially provided free of charge, this studio was subject to a withholding from their salary, a clandestine form of rent that was much higher than what was provided for in the collective agreement (300 euros per month instead of the 4 hours of work stipulated in the law). On top of this, there were additional fees for water and electricity, which again gave the employer with the opportunity to "scratch", to "cut"—to use the *emic* terminology—i.e., the opportunity to reduce, through theft, the cost of their workforce.

played a central role in her resignation to "deal with it." The main reasons for this were the aforementioned difference in salary, Ayoub's status as breadwinner for the family in Morocco, and their recent marriage, which meant that the young couple were still trying to settle down (in 1997–1998, they bought a small apartment in the Bab Sidi Boujida neighborhood of Fez by taking out a loan from Malika's father and a friend). [12] The other form of compensation was more on the order of the promise and belief, and concerned her "papers." Like many seasonal workers, the young woman hoped one day to convert her seasonal status to a more permanent residence permit and thus be able to change jobs and employers. Although in practice, this change of status has been practically impossible since the abolition in 1974 of the so-called "permanent status" procedure,[13] the employer's wife made sure to keep this dream alive for Malika. She signed two written promises to hire Malika on a permanent contract, one in 1997—in the midst of Chevènement's legalization campaign, which excluded seasonal workers despite the local mobilization of the CGT [Décosse 2011]—and one in 1999. Malika even applied to the OMI to change her status so that she could be legally employed as a housekeeper.

These individual and collective systems for curbing resistance would, however, eventually break down in 2000 under the influence of two factors. The first was the deepening rift between the employer's expectation of availability and Malika's growing resistance to working weekends. This tension should not be understood only in the material terms of a struggle to preserve or, on the contrary, to limit the maximization of the (absolute) surplus value obtained through the expansion of her working time. In addition to this material issue, personal power relationships were at play that could not be reduced to this simple calculation. After the departure of the employer's wife and children in 1999, Malika reported to the employer's mother, who felt that Malika was now "paid to do nothing". In addition to forcing her to clean her own house in addition to her son's, she regularly "lent" Malika to family friends, for whom she did housework. This testifies to a patrimonial vision of the work provided by the employee, a private appropriation of her labor force, conceived of and managed as a personal resource that can be shared with her entire "clan". In this way, Malika's status was downgraded: on the one hand, because her work, which had been diverse and rewarding in some respects (the role of *nounou* in particular), is now reduced to that of a housekeeper; and on the other hand, because she had become "commodified," in the sense that she as seen as a resource that could be mobilized indiscriminately, and the employer's mother treated her in an authoritarian and degrading manner, thus asserting her status as mistress of the house and making her pay for her supposed intimacy with her former daughter-in-law. A single example should suffice to illustrate the treatment

[12] Interview with Malika Amrani, recorded, approx. 120 min. Conducted at her home by Emmanuelle Hellio, on 10/06/2015.

[13] Moving from a temporary residence permit to a long-term residence permit.

reserved for the young woman: one weekend, Malika was told at the last minute that she must care for the maternal grandmother that weekend. Malika refused, having already planned to go away for the weekend with Ayoub. Her refusal led to the intervention of the "big boss," who threatened retaliation against her family and told her to get on her knees before his wife to beg for her forgiveness. It can thus be seen that more than simply an issue of being on call, what Malika was accused of was the failure to fulfill her duty of social hyper-correction (Sayad, 1999), an emancipation that, in a dialectical manner, provoked in return the symbolic restoration of authority, put on display through a "ceremony of degradation" (Garfinkel, 1956). The second event that led up to this rupture occurred by chance: in August 2000, Ayoub had a serious fall in the orchard and fractured his hip. The work-related accident occurred during the harvest period, i.e., at a time when seasonal workers work up to 300 hours/month. That day, the rain had made the ground slippery to the point that the workers did not want to enter the orchard in the morning because of their "expertise in prudence" (Cru & Dejours, 1983). Perched on the fifth step of his stepladder, Ayoub leaned on a branch of an apple tree to reach some apples that were up high. He had a crate weighing 20 kg hung across his body, which shifted his center of gravity outwards His precarious balance was thrown off when the foot of the stepladder abruptly shifted. Pulled down by the weight of the crate, Ayoub fell almost 1.5 meters onto his back.

The fire department was called and Ayoub was taken to the hospital, forcing the employers to declare the work-related accident,[14] which went against the habitual practice of non-declaration, allowing the injuries and the cost of their care to be externalized to the OMI worker's country of origin (Décosse, 2013). Ayoub had surgery on his hip and received a prosthesis. His contract expired on October 15 and would not be renewed in 2001. Neither was Malika's, nor those of the other members of the Hassani clan (including her father and brother). The termination of the (employment) relationship was announced in early October 2000, a few days before the end of Malika's contract. The accident would prove to be a catalyst for her. It was the external and irreversible event that put an end to a situation that was untenable for both parties. Ayoub's brutal decline in health shattered the couple's adherence to the norm of collective obedience and individualized their logic of action. Repairing the physical damage and accumulated injustice became their priority, at the same time that the employer evicted them from their home and reported them as undocumented migrants to the gendarmerie, which called them in on several occasions. With the support of the MRAP and the CGT, Ayoub and Malika contested the successive work-related accident evaluations of the doctors of the *Mutualité Sociale Agricole* and, after two counter-evaluations, were awarded a declaration of 20% permanent

[14] Interview with Ayoub Amrani, recorded, approx. 60 min. Conducted in his home, Saint-Chamas (13), France, June 2004.

partial disability statys. This entitled them to a residence permit, which was finally issued in 2004. In early 2002, they filed a complaint with the *Conseil des Prud'hommes*. The couple's disobedience and the retaliation against the clan were to have a lasting impact on the young woman's relationship with her family. At the employer's behest, her father urged her to drop their lawsuit. With 93 of his compatriots, her brother Mokhtar even signed the following false statement to his disadvantage, in an attempt to be rehired by the company:

> We are very satisfied with our relationship with our employers. We have appropriate accommodations, are properly paid and are treated well. We have learned that one of our compatriots, a former employee, is wrongly making defamatory comments. We disagree with her actions and we are afraid that all these made-up stories will cost us our jobs.[15]

It is clear that the seasonal OMI contract system, as it combines unstable employment and residence status, discretionary contract renewal, recruitment through sponsorship (on a clan basis) and paternalism, is a limited wage system that forces migrant workers to be loyal to their employers. In this constrained universe, Malika's trajectory emphasized the existence, despite it all, of a certain "autonomy of migration" (Mezzadra, 2004), where Ayoub's accident led the couple to break the pact of collective obedience and to openly contest both the employer's discipline and contract migration in general. This event caused a rupture in their biographical trajectory, perceptible on the professional level (non-renewal of their contract and those of their relatives), administrative level (undocumented situation and expulsion), and family level (the long quarrel between Malika and her clan). This rift gradually faded over time. After regularizing their situation, the couple settled apart from the rest of the Moroccan community. Ayoub returned to his job as an autobody mechanic, while Malika spends her time raising her niece, Mouna, Amal's eldest daughter. Just like Malika did 40 years ago, the young girl was entrusted *(kafala)* to the childless couple so that she could go to school. She now attends a vocational high school. Furthermore, the couple actively plays the role of breadwinner for the family in Morocco, sending them savings earned with Ayoub's modest salary on a regular basis. Malika says she has forgiven her brother and her father, whose pension she has taken care of with the MSA (a little less than 400 euros/month, including the minimum contribution for 100 validated quarters). Their material and financial support has largely contributed to the gradual pacification of relationships within the Hassani clan, most of whom still work for the same employer. Malika and Ayoub have also participated in the fight for seasonal workers' rights, playing a key role as translator and intermediary between workers, trade unions and non-profit activists. Fifteen years after the incident, Malika's case before the Conseil des Prud'hommes has still not been settled, as a simultaneous action before the Criminal Court interrupted the

---

[15] *Submissions before the Conseil des Prud'hommes of Aix-en-Provence.* Memorandum written by H. Gouyer, CODETRAS internal documentation, unpublished, 2016.

course of the civil proceedings. The former rebellious worker is losing patience and finds it hard to believe she will find justice under the French system.

References

Bossard, R. 1979. « Un espace de migration. Les travailleurs du Rif oriental (Nador) et l'Europe. » Ph. D. Dissertation in Geography, Université de Montpellier.

Cru, D. & Ch. Dejours. 1983. « Les savoir-faire de prudence dans les métiers du bâtiment. » *Les Cahiers médico-sociaux* 3: 239-247.

Décosse, F. 2013. «Entre 'usage contrôlé', invisibilisation et externalisation. Le précariat étranger face au risque chimique en agriculture intensive. » *Sociologie du travail* 55: 322-340.

Décosse, F. 2011. « Migrations sous contrôle. Agriculture intensive et saisonniers marocains sous contrat "OMI". » Ph. D. Dissertation in Sociology, EHESS, Paris.

Décosse, F. 2004. « Conditions de travail et accès à la santé des saisonniers agricoles étrangers en agriculture intensive. L'exemple des contrats OMI dans le département des Bouches-du-Rhône. ». Mémoire de DEA (RCD), EHESS, Paris, 2004.

Garfinkel, H. 1956. "Conditions of Successful Degradation Ceremonies." American Journal of Sociology 61: 420-424.

Hellio, E. 2014. « Importer des femmes pour exporter des fraises? Flexibilité du travail, canalisation des flux migratoires et échappatoires dans une monoculture intensive globalisée: le cas des saisonnières marocaines en Andalousie. » Ph. D. Dissertation in Sociology, Université Nice-Sofia Antipolis.

Herman, P. 2008. Les nouveaux esclaves du capitalisme. Agriculture intensive et régression sociale: l'enquête. Vauvert: Au Diable Vauvert.

Hubscher, R 2005. L'immigration *dans les* campagnes *françaises (XIXe-XXe siècles)*. Paris: Odile Jacob.

Jounin, N. 2006. « Loyautés incertaines. Les travailleurs du bâtiment entre discrimination et précarité. » Ph. D. Dissertation in Sociology, Université Paris VII.

Lautier, B. 2010. « Introduction. » In J. Falquet, H. Hirata, D. Kergoat, B. Labari, N. Le Feuvre & F. Sow (eds.) Le sexe de la mondialisation. *Genre, classe, race et nouvelle division du travail*,. Paris: Presses de Sciences Po: 21-25.

Lazaar, M. 1987. « Conséquences de l'émigration dans les montagnes du Rif Central (Maroc). » Revue européenne des migrations internationales 3 (1-2) :97-114.

Lefebvre, H. 1968. *Le droit à la ville*. Paris: Anthropos.

Mernissi, F. 1981. Développement capitaliste et perceptions des femmes dans la société arabo-musulmane. Une illustration des paysannes du Gharb, Maroc, Non published paper presented at Séminaire Régional Tripartite du BIT pour l'Afrique « La place des Femmes dans le Développement Rural ». Dakar, Senegal, 15-19 juin.

Mezzadra, S. 2004. « Capitalisme, migrations et luttes sociales. Notes préliminaires pour une théorie de l'autonomie des migrations. » *Multitudes* 19: 17-30.

Morice, A. 1996. « Des objectifs de production de connaissances aux orientations méthodologiques: une controverse entre anthropologie et psychodynamique du travail. » *Revue Internationale de Psychosociologie* 3 (5): 143-160.

Morice, A. 2004. « Le travail sans le travailleur». *Plein droit* 61: 2-7.

Moujoud, N. & J. Falquet. 2010. « Cent ans de sollicitude en France. Domesticité, reproduction sociale, migration et histoire coloniale. » Agone 43: 169-195.

Moulier-Boutang, Y. 1998. De l'esclavage au salariat. Économie historique du salariat bridé. Paris: PUF.

Sayad, A. 1999. La double absence. Des illusions de l'émigré aux souffrances de l'immigré. Paris: Seuil.

Terray, E. 1999. « Le travail des étrangers en situation irrégulière ou la délocalisation sur place. » In E. Balibar, J. Costa-Lascoux, M. Chemillier-Gendreau & E. Terray (eds.) *Sans-papiers: l'archaïsme fatal*,. Paris: La Découverte: 9-34.

Virolles-Souibes, M. 1986. « Du pécule au salariat. Travail et stratégies féminines en Algérie. », In M. Virolles-Souibes (ed.) Côté femmes. Approches ethnologiques, Paris: L'Harmattan: 193-208.

Weber, M. 2014. *La ville*. Paris: La Découverte.

'SUZANA'S CHOICES'

WORKING IN THE MAQUILADORAS, MIGRATING TO SURVIVE AND LIVING TRANSNATIONALLY

Delphine Mercier

Suzana: an exceptional trajectory from Azumbilla to Mexico...

Suzana was 47 years old when I met her. She comes from an Azumbilla village in the state of Puebla, Mexico. Her whole family is still there: her mother, her siblings, her husband, and two of her daughters. She left her village 10 years ago to go to work in Mexico City, the capital of Mexico, in the domestic work sector. Before arriving in Mexico, Suzana worked in the maquiladora textile factories[1] of Azumbilla. These precarious factories assembled clothes (shorts, trousers, shirts, etc.) for the US army. The factories were set up near[2] La Bestia railway line, La Bestia being the freight train that traverses the length of Mexico and transports illegal migrants from Central America or other regions of Mexico. The train passes by very close to Azumbilla. Migration in their village is part of the history of every family; everyone has an episode of migration to the United States in this village. Suzana married very young and had two daughters. Her first husband left her and moved in with the neighbour with whom he had eleven children. Following this traumatic moment in her life as a wife, woman and mother, Suzana decided to work in transnational companies, no doubt hoping to get closer to the United States. She then met someone else while she was still married to her first husband. Her fiancé left for the United States to earn money and to bring her there later. Suzana was pregnant and waited several months without any news. One morning her fiancé's mother told her that she should not waiting any longer, that he will not come back and that he has found another woman there. Suzana lived through her second trauma. She left to go to Mexico (internal migration) where she stayed at her cousins' house. Initially, her daughters stayed in Azumbilla with their grandmother. The eldest had already reached adulthood and joined her mother, and the two youngest stayed in Azumbilla. The second youngest married a local, Oscar who also migrated for two years to build up capital. The youngest daughter stayed in the village in the small house that Suzana managed to build little by little over time. Her youngest daughter was also in a relationship, much too young according to Suzana. Aged 17 years old, her boyfriend

---

[1] Throughout this text, we will use the term maquiladora to describe foreign *capital* companies established in a country to benefit from an exceptional system, whether in Mexico or elsewhere in the world. We will also use the term export processing zone.

[2] La Bestia, the train that traverses the length of Mexico

almost migrated on a whim while her daughter was expecting a baby. Suzana intervened; she found work for her third son-in-law in the textile maquiladora. Her eldest daughter married a local who found a job in Mexico City. He is a building caretaker; it is better than nothing. This situation highlights a trajectory of precariousness during which migration appears as a possible step, a possible job in the precarious "career".

La Bestia also passes by Azumbilla

During a trip to Azumbilla in the Puebla region, I met Suzana. She had just bought a small piece of land in her village and had started to build her house. Her house was her dream; the other dreams were forgotten in the long lonely nights. She put her woman's ideals aside. A true builder, Suzana spent these last years making choices, to leave her first husband, to work, to fight to survive, to support her daughters and to help them build their lives. She kept repeating: "I don't want them to end up like me, having to choose when there is no longer a choice". For 10 years, she put money aside every month. Along with the other female 'de planta' domestic workers (home domestic workers), she set up a tontine (tanda in Mexico). The 'tanda' became central for Suzana because it allowed her to build projects and make choices. This form of economic action favoured the collectivization of resources for the benefit of everyone. Such a contribution system appeared to be efficient and independent for Suzana. Although Suzana had not always trusted life, she trusted the 'tanda' to which she belonged. There, she was able to think, plan and build projects for her house, help her daughters, train herself to be able to create her individual company in embroidery and fashion clothing.

Choosing to work in a maquiladora: migrate or work in a "transnational" company in the context of the 1980s in Mexico

Her first step towards independence was a forced choice as her first husband had just left her and Suzana had only one possibility left to work. In Azumbilla in the 1980s, maquiladora factories developed in the textile sector. The industrial export processing zones developed from the 1960s in Mexico, based on the Shannon model in Ireland developed in 1958, with the central idea of producing under customs control. These free zones were quickly appreciated as the new development model for developing countries. It was a question of bringing together attractiveness conditions sufficient for multinational companies to relocate part of their production to developing territories, where labour was cheap, and especially to complementary territories, which could respond to migration issues. This is how the free zones in Mexico developed, known as *maquiladoras*, in the 1960s. The development, accompanied by multinational companies in the textile sector, was intended to complement seasonal activities carried out in the United States and put an end to plans to settle Mexicans in the United States. The objectives were producing at low cost and building a second internal frontier, the one that would make it possible to retain a seasonal workforce.

This development of the 1960s has not yet stopped in 2021, and it has experienced expected and unexpected trajectories. The expected phenomena have involved the development of *maquiladora* factories in all types of sectors and the unexpected phenomena are the diffusion of these devices in many countries with economic advantages (and especially emerging countries), either in terms of the use of resources, workforce qualification, geographic proximity, or labour cost.

Conform or liberate? This chapter will be articulated through a reduced prism, which refers to two productive formats and also two possible postures of the dynamics of capitalism in the context of globalisation. Michael J. Piore, in 1979, wrote the book Birds of passage: Migrant labor and industrial societies, which discusses labour migration. He demonstrated that, firstly, migrants were recruited by the industries of rich countries and that their objective was to come for a limited time, save their wages and return to their countries of origin. He then specified that the industries recruited foreign workers to fulfil the missions that the native workers did not wish to carry out, which was the result of a complementary duality between the workers' unions and the monopolistic companies. Finally, the migrants who occupied these rejected jobs created the complementarity conditions necessary for the functioning of this triangular system stabilising the recruiting intermediary (workers' unions), the employers (large monopoly industries) and the workers (migrants). In this context, migration became a problem because the children of the settled migrants found themselves in competition with native workers and no longer fulfilled their subordinate roles. Following the field work consulted since the mid-1990s, we witness a crossbreeding between migrating birds and swallow capitals. In particular, through the study of southern countries, we observe the most emerging and contemporary forms of economic and social globalisation. In the border areas to the south, a double process is observed: the first is a transnationalization of productive territories and the second is the informalization of industrial sectors specifically with a connection to the commercial, artisanal and local sectors. The connection to the national commercial sector (Peraldi, 1999) blurs the lines and borders between a global northern economy on the exploitation of workers from the south who move north, and a northern economy moving to the south (globalisation from the bottom up) to control the influx of populations, towards globalisation in situ that bases its development on transnationalization of productive territories, informalization of industrial sectors and superposition of legal, fiscal and social scenes within the same territories.

As I have emphasized several times in my work, the example of border industrial export processing zones is therefore rich in lessons, particularly when one analyses it as a device for the management of globalised capitalism, i.e. a device which consists in freeing oneself from certain common customs and commercial rights and then reintegrating, through various exceptional regimes, the economies to which they must export. The general principle of this device is to suspend, for a possibly determined period, the common rights of a country within enclaves, with the aim of making the most of the local and international environment. They are therefore true globalisation laboratories.

In this article, we will not discuss again the context of globalisation that has hit the southern countries since the mid-1960s. The rest of our discussion will focus precisely on two phenomena that have been well-studied, but not necessarily always articulated in their implications. We will focus on the establishment and development of the workforce management policy by linking it to the evolution of the transnational and border companies' model.

In the 1990s, we observed a certain integration of these freed border areas into the local economy and therefore an enhancement of the workforce and its development, in particular with the improvement of the production process. We demonstrated that the rise in technical skills of these companies guaranteed, through the standards to be respected, an improvement in working conditions and allowed qualification of the workforce and especially the establishment of collective demands.

Since the 2000s (more precisely since 1995), situations have deteriorated enormously in terms of employment management, fundamentally because the workforce, which was the number one ally of these offshore companies, has become the indispensable enemy. This degradation of professional relations in these border areas poses two major conclusions from the outset:

- The epiphenomenon of the implementation of quality policies at the end of the 1980s (1983-1994), consisting in putting the worker and the customer at the centre of the process, is definitely over or was only an ephemeral additional fad;

- The *maquiladora* model (which was originally developed at the borders of countries with a strong economic differential only) has spread to the territories and is no longer limited to border areas. It has become the model for companies around the world and not just in southern countries.

We will first present the beginnings of this relocated company and workforce management relationship (the maquiladora model of workforce management), the standardisation phase of the relationship, and we will then describe the professionalization phase of the relationship (the total quality model of workforce management). Finally, we will present the outsourcing phase of the relationship (the offshore model of workforce management).

In view of the work that we have carried out in recent years, we present these three phases chronologically. The first phase corresponds to the period 1965-1983, the second from 1984 to 1994 and the third from 1995 to the present day. This chronology allows us to better contextualize the phenomenon. However, our observations in the field[3] have always shown that certain stages in the development of international companies are often concomitant and situated. Time is a necessary but not sufficient variable, and the question of space must also be taken into account. The characteristic of these human resources management practices is precisely to play on the deterritorialization and re-territorialization of production. The complementarity of the territories in time and space is the main added value, but in order not to complicate the text too much, we will adopt a chronology.

The main objective of human resources management is "a temporary and limited freedom from common rights" (Mercier, 2008). At the origin of *emancipation* (Mercier, 2008), labour law (which is not necessarily explicitly granted by the international mechanism, but which can be an advantage specific to the country or to the zone) is not necessarily at the centre of attractiveness. During the development process of the free zone, through different mechanisms (social conflicts, the need for a qualified workforce, competition) common law, social policies and the skillset of the territory prior to the definition of the zone are reintegrated voluntarily or not in the zone.

The maquiladora model of workforce management

As early as the 1960s, during the development of industrial export processing zones in Mexico[4], in particular, a management system of artisanal labour was set up and then standardised, leaving little room for employee autonomy. These (simple) assembly companies, located at the borders of countries with a strong economic differential to benefit from cheap labour, first of all, faced a mainly female and young labour force that had never or little worked in industry.

The worker was interchangeable, managed by a single union that signed a contract with the company (parent company) guaranteeing the management and organisation of the workforce, on-the-job training, selection of candidates, and the management of life inside and outside the company. Moreover, practically in all the countries of Central America but also in North Africa, an operator was above all a "union member". This term used to name them did not mean that there is union activity, but simply that the union carried out the recruitment.

They were no longer labourers, a term referring to heavy industry, but operators with two statuses: full-time unionized plant operators or potential operators. The hired operators were recruited from neighbourhoods near the factories, showed up in the morning and were interviewed, which consisted

[3] Field studies in Central America, South America, Spain/France/Italy, Morocco, Mexico...

[4] Mexico was one of the first countries in the world to develop this model almost at the same time as the one in Ireland.

rather in determining their personality and reliability. The question of competence was hardly addressed. As soon as the person passed the psychological tests, they were trained on the job. Very quickly, they were assigned to a production line and became part of the team.

In the 1970s, these factories hired every day and there were banners permanently on the walls of the companies. The signs "here we recruit" were the only inscriptions on these "invisible and clandestine" factories. One of the guarantees to get a job was the recommendation of a friend or a neighbour who already worked in the company. As soon as they were employed, they were supported by a union, which ensured the socialisation of operators. As a result, there was often confusion in factories as the supervisor was most of the time the union representative.

This "archaic" mode of labour management is well known in the agriculture and construction sectors, but it is the one that has always prevailed in the context of organised work with migrant populations. For the managers of the parent companies in the United States, for the most part, a very efficient calculation was made: the working tool was replaced by a standardised, interchangeable, docile workforce. The parent company chose a human resources director who facilitated the hiring of the technical team and in particular the manager, who was most often a production engineer from the local industry. Supervisors, experienced, older and exclusively male, were also drawn from traditional local industry.

Operators were female except in factories that require a certain force to handle assembly lines. The operators were all chosen according to the same profile, the same age and from the same neighbourhood, which allowed extremely homogeneous management of life inside and outside the factory (between 16 and 18 years old, single, high-school-level). Bus transport was is facilitated, as was internal management. For more complex *production processes*, slightly older women were hired (30 years old, single mothers). This standardised model of workforce management functioned quite stably until the late 1980s. If an operator did not show up, there were dozens of others looking for work. It was a permanent offer on both sides. The factories operated in three shifts and as soon as there was a problem or illness, it was very easy to break the contract, especially since the union, being so internalised in the hierarchical functions, made any complaint disappear. Moreover, there was usually no employment contract, only an implicit contract that could be broken due to absenteeism, delays or slowness.

For many of the operators who worked in these factories, the company very quickly became the only place to socialize. Migrants from the neighbouring state or from the neighbouring region, which was in general poorer, or fleeing a certain form of rural life, the operators also found in the factories the first possibility of earning a salary, living independently and postponing the moment of migrating to the United States, in the case of

Mexico, or to Europe.

This phase of the first wave of globalisation, which also corresponded to the phase of opening up the borders of the *southern countries,* lasted until the end of the 1980s. At the end of these years the *maquiladora* model, which was to have a limited duration, began to spread around the world. Becoming a real alternative for many regions of the world, this *globalised capitalism* model developed and took different names depending on the contexts in which it was implemented.

For the International Labour Organisation, the first surveys, carried out to understand the working conditions in these free zones, dated from the end of the 1980s. The interchangeability of the workforce was a strong and central point because the gesture to be performed could be learned in a few hours. For the rest, it was more a question of physical skills, resistance and speed. Once a year, the union brought together staff around a rather festive event. There was no in-house training and an extremely simplified salary grid in four categories (operator, supervisor, technician and employees) was applied. Employees designating administrative staff, generally called "trusted employees", guaranteed its operation. Many of them were working for the first time in the industrial world.

Also, in a context where hardly anyone except the managers (engineers) and the supervisors had references and experience, the work and its content were never questioned or very little. The pace, the forms of employment and the non-negotiation finally appeared as "normal" conditions of industrial work[5].

The total quality model of workforce management

At the end of the 1980s, the industrial export processing zones, despite their exponential development putting the territories in competition with one another, experienced a fairly short period of development in human resource management. Faced with a process of integration of the border industry with local businesses, labour standards were disseminated. These working standards were more marked by an international culture than a national one. This essentially consisted of developing quality methods in the factories, and in particular those which were applicable to the production process. Despite the essentially industrial and commercial aspect of this system, its impact was notorious on the management of human resources.

Any form of liberalized competition was gradually constrained by regulatory frameworks in order to limit competition and product circulation. As the products of the *maquiladoras* were mainly intended for export, the

[5] The *maquiladora* model of the workforce management written for implementation synthetically is the result of readings of a few sociologists and anthropologists, who carried out field studies in factories at the border zones, my analysis of the corpus of the recording complaints to international unions and the ILO and my own in-situ or participant observations.

maquiladoras found themselves obliged to certify their *process* in order to give guarantees of production. During the development and implementation of these standards, we witness a short period of real workforce management professionalization.

During this period, *maquiladora* companies settled outside the border areas, and this tax-free mode of production became a new possibility of production, making it possible to face various situations: countries with economic differentials, areas undergoing industrial reconversion with saturated employment areas, development models, model of transition from national economies to capitalist economies, etc. The *maquiladora* model spread, sometimes taking the name of a free-trade zone, a business zone or a special economic zone.

Within this framework and this context of regularisation, human resources management developed, based on the improvement of working conditions and employment conditions, and most of the time putting aside the question of training and qualification. For about ten years, human resources management was structured by trying to reintegrate the local labour standards of the countries where the export processing zones were established. In addition, union plurality developed in some companies, allowing social dialogue to begin and complaints to be registered. Everyone played their part, including international organisations, in trying to update the different forms of employment practised. Companies developed internal careers and vocational training with the aim of retaining the workforce and improving production conditions.

At the end of the 1990s, the terms of management in the first countries that had developed this mode of globalised capitalism had changed, transferring to their "poorer" neighbours and recently entered the world of globalisation and the policies of exploitation of the workforce. In the 1990s, at the height of the development of *maquiladoras*, the trend was quality standards (ISO 9002 to 9004). All companies whose vocation was to export had to pass under the Caudine forks of certification, in particular, to ensure the routing of products on the international market. The wave of certification considerably transformed production conditions in factories and, in particular, working conditions. This certification was implemented very assiduously in these companies and by the local managers who saw it as an opportunity to consolidate the production process, improve production conditions, justify the use of suppliers' premises, and organise the training of supervisors, technicians and operators. Certification enabled the consolidation of human resources and engineering departments in companies. In this context, the unions weakened, because often they were not able to relay the demands and became practically absent from the companies. This negation of the unions was well supported by the managers and engineers, but also by the operators who found, through quality standards, much more effective possibilities to negotiate their conditions of employment, prescribed immediately in the various manuals and evaluated. However, the wave of certification, which ended in the late 1990s, was not relayed by other systems ultimately as complete as those concerning quality. The management tools, which were introduced into companies, consisted of financial tools and inspections, without the approval of the unions, which had already left (the scene of negotiation) the companies concerned.

The offshore model of workforce management

At the end of the 1990s, the crisis and the devaluation again implied a diversification and a specialisation of the industrial system. Once again, it was a question of lowering the cost of labour. It was a struggle of the industrial sectors, which implied mutilation of the collective agreements formed. This enhanced flexibility, but also fragility. Weakening of the paternalistic relationship that had prevailed. The new shareholders did not necessarily have an interest in maintaining production conditions as they were. The vulnerability of work developed again, in particular by distributing the risk of work on the subcontractors. Outsourcing began to develop and at that time, the *maquiladoras* once again joined the industrial system under another more modern name: international companies or the international technology companies' programme.

In the oldest countries *maquila,* the most traditional and labour-intensive sectors of activity, such as textiles or the manufacture of toys, totally disappeared in favour of sectors more intensive in technology and with the need for skilled labour such as electronics, household appliances, equipment and the production of automotive parts. The latter was mainly in the hands of foreign capital (American, Japanese or Korean) and together account for more than 70% of the workforce.

The production *process* culture transferred to the *project* culture, which was ultimately quite devastating for employment conditions. The workforce became older, qualified, specialised and the activities evolved. This project culture, emphasising short processes, also involved the development of outsourcing, which consisted of considering labour as another raw material that is interchangeable and manageable by a unique subcontractor. It also concerned the development of industrial parks with the "all-inclusive" period. In our daily life, holidays and work, we live in a culture where the definition of the base is made upstream. The structure and management methods are predefined and the parent companies compare countries to obtain the best turnkey service offered by those countries.

Recruitment agencies developed in industrial parks, ensuring for companies' selection, management, pay, contracts, day-to-day negotiation, complaints and termination of the contract. In the 2000s, human resources management (HRM) services or departments in companies practically disappeared. The only traces that can be found of HRM in these areas are in the mandatory committees on health and safety, where the unions and the few representatives of traditional human resources management persist and share the remains of reflection on working conditions.

Human resources management activities were replaced by indicator tables and various contract management tools adapted to production needs. The manager established his order book for raw materials, spare parts and labour at the start of each production cycle. This practice of zero stock completely changed professional relations. Also, during this period, individual conflict grew and the collective struggle system disappeared, thereby transforming professional relations.

At the time of setting up these companies, it was not only the production *process* that was outsourced, but also the professional relations within the company. As long as the *maquiladoras* negotiated their settlement in the territory while maintaining a local manager from the receiving town and aware of local practices in terms of labour law in its legal practices and also in its legitimate practices, a relative improvement in employment conditions and possible negotiation spaces was observed. The "recolonization" of the entrepreneurial class of *maquiladoras* by the parent companies, dramatically changed the conditions for setting up these businesses, including their integration and the conditions for integration into a local system. Today, the *maquiladoras* are set up in industrial parks reserved for exporting companies, almost exclusively at odds with the local industrial system, the latter being located in the old industrial spaces of the town. Apart from infrastructure, an office takes care of all administrative and fiscal matters of setting up businesses, including the function of human resources management, recruitment and sometimes even payroll. This excessive outsourcing helped with the concerns of the employees in the factory because the absence of an internal interlocutor made it possible to delegate the social responsibility of the company in terms of training, wages and working conditions. In addition, it made it possible to pool information about the employees likely to work in these companies (their trajectories, the companies in which they worked, dismissals, conflicts and their union membership). As a result, this externalisation severely damaged the previous professional relations model by outsourcing it and reducing it only to hiring and wages.

An offshore workforce management model installed for how long?

We have described three phases of the development of human resources management in transnational companies, particularly border companies and those founded in areas of tax-exempt zones. All along, we have called this global capitalism device *maquiladora*. The *maquiladora* is the initial model that spread to low-wage countries to respond to different country transitions, whether transitions to capitalism for formerly socialist countries or transitions to cope with the very brutal reconversions in Europe. We have shown that the first wave of this development was organised essentially in agreement with the States and the unions of the host countries, but today the regulatory actors of the 1970s are no longer present. They have been replaced by private actors, intermediaries who manage the employment relationship from start to finish. We would prefer not to give too chronological a view of these policies. Subcontracting of the 1970s is very different from that of today. It is nonetheless true that these transnational companies are subject to international requirements and standards, which tend to homogenise both the criteria of productivity and employment management. The territorial question is also at the heart of this development, the globalised capitalism devices causing the territories to vary according to the interests and advantages that the settlement territory offers.

The main displacement since the 1970s has been that of the actors of wage regulation and employment. At that time, this regulation was still marked by a traditional and triangular form (State, Union, Patronage). In the 1990s, new players emerged: associations of business leaders and quality management tools with production as the workforce organiser. In the 2000s, the advent of project management, employment intermediaries and industrial parks made human resource management one dimension among others of the production. In this last phase, the operator was ultimately the most subject to uncertainty and found themselves confronted with a single interlocutor who capitalised total knowledge of their trajectory and from whom they could not deviate.

The choice to migrate to Mexico City

Suzana made choices. In the context of gender, work and migration, Suzana made life choices by alternating production and reproduction by and for work. This iteration between liberation and submission was part of Suzana's journey.

Mexico: a transnational model of workforce management

The case of the maquiladoras is interesting because it is a sector that plays at the same time on the transnationalization of the labour markets, not only from the point of view of the activity, but also on the capture of a labour force endowed with transnational capital (ability to mobilise skills and networks on both sides of the border), whether in terms of qualification or mobility experience. In this specific case, we are not concerned with the transformation of material, but with management and the circulation of information. Transnational labour markets are double-rooted in the national contexts of labour markets and in the lines developed by two States to regulate relocations or activities organised transnationally. The national institutional factors that were once at the centre of sociological labour market theories do not allow an understanding of these new emerging transnational labour markets. There is a need to go further. If we focus on the debate on the impact of economic globalisation (which does not mean transnationalization) on labour markets, two contradictory arguments arise: that of "strong" globalisation and competition, increasingly intense globalisation, combined with the globalisation of production, creating a de facto convergence of corporate strategies and organisational styles, as well as a convergence of different national models of capitalism and employment systems; that in contradiction with the proponents of such a "strong" thesis on globalisation, the argument which puts forward that the degree of globalisation could be exaggerated and that its effects are more moderate, arguing that the employment issues still need to be scrutinized under national hiring orders. However, neither of these approaches provides a sufficient analytical framework for the many examples of so-called transnational labour markets, for example, platform workers. In these cases, national employment systems and governments retain their importance as providers of the institutional contexts in which labour markets are embedded.

Conclusion: a transnational territory streaked with strong inequalities

In this article, we presented the maquiladoras and their development in Mexico, positioning this development in a cycle of technical transformations. We focused on transnational operators and transnational workforce management. We developed a cross-analysis of transnational labour markets and the Mexican case to understand its role as a laboratory.

In terms of labour analysis, we hypothesised using a central assumption that transnational companies and operators *walk and cross the line* of sharing, one foot in a globalised economy, and the other in a nationalized economy. This game on borders creates alternations between a nationalised (place of activity), globalised (the type of industry in which the operator works) and transnationalized (by crossing borders, by exceptions, depending on competitive situations) operator.

Transnational work is, above, all dematerialized work and the key to spatialization is apart from the question of geographical proximity. The transnational workers of Mexico are generally precarious workers and their parents were temporary workers (Piore, 1979), migrating birds, as described by Mikael Piore. Until the mid-1960s, it was the reign of temporary work, organised by the States. In 1965, when globalisation sounded the death knell for seasonal workers (organised under bi-national programmes), workers in invisible occupations became transnational workers, and the organisation of this transnationalism was implemented by intermediaries, which are no longer the responsibility of the nation-state and its regulations. This transnationalization involves new intermediaries and new standards. The maquiladoras have been the spearhead of this transnationalization of the economy quite simply because they made visible the transnational links (of the ex-colony type, etc.) between two or even three countries where the work was outsourced.

A service area in the incessant migration of "swallow factories" or foreign capital flows, Mexico and Central America - and this is our hypothesis - appear to us as a for the assembly of activities and the connection of legal and illegal, highly hierarchical, dysfunctional and subordinate spaces.

References

Mercier D., 1997, « Les capitaux hirondelles ». Les formes d'organisation des entreprises *maquiladoras* du Nord du Mexique (Monterrey). La circulation des Hommes et des techniques. Doctoral thesis, Paris, Université de Paris XII.

Mercier D., 2008, « L'industrie *maquiladora* d'exportation mexicaine à 40 ans : modèle économique, modèle juridique, modèle social ? », in Virginie Baby-Collin D.M. (dir.), *Sud à Sud : dynamiques sociales et spatiales Amérique Latine/Méditerranée*, Aix-en-Provence : Presses Universitaires de Provence (Monde contemporain), p. 133-151.

Peraldi M., 1999, « Marseille : réseaux migrants transfrontaliers, place marchande et économie de bazar », *Cultures & Conflits*, 33-34.

Piore M.J., 1979, *Birds of passage: Migrant labor and industrial societies*, Cambridge, UK, Cambridge University Press.

Portes Alejandro. La mondialisation par le bas [L'émergence des communautés transnationales]. In: *Actes de la recherche en sciences sociales*. Vol. 129, septembre 1999. Délits d'immigration. pp. 15-25.

PART FOUR

FROM EXPATRIATE TO MIGRANT?

FROM "EXPATS" TO MIGRANTS: MANO'S WORLDS IN MARRAKESH

Michel Peraldi

Mano was one of the first people I met in 2011 in Marrakesh, where I had moved for two years of fieldwork with the aim of conducting research into the history of the city and its urban development against the backdrop of a tourism-based economy (Peraldi, 2018). He immediately told me his story without pouring his heart out too much, then soon kindly and spontaneously offered to help me with my personal and professional paperwork. He came at the right time, as I was looking for a place to live and he worked at a real estate agency; above all, he knew many people in Marrakesh. He quickly found me a property to rent that suited me perfectly, then opened his social calendar to me and brought me with him to parties and dinners hosted by friends, and friends of friends. His world was nothing like that of the European jet-set featured in magazines that has given Marrakesh the reputation as a "place to be." On the contrary, his was a social world where you met unknown people on the younger side, the vast majority of them French, often newcomers, and far from rich. There were also a few Moroccan men and women, all from the same generation and cultural and professional spheres as their French friends, many sharing a home with a French partner. Finally, many young children would run around among the dancers or fall asleep on the sofa at the end of the evening.

They were restaurant owners, artisans, IT technicians or foremen, real estate agents and tour organizers. They drank alcohol, but only at these occasional parties and dinners, and smoke a little hash; regular young people in short, whose time is already largely dedicated to work and family life.

Growing steadily since the 1990s, the French population that the Ministries refer to as "expatriates" worldwide has increased considerably. It has been estimated that in 2014, the most recent year for which figures are available, there were just over 1.7 million expatriates, but as they are not required to declare themselves at the Consulates, the true figure is likely to be well over 2 million. France has some of the lowest levels of expatriation of any European country. The United Kingdom had more than 5 million expatriates during that period; Italy had 3.6 million, part of a "brain drain" trend that is increasing from year to year,[1] and Germany had 4.2 million expatriates. The vast majority of these European expatriates settle within Europe, as is the case of 51% of French people who have relocated. However, the phenomenon is fairly recent. There is increasing expatriation to the countries in North America, especially the U.S. and Canada, and even

[1] OECD figures, cited by Biacabe and Robert, 2014.

more recently, significant numbers of expatriates moving to countries in the Maghreb. Morocco, which receives most of this movement in population, is today the tenth most popular destination for French people who settle abroad; it is a country where there are also many other Europeans, especially Spaniards, Italians, and Germans. Here again, the official figures are only a low estimate of the real scale of these movements. The number of French people settling in Morocco was estimated at 41,129 in 2010, 44,400 in 2011 and 49,195 in 2014, according to consular figures. According to both French and Moroccan officials, an additional 25,000 to 30,000 people should be added to these figures, which corroborate our own investigations in Marrakesh.[2] The majority of these French people are based in Casablanca, the economic and industrial capital of the country: 48% of them live there. Rabat and Marrakesh are tied for second most popular destinations for the French, 15% of their population, but for very different reasons: Rabat, the administrative capital, mainly receives seconded French government employees and humanitarian organization staff. Marrakesh, on the other hand, attracts a population that is more difficult to identify as a professional group, which includes tourism entrepreneurs and retirees (Therrien, 2016; Boudarssa, 2017).

These professional worlds and the corresponding life journeys thus raise two types of questions about these Europeans' migratory mobility. To start with, what can we call these movements and their protagonists? Indeed, it is now clear that an ever-growing proportion of those whom the authorities call "expatriates" no longer really fit this description, but can they be called "migrants"? Admittedly, in law, the term expatriate, like the term "seconded," refers to persons sent to live abroad by their state of registration or by large firms, which provide them with protection and social security cover independent of the local protection system, which for some third-world countries is lacking or simply non-existent. Yet this category is declining very sharply among French people who have relocated around the world. They made up 36% of this population in 2003, by which time the decline had no doubt already begun, and only 19% in 2013, with a steep increase in the number of entrepreneurs and members of the liberal professions (Biacabe & Robert, 2014). We are therefore witnessing the emergence of a new population, generally made up of entrepreneurs or freelance workers, sometimes employees of local firms, who have no relationship of protection or dependence with their state of registration. They are no different from "migrant workers" in the strictly economic sense of the term, but can we really use the word "migrants" to describe economic actors generally endowed with incomes or wages that are—compared to the conditions in the countries where they live—generally comfortable?

Many researchers indeed consider that the term "migrant" should be

[2] In the survey that we distributed in Marrakesh, the findings of which are analyzed in this article, 70% of respondents said they had registered with their national consulate.

reserved for subordinate forms of mobility that characterize workers whose state of professional and statutory precariousness, living conditions in migration, and often even travel conditions place them in a situation of inferiority and fragility in the societies to which they migrate. Even if they have lost the protection of their state of registration, this is obviously not the case for European expatriates in the former colonies, who generally have middle- to upper-class social status. However, focusing the debate on the social condition of migrants obscures the economic transformations of which these new "migrations" are the consequence and the manifestation, precisely within these dynamics that are characteristic of the middle classes and the economic sectors that they dominate.

Mano's experience is evidence of a professional precariousness that in many ways is personal to him and is the consequence of his own way of combining a range of possibilities and ambitions. However, his precariousness is also the hallmark of the professional worlds which, like him, a large proportion of these European "migrants" inhabit, signaling a very particular socio-professional dynamic where migratory mobility is a way to escape the social downgrading to which this precariousness could lead. In a nutshell, this is a kind of migration whereby the migrant tries to "save their honor" by leaving a European society that exposes them to the risk of generational downgrading, rather than one that changes the social condition of those who experience it.

Mano was born in 1966 in a municipality of Seine-Saint-Denis, in France. He was a suburbanite but spent his childhood and adolescence in one of the small housing developments that never riot their way into the news headlines, inhabited mainly by families of employed people, mostly from the French West Indies, who are very keen to appear respectable and ensure that their children behave well. This was the case with his family, originally from Guadeloupe. His father was an employee of the French postal service and is now retired. His mother, also retired, was a primary school teacher. In these families, academic success is central to an education driven by the need to differentiate oneself from the pejorative social image that *la banlieue*, suburbia, has in France. And because he did not follow this virtuous pattern, despite not being a "delinquent," Mano did not share these family values and was regularly in conflict with his parents or brothers and sisters, who conformed to the family model by pursuing public sector careers. Mano was soon banished from a school system that did not tolerate what teachers called his unstable, impertinent, and agitated behavior. He still passed his vocational baccalaureate, earned a BEP (*Brevet d'Etudes Professionnelles*), a vocational diploma in sales, and quickly joined the post office administration through the family network, though he could only take temporary jobs there, with no motivation to take the public sector exams that would have led to a stable position. Moreover, these jobs are far more difficult to obtain than they were for Mano's parents' generation. He very soon tired of the jobs he had and spent time in the world of parties and nightclubs in Paris. He dreamed of being a dancer and tried to train for it but gave up on the program just before he was able to gain a qualification. Despite not being rejected or abused by his family, he "was a cause for concern"—as he quotes his mother saying—for his relatives, who believed that much of his instability and difference was due to him being openly homosexual.

His friends soon became a substitute family, where unlike the biological family circle, bonds are chosen and consented to, formed through mutual help and being there for each other, as well as partying together. One of his friends inspired him to go to Morocco. He thought that it promised fulfilling jobs, landscapes to explore, and maybe also the hope of living more fully as a gay man due to a more tolerant environment. In those areas, as he would later acknowledge, his expatriation was a total fiasco.

He arrived in Rabat and found a job as a manager at a restaurant, then later at a late-night bar. He spent two years there and managed to turn it into a sought-after and fashionable place where he flitted around, brilliantly practicing the art of connection and worldliness that he had learned by mimicry in the nightclubs of Paris. That is, until the boss married an Ivorian woman who intended to run the place herself and deprive him of his management role. Tensions and disputes turned nasty, a pattern that would recur quite often in his career. He started to feel restless again. Everyone was talking about how Marrakesh was booming.[3] He easily found a job there as a guesthouse manager[4] in Palmeraie;[5] but the boss turned out to be a "jerk," authoritarian and temperamental, racist—all this from Mano's point of view of course. Moreover, his employer refused to declare him as an employee; out of the ten or so jobs he has held since arriving in Morocco, none of them have declared him in fact. They got along badly, argued often, and it was especially easy to leave since there was no contract between boss and employee. However, Mano had time to make a name for himself in the small world of the Marrakesh hospitality business, and another job opportunity at a riad in the medina[6] was offered to him, until his employers eventually decided to sell it.

One might imagine that the whirlwind he was caught in, his inconstancy, the fact that, as his teachers told him, "he can't stay still," were nothing more than a way to remain mobile; having failed to succeed in upward social

---

[3] From the 2000s onwards, Marrakesh experienced very spectacular economic and urban development, driven by improvements made by the Moroccan state (a new airport, a railway station, a freeway), which would turn it into a major tourist destination (Peraldi, 2018).

[4] The originality of the tourism offering in Marrakesh lies in the development of "guest houses" (new villas with gardens) and "riads" (renovated old houses in the medina). In these houses and riads, always made up of four or five rooms, tourists find personalized accommodation that plays on authenticity and a simulacrum of orientality.

[5] Palmeraie, a district on the outskirts of Marrakesh, is a kind of local Beverly Hills where the most sumptuous villas, golf courses, and a few luxury hotels are clustered together.

[6] Medina, *m'dina* in Arabic, means "town." It is Marrakesh's old town, still surrounded by ramparts, the part of town that the tourists visit.

mobility, the act of changing jobs often gives him the illusion of being in motion, always available for the next "dream job". This is a kind of horizontal mobility that is a substitute for upward mobility, the type that he would have pursued if he had followed in his family's footsteps. In short, instead of progressing, he becomes agitated, inconstant, unstable, impatient, easily bored. And yet it would be a mistake to individualize this type of career and see it as the consequence of emotional instability or a particular psychology. For his instability was also greatly heightened by the precariousness of his status in the jobs that he occupied. Light as a feather, he as never officially declared, or only part of his employment was, but he was often given a share of the profits, so that he occupied a rather paradoxical position: having a job with responsibility gave him the moral right to give his opinion on the management "politics" of the companies where he worked and let him feel a little like a "manager," without having the "statutory" rights or of course the income of a manager.

When we met, he had just joined the real estate agency owned by M., also from the French suburbs, born to a Nigerian father. He was an agent there, paid on commission. But of course, his employment was not declared. The agency was based in an industrial park. The premises set aside for artisanal activities were huge, as they occupied a whole floor, "semi-finished" as real estate agency brochures say euphemistically. Behind a pair of makeshift curtains, Mano created a sleeping and washing area for himself at the agency.

A few months later, Mano's financial situation went beyond the limit that he had often come close to, like a tightrope-walker balanced between precariousness and true destitution. He had just lost his RSA benefits that he had continued to receive despite his expatriation, forcing him to make some express trips to Paris.[7] This time his bank account was truly empty, his credit card was blocked, and finally the person subletting the student room that Mano had continued to rent through the City of Paris' HLM program (social housing) was no longer responding to any communication and had stopped paying the rent. Mano had just learned that another riad that he had been asked to manage would finally be reopened without him; the few real estate "deals" that he had kept up his sleeve upon leaving the agency did not go through, and some kind of disagreement heralding arguments and misunderstandings had set in between his boss and him. Lastly, the property development in which G. had promised him a sales job had fallen through, due to the failure of a Saudi lessor. Basically, Mano was in a mess, for real. He went to live with Stéphane, the friend who had encouraged him to come to Morocco. He too is an interesting case. He lives between Paris, Lisbon, and Rabat, works as a freelance IT maintenance technician, and earns a very good living. He travels widely, parties quite frequently, and has invested some of his income in property. He had just bought an apartment in Marrakesh,

[7] *Revenu de Solidarité Active* (Active Solidary Income), the minimum social security benefit paid by the French state to those who have no other income. In Mano's case it was around 500 euros a month.

which Mano looked after in exchange for accommodation. The relationship was ambivalent, between friendship and housekeeping: Stéphane regularly traveled from Rabat to spend the weekend in Marrakesh with friends, and when this happened, Mano was asked to find other accommodation for the weekend, while making sure the guests found the apartment clean, with a full fridge and cupboards.

His situation thereby gave me the chance to pay back what I saw as a debt for the many favors he had done for me and the constant and sincere interest that he had shown in my work.

Since I arrived in this area, I had indeed been wondering how to check the regularity and representativeness of some of the information yielded by the interviews and life stories of a population that is fluid, "liquid" (Bauman, 2006), changeable due to being mobile, and segmented at the same time.

I was surprised by how easy Mano found it to get to know people, his availability, and his helpfulness. With no ulterior motive, he had therefore built, like other people I also met in Marrakesh, a dense network of relationships establishing him as someone who flirts with codes and norms and is curious about people, although this relational flitting about is also a professional necessity, he makes a living from it. He was exactly how I pictured the marginal man described by Park (1928).

He knew many people and his circle of acquaintances grew almost daily; his life was made up of meetings. He often talked to me about it, but I was lost in the plethora of portraits that he painted for me. Hence the idea that I pass around a survey that was quick to complete, designed without excess sophistication in terms of interactions, which would nevertheless allow me to systematize the information collected. This would be done without going beyond what the implicit rules of conversation and superficial encounters made it possible to ask; "Without seeming like a cop or a sociologist," he said, with one of the bursts of thunderous laughter that regularly punctuated his remarks.

We devised a survey that could be completed in half an hour by even the most talkative people, did not require lengthy training in coding to fill in, and contained no tricky questions that would require deep interactions. The general idea was that Mano could pass the survey around in public places, bars, restaurants, even parties or the pop-up venues where he socialized. We soon agreed that he would be paid a flat fee. In two months, he would gather just over a hundred surveys from around 200 people, before finding a new job that would take him away from Marrakesh, which he said he had seen enough of.[8]

[8] At the end of 2014, Mano returned to Rabat, where he took over the running of a restaurant which was a local institution in that city, frequented by the Moroccan and European bourgeoisie. But there again his employment was not declared, the management of the establishment proved catastrophic, and the

The instrument is therefore very imperfect from a strict socio-demographic point of view. It has loopholes which a life story or in-depth biographical interview would not: the depth of personal genealogies, the journeys, "careers," doubts, detours, etc. The story of each person he met is reduced to a few laconic mentions of the previous steps along the way. On the longitudinal level, the survey is short on questions about professional careers, silent on education and qualifications earned, which turned out to be a very tricky subject to discuss, and obviously, like any instrument of this type, it forces us to take people at their word, in areas where people tend to "blur" or hide information: income, property, savings, and debts.

With these precautions taken and these weaknesses admitted, the instrument gives a fairly precise snapshot of a population that is known only very roughly in the institutions through which it passes (associations, consulates) or in an overly fragmented way through its life stories and biographical accounts. Lastly, the sample is in no way "representative," both because it is composed randomly and circumstantially— Mano's socializing—and more fundamentally because the idea of representativeness presupposes something of a community which is nothing less than random in the European milieu in Marrakesh. It is simply a world, that is to say a set of people who do not necessarily know each other (although many do, at least from sight) but who, sharing a certain number of common professional, leisure and family activities, also share circles of opinion and socio-demographic categories. For lack of anything better, I call them "Mano's worlds," since they are people who resemble him.[9]

Most of them are of French nationality: this applies to 89% of them, and 75.8% of these French people were born in France.[10] In descending order, they come from Paris and the Ile-de-France region (30%), a large group from the West (23.7%) or South-East (15.7%), and finally the North (12%). Urban France in short, or more precisely the neo-urban France of suburbs and developments with single-family homes, of attractive medium-sized cities, like Nantes, Poitiers, or Toulouse, rather than outright rural areas or long-urbanized parts of France.[11] Paris, Lyon, and Marseille are less commonly cited than their metropolitan peripheries. The other Europeans are, in order of number of respondents, Italian, Belgian, Spanish, and Swiss. In this respect, at least we can say that this sample of nationalities is quite consistent with the social composition of the inhabitants of Marrakesh, where the

restaurant closed in 2016, sold to a restaurant chain.

[9] Here I have to thank Patrick Perez, Lecturer in Sociology at Aix-Marseille University, who developed the data processing protocol.

[10] The survey was administered individually to 107 people, and to the extent that some questions relate to the family when there is family, sometimes in the presence of the spouse, we questioned a total of 176 people, with a total of 129 children. In the sample, 60% of respondents were men and 40% were women.

[11] To the question "How would you define yourself if you had to do so?", the most salient regional identities expressed are "Parisian" (9 people) and the Breton (8). This is in no way a dominant group: as we will see, what dominates is rather a proclaimed "universal citizenship"; this is just a salience that further highlights the dominant regional origins.

French are by far the biggest group of foreigners. A handful is Franco-Moroccan, and more frequently Euro-Moroccan, all in a relationship with Europeans.

Mixed couples are not an exception, but a very significant minority, nearly 30% of the couples we met. All adult categories are represented, but the vast majority are over 30, with two troughs in the age pyramid: the under-30s (9.7%) and the 50-60s (15.9%), the best-represented generations being those aged 30-40 (31%) and those over 60 (23%). This distribution of ages is not so random: on the one hand, people starting or restarting a professional career at an age when it is still socially possible to do so, because their commitment and roots in their profession are not yet that deep, and retirees on the other. To complete and refine the picture, we must add that 23.9% are single, 55.7% married or in a couple, and finally 19.5% widowed, separated or divorced.[12] If we add that 31.2% of the couples are childless, we can deduce a majority of people without family responsibilities (counting singles, separated people, and couples without children, they make up 61.2%), who are therefore more available to build or rebuild their lives. However, this is only a relative majority, as 39.0% of people in our sample came to Marrakesh with children: two, three, or more sometimes,[13] rather than just one.

One-third of these couples are couples in which one of the spouses is Moroccan; in the vast majority of cases, 69%, a Moroccan woman in a relationship (married or not) with a French, Belgian, Swiss, or American man. Non-French people are more likely to be in mixed relationships than the rest of the sample as a whole.

At the professional level, even if, as we must humbly point out, this picture is very vague, instantaneous, and even controlled by the people themselves, it nevertheless offers a certain coherence that raises questions: employees only represent 17% of respondents, or 25.6% of workers,[14] while "freelancers" make up 49% of the sample and 64.7% of workers, to which we must add the group of those who declare themselves "bosses," 5.0% of the sample and 9.7% of workers. Of the employees, 57% are "expats," according to the definition we gave of this term, that is to say at least employees of the civil service of their country (France mostly) or a large firm; there is not much point being more specific because in this case, most of these ten or so people are teachers at French schools. Among the "freelancers" (who prefer to say they "work for themselves"), about thirty are shopkeepers, 31.7% are workers, and 49.0% describe themselves as

[12] Observant readers will notice that 0.9% are missing. These are people who did not answer this question.
[13] Just one family of five children, most have two (28.1%) or three (20.0%). Two families have children that they adopted in Morocco.
[14] Workers are those who describe themselves as being employed, except for retirees, non-respondents, and evasive responses which indicate odd jobs that are difficult to define as a profession... Thus, workers make up 72.5% of the sample, while the others, mostly retirees, make up 27.5%.

"artisans," even if the term is ambiguous in Marrakesh since it seems to suggest a connection with traditional crafts. In actual fact, they tend to work in service professions, from "heavy" building services (plumbing, gardening, masonry) to maintenance jobs (computing, for example) and what would be termed the "liberal" professions in Europe: accountants, architects, and increasingly the paramedical professions.

The most common activities among freelancers, "bosses" included, are food service, decoration, and technical services such as computer maintenance, for example.

This situation of freelancing, being "self-employed," therefore encompasses a very varied range of professional statuses: conventional entrepreneurs, business owners, usually commercial and officially declared; artisans who are also declared; freelance workers or liberal professions, such as those engaged in para-medical activities; and finally a whole fringe group of people involved in very precarious, very imprecise activities (they say "doing business"), or very casual work (they also talk about "doing odd jobs"). Mano's different jobs are an example of this, which may seem extreme but is ultimately quite representative.

Logically, this diversity has repercussions on the scale of incomes, which for the most part are rather modest; we say this as they are described as such by the respondents. Nearly 60% of the people in our sample say they have monthly incomes of less than 2,000 euros, just under 27% "admit" to incomes between 2,000 and 3,000 euros, and just under 13% say they receive an income of over 3,000 euros. For a more accurate picture, we should specify that the poorest, who earn less than 1,000 euros a month, make up 23% of the group and include two retired people living on less than 500 euros a month. Among the higher incomes on the other hand, just one person told us they earned 7,000 euros a month, with the bulk of incomes above 3,000 euros not exceeding 5,000 euros a month.

If we focus on retirees, 40% have monthly incomes below 2,000 euros, and among these, only one-third has revenues of less than one thousand euros. The majority of retirees in our sample have incomes between 2 and 3,000 euros, 48%, and 12% even have incomes of more than 3,000 euros. Bearing in mind that 75% of our retirees live alone, we have here a population with very comfortable incomes, quite consistent with the idea that the media create when presenting Marrakesh as a gilded retirement home. On the other hand, it is the employees who have the most comfortable financial situations, since 30% of those in our sample have incomes of more than 3,000 euros, 18% have incomes between 2–3,000 euros, and the majority, 52%, has an income below 2,000 euros (two of them claiming to earn less than 1,000 euros a month). This financial comfort must be qualified however, because for 44% of this group, these incomes are household incomes, earned jointly by couples with children (two-thirds) or without children. Overall then, a real dividing line appears, a social boundary, between a small minority of these migrants, consisting of well-to-do retirees and "expat" wage-earners, and a majority of freelance workers in precarious circumstances, to say the least, and therein lies the social key to their situation, from the point of view of the norms prevailing in the European societies that they have left behind.

The group of "freelancers" is where we find the most contrast in financial situations and especially the most relative precariousness: 68.5% of them claim to earn a monthly income, per individual or family, of less than 2,000 euros, and we must bear in mind that 72% of these low incomes are couples with children (two-thirds) or without children. This is also the group where we find the highest proportion of low incomes: indeed, 31% of this group claim to earn less than one thousand euros a month. In this group, 7.5% claim to earn a monthly income of less than 3,000 euros, and 24% earn between 2 and 3,000 euros. Here again, this group contains a high quotient of families (72% are families).

When we met them, just over 20% of people in our sample had lived in Marrakesh for over ten years (21.2%). The arrival dates of the others are spread evenly over the last ten years. Around 18% had been settled in Marrakesh for less than two years when we surveyed them (17.7%). It seems that Europeans have not been moving there continuously since the city began to develop, but rather most of them arrived in the last ten years, in regular waves. Their relocation, therefore, has all the signs of a migratory cycle.

How do they live in Marrakesh? Let us first dispel a myth: they do not live in the medina in huge numbers; they are not the "gentrifiers" of a "colonized" urban space.[15] Only 7% of the people we met live in the medina, and two-thirds of those are tenants there. A clear majority, 52%, live in Gueliz or Hivernage, neighborhoods invented and built by and for Europeans after colonization.[16] Nor are they members of the "rich people's ghetto" that is Palmeraie: just 8% of them live there, and 85% are tenants. Lastly, 26.5% of them live in the new extensions of Marrakesh, in areas alternating between housing developments and tower blocks in the north-west of the city. There again, they are overwhelmingly tenants, around 85%; in general, rented accommodation is indeed the most common type of housing, for 71% of respondents. The vast majority of them lives in "villas," a term commonly used in Marrakesh and Morocco, in general, to refer to detached houses surrounded by small gardens. The homes closest to downtown have minimal gardens, often no more than a patch of lawn, while the most luxuriant include a swimming pool and enough vegetation to require a paid gardener. The vast majority of our Europeans live in this type of housing, 66.4% of them versus

[15] This theme of post-colonial gentrification has been the subject of many articles in the local media but also, strangely, the international media, sometimes backed by researchers' work. See for example Coslado E, Mc Guiness J, Miller C (dir) Médinas immuables ? Gentrification et changement dans les villes historiques marocaines (1996-2010), Rabat, Centre Jacques Berque, 2013.

[16] For more details about the urban history of Marrakesh, see Peraldi, 2018.

24.8% who have chosen older housing, either in the medina or the "urban" apartment blocks in the Gueliz district, generally built before independence. Lastly, 6.2% of them live in the modern apartment blocks of the immense suburb that Marrakesh has become. Whatever type of residence they choose, a dream home or a more pragmatic option, our Europeans prefer to live in villas rather than traditional Moroccan housing. We can even go further by affirming logically that this is exactly what they come to seek in Marrakesh; not the exoticism of a "traditional" home but the virtually universal dream of the French: a detached house with a patch of garden.

Many were evasive about their professional life before they came to Marrakesh, or perhaps we should have been more persuasive and insistent. The fact remains that we only know a little about a few people's previous professional activities. Logically, the younger ones were students and say so. Some also say they have experienced a period of unemployment. Therefore it is not unusual for their job in Marrakesh to be their entry into working life, so most are "self-employed." Another large group of our respondents came to Marrakesh to do what they were already doing in France. The only changes are tiny shifts in professional position, and there again in the direction of entrepreneurial autonomy. Let us also destroy another myth: even though there are numerous, highly publicized cases of radical changes in career or professional status, they are not the rule.

This is surely the characteristic that most singles out the population that we met: 56% of them have experienced international mobility at least once—non-tourism expatriation in other words—for varying lengths of time. This mobility obviously covers a wide variety of experiences, from an internship at an NGO lasting a few months to recurring expatriation for a sales executive at an international firm, or even the children of managers or diplomats who spent no more than four years in the same country during their childhood. However, we must not exaggerate the exoticism of this experience: this mobility mainly takes place in Europe, including Switzerland, a country regularly mentioned when talking about professional mobility, followed by the U.S. and French-speaking Africa, where equal numbers of our respondents have lived. Next are Asia, in particular China, Japan and Thailand, for a significant number.

66% of the people that we questioned have kept no residential connection to France or their country of nationality, though 65.5% are registered with the Consulate of their country, and just over 65% have applied for and obtained a residence permit. Indeed, Morocco allows holders of a tourist visa to stay in the country for three months, and the visa is automatically renewed each time they come back. Most of the European "migrants" therefore make regular trips to Europe before their visa expires in order to renew their residence rights. This is the case with Mano.

This situation, however, attests to a particular form of precariousness and social integration, because it means that these "migrants" de facto deprive themselves of any participation, other than economic, in the social life of the country where they live. In short, they are city-dwellers but not citizens.

Thus, we have a large proportion of "illegals," although the term should be taken with a little irony. About 35% of these European migrants are indeed neither declared at their consulate nor in possession of residence permits. In fact, the figure is much lower if we subtract those who have been in Morocco for a few months and have not yet completed the formalities or are in the process of doing so. On this basis of calculation, only 22% of them are "illegal."

To conclude, let us return to the debate presented at the beginning of this article on the migrant condition and its social forms. It is clear that the settled population of European migrants—the term should no doubt be clarified, for as we will see, it is one of the theoretical keys to this debate—in these formerly colonized countries enjoy a position of privilege. This privilege is in large part due to the existence of a weak social state that enables them to live in precariousness without suffering legal consequences or administrative worries. In short, this is an inverted condition of precariousness. While workers migrating from South to North experience their precariousness as a situation that weakens them directly because they are under the constant threat of a "criminalization" of their condition (Le Courant, 2015), Europeans benefit doubly from their legal "precariousness." It allows them, on the one hand, to not have to submit to normative and contractual rules in exercising their economic activities, while on the other hand maintaining the "liquidity" of their condition by returning regularly to their country of origin. We must therefore conclude that their situation sheds new light on sociological reflections and theories in the field of migratory dynamics. Indeed, here it is no longer a question of considering migration as a form of exile, of even a relative abandonment of one national condition for another. Migration here is a form, a modality of a general condition of mobility. Before they are migrants, our Europeans are mobile people. They are primarily so because of their situation as permanent "tourists," more fundamentally because their personal journey is often made up of mobility rather than being sedentary, and finally because their migration is indeed a moment in a cycle which incorporates, and which will incorporate throughout their professional life, other moments of settling in foreign countries. The difference which then appears—which then becomes discrimination, placing two types of mobility on either side of a clear, impassable border—lies in the institutional and legal frameworks that either make this "fluidity" possible or, on the contrary, very arbitrarily prevent it. On one side of this border, migrant workers moving from the South to the prosperous North, to whom the legal and institutional barriers and "walls" assign the status of exploited and expellable undocumented migrants, whose mobility is a condition of their fragility and vulnerability, aspects which are simultaneously the conditions of their employability. In other words, this is the mobility of subordinates. On the other side, on the contrary, is a privileged mobility, because it is indeed a "privilege" granted, a liberation from the local rules of law, which enables people to develop economic activities under economic conditions with a profitable differential.

References

Bauman, Z. 2006. *La vie liquide*, Chambon: Ed. Le Rouergue.

Biacabe J.L. & Robert S. 2014. Les Français à l'étranger. L'expatriation des Français à l'étranger, quelle réalité ? Paris, CCI.

Boudarssa C. 2017. Entre travail et engagement, les acteurs expatriés et nationaux de solidarité internationale au Maroc: volontaires, salariés, bénévoles et stagiaires. Le cosmopolitisme à l'épreuve ? Ph. D. Dissertation in Sociology. Nanterre: University of Sorbonne .

Department for French Nationals Abroad and Consular Administration (DFAE). 2013. *French expatriation survey*. Paris: Ministry of Foreign Affairs.

Le Courant, S. 2015. Vivre sous la menace: ethnographie de la vie quotidienne des étrangers en situation irrégulière en France. Ph. D. Dissertation. Paris: EHESS.

Park, R.E. 1928. "Human Migration and the Marginal Man", *American Journal of Sociology*, 33 (6): 881-893.

Peraldi M. 2018. Marrakech, le souk des possibles. Du moment colonial à l'ère néolibérale, Paris: La Découverte.

Peraldi M & L. Terrazzoni (eds.). 2016. « Mobilités et migrations européennes en (post) colonies ». *Cahiers d'Etudes Africaines*, 221.

Therrien C. (dir.) 2016. La migration des Français au Maroc. Entre proximité et ambivalence, Casablanca, La Croisée des Chemins.

THE AERONAUTICAL ENGINEER IN FLIGHT: TURBULENCE AND THE CAPACITY FOR AGENCY ACROSS BORDERS

Alfredo Hualde[1]

Introduction

This paper examines the story of an engineer's career and life in the aeronautical industry. Our engineer is 55 years old and has three children, all of them grown and successful. He is currently planning his retirement. As a Mexican born on the border with the United States, he's been familiar with the American way of life since early childhood. Little by little, as his career unfolded, he had to adapt to it completely, experiencing the work customs and the instability of the aeronautical industry first-hand, and repeatedly going through the turmoil of changing jobs. On several occasions, he was forced to start all over again from the ground up.

Despite all these vicissitudes, the engineer—whom we'll call Lindbergh—and his family were not disheartened. Driven by his fascination for aircraft, and inspired by his father, who'd been a flight engineer, Lindbergh studied at the National Polytechnic Institute of Mexico City, a public institution that has been providing Aeronautical Engineering training since the 1930s. Although he found the capital city mesmerizing, he soon returned to the border, to work with U.S. companies. Over the course of his career, he founded a helicopter repair company on the border and worked for large companies such as Boeing in Wichita (Kansas) and Bombardier in Montreal (Canada). All of this served to broaden his experience, which was marked every five or six years by economic crises, mergers and restructurings, both in the aeronautical industry as a whole and in the companies where he worked. His career has been a real roller-coaster ride, exacerbated by upheavals in the wider world that significantly affected the industry, such as Mexico's debt crisis in the eighties, the environmental regulations implemented in California that scared off aeronautical companies, and the crisis that followed the attack on the World Trade Center.

Lindbergh's trajectory was punctuated by distinct periods of movement, away from home and back again. When the ground fell away beneath his feet in distant lands, he'd return, seeking shelter on the border between Tijuana, Baja California, and Chula Vista, California, where he had friends and business contacts, and where his wife could pursue her own engineering career. Here, he started up small businesses that helped him make it through

[1] I would like to thank Verónica Carrión for generously granting me to use the interview she conducted for her doctoral dissertation.

the hard times. It is this constant struggle, the continuous need to learn and adapt to new situations, which truly defines both Lindbergh's life and his career.

The path taken by this engineer is a world away from the classic "lifelong employment" model of the "organization man" as defined by William White. Lindbergh is, by contrast, much more of a 21st-century man, facing continuous trials and tribulations both in his professional life and in his family life, brought about by globalization and the continuous restructuring of his chosen industry—the huge, complex, demanding and, to a certain extent, unpredictable, aeronautical industry. Eventually, after long years of uncertainty in the U.S., working, like so many others, as a migrant on a temporary U.S. work permit, Lindbergh's efforts were rewarded. Bombardier, an aerospace company based in Montreal, helped him obtain a Canadian passport, which paved the way to obtaining U.S. residency. Was this the culmination of a career fraught with obstacles and dangers? Not yet, perhaps: at the time of our interview, Lindbergh's career hadn't quite come to an end, and, although the idea of retirement was trotting through his mind, it had yet to mature into a concrete plan. In any event, the new legal status Lindbergh received in Montreal took a heavy load off his back, easing the pressure and giving him peace of mind. It gave him the satisfaction of being able to provide a promising future for his children, who'd crossed borders, learned different languages, adapted to new schools, made new friends in new cities–who, in short, had adopted a whole new culture. It's clear from Lindbergh's story that his career trajectory abounds with challenges, transformational changes, tricky situations and risky decisions. The driving force behind his actions, he tells us, is a kind of life philosophy inspired by Newton and Einstein. "In order to keep going forward, individuals must move, producing a sort of imbalance..."

The Biographical Method in the Context of Professional Migration

Lindbergh is one of thousands of Mexican engineers who migrated to the United States, a country in which the significant presence of highly skilled migrants has been overshadowed by the vast number of migrants without university degrees. In the case of Mexico, research has largely focused on the mass migration of millions of Mexicans, who found employment in agriculture for a hundred years or so, and then, in the seventies, turned to construction, kitchen jobs in restaurants throughout California and Chicago, or gardening work for predominantly white families. Paradoxically, the other migrants, those with university degrees, are much less visible. However, a number of research papers have been published over the last few years on the theme of university-educated migrants, a subject which is gaining ground partly because of the considerable number of this type of migrant.[2] In 2011,

[2] On this subject, see the works of Calva and Alarcón (2015), Hualde and Rosales (2017), Lozano and Gandini (2012), Lozano, Gandini, and Jardón (2015).

there were about 300,000 university-educated Mexican migrants, of which approximately 60,000 were engineers (Calva & Alarcón, 2015; Carrión & Hualde, 2013).[3]

Little attention has been paid to professional migration in Mexico, in contrast to other parts of the world, where the phenomenon is increasingly and extensively documented. After the seventies, when research concentrated on the "brain drain," the international debate took a different track, emphasizing the positive effects of professional migration on the country whose "brains" are emigrating (*brain gain*) (Stark & Fan, 2007). This idea is perfectly illustrated by the case of Indian engineers (Iredale, 2001) who, after studying and working in the United States, return to India to create high-tech companies, supported by the network of business contacts established between the two countries. And India is far from being the only country in which the brain drain phenomenon has significantly progressed: young people educated in other countries do indeed return home with new skills and capabilities (Lazonick, 2007).

But that is just one aspect of highly skilled migration; there are many more to consider. Research shows that from the 1980s onwards, new issues cropped up alongside new methodological approaches. Firstly, the growing heterogeneity of migration became more and more apparent. Secondly, migration policy and its consequences came into the spotlight, along with the quality of work and the skills of workers. Thirdly, attention turned to the corporate sector, examining migration in a field that had greatly expanded with economic globalization and the growth of transnational corporations (Koser & Salt, 1997).

With this in mind, these "new professionals" can be seen as actors in globalization. There are now a number of distinct new factors to consider that do not fit into the classic career model: mobile skills and, consequently, knowledge and capabilities acquired in various companies; identifying oneself with a particular job; learning experiences at work and among peers; the development of multiple networks and the responsibility of individuals to take charge of and steer their own careers (Sullivan, 1999). This new career style is much more flexible and open to change, but it does not blur the differences between professions. The qualification requirements for medical professions, for example, are much stricter than for some of the technical professions associated with information technology, an industry that is much more flexible, since the capacities it requires are international skills that make any particular cultural context almost irrelevant. English, as the *lingua franca*,

[3] In terms of migration, Mexico has particularities that make it a unique case study. The 3200-km northern border both separates the country from and unites it with the world's biggest economic power. The North therefore exerts a powerful pull: there are currently 12 million Mexicans living in the U.S. For decades, this was the only destination that Mexicans thought of migrating to, but in recent years, migration to Canada has been on the rise. The 2007-2008 crisis marked a change of tide, gradual yet inexorable. The number of Mexicans crossing over the border to the U.S. started to drop, while the number of Mexicans returning rose, either as a result of the U.S. government's deportation policy or through personal choice.

dominates the sector; work experience is the surest way to obtain capital and to become more versatile; there is a high level of mobility between regions and countries; there is potential for return on investment and migration; and the professions are only loosely regulated by trade unions or other mechanisms (Iredale, 2001).

Lindbergh is a good example of the new professional globalization while also being a Mexican from the border. The border area is his home turf. Although Lindbergh's narrative obviously tells only one individual story, its significance lies in the fact that this story is so characteristic. As such, it provides useful insights, deepening our understanding of an era (the era of globalization), and a region (the U.S.-Mexico Border), a complex and ever-changing global industry (the aeronautical industry) and a family environment in which the division of the sexes at work, far from disappearing, takes on different shades.

In the description of Lindbergh's career, we shall examine the ways in which the engineer responds to unforeseen events, mainly linked to global economic crises, industry crises or austerity measures in the companies that he's employed and dismissed by. The aim is to determine his capacity for agency from a longitudinal perspective (Ebirmayer & Mische, 1998). In order to do this, we will try to pinpoint the most important sections of the career path and highlight the disruptions and bifurcations.

We have chosen to use the biographical method because it allows the changes and continuities in the factors that influence individual careers to be examined side by side. This juxtaposition of change and permanence is particularly relevant, in view of the documented fact that career paths have become much more unstable since at least the 1970s. Some traditional professions had already forewarned us, decades ago, about the sinuous new roads a career may take, even in times of relative calm:

> Hence, although a man's work may indeed be a good clue to his personal and social fate, it is a clue that leads us – and the individual himself – not by a clear and single track to a known goal, but into a maze full of dead-ends and of unexpected adventures (Hughes, 1964, p. 8).

Analyzing career trajectories opens up the analytic potential of observing, documenting and interpreting events of all different kinds, events that can produce either a progressive or sudden deterioration in living conditions and work conditions, or a steady improvement, paced by advances and setbacks. The paths are punctuated by disruptions and turning points that sometimes get in the way of work achievements, hindering a career, and other times can actually have a positive effect.

Therefore, although the chronological timeline is important to our understanding of a career, what some authors deem of greater importance is the biographical dimension, the "lived" time that flows faster or slower according to how the subject experiences significant events:

> To approach time solely as a chronological sequence is to strike out any advance in the study of times, since the clock does nothing more than count and measure, rejecting the existence of a multiplicity of times. Temporalities cannot be reduced to such measurements. The phenomena experienced in the duration have a temporal "thickness" and it is this thickness that can be approached and recreated through process-based analysis (Méndez, 2010, p.12).

Moreover, this type of analysis examines individual life stories in the context of other types of social structures, such as the family, or the specific geographical environments such as a city or region; the aspects of dynamics and of relationships are thus reintroduced into the analysis (Bidart et al., 2013, p. 745). Finally, the trajectories of individuals are influenced by macro events such as economic crises or profound political changes. As has been noted, "life stories are global constructions, through which individuals build a defined present within the specific horizons of past and future" (Bertaux & Kohli, 1984, p. 222; Demaziere & Dubar, 1999). That is not to say that this is a psychological analysis, but rather a sociological one, in which one of the most complex challenges consists in bringing individual characteristics and preferences into the context of a collective background.

A Life Across the Border: The Challenges of the Industry and the Responses of the Engineer

The First Steps: Studies and the Beginning of the Career Path

Lindbergh was born in Mexicali, a town on the border of Mexico and California. In his early years, the family moved to Tijuana, another border town, where he spent a happy childhood, in relative comfort—partly because people could obtain goods from the U.S. without having to pay sales tax. Although it would have made perfect sense to attend a university in San Diego, the nearest city, Lindbergh chose to study in Mexico City instead. He was one of six children and he felt that studying in San Diego would cost his family too much money. This decision was also influenced by the fact that his grandfather, who also belonged to the world of aeronautics, lived in Mexico City. Lindbergh's grandfather had wanted to be a flight engineer, but as this was beyond his reach, he worked as a mechanic instead; his son, however, did manage to become a flight engineer. Looking up to his father and his grandfather, the young Lindbergh dreamed of becoming a pilot.

He was determined to study and carve out a career in the aeronautical industry. Firm in his decision, he paid no attention to the sarcastic comments of his colleagues in Mexico City. According to Lindbergh, Mexico could not build any planes at the time because of the 1923 Bucareli Treaty with the U.S. His future, these colleagues would tell him, would consist in "cleaning the bellies of planes because any old mechanic will have better skills than you."[4]

[4] The interpretation of these treaties is not accurate, as Mexico built a number of aircraft in the 20th century. The Treaty's restrictions did not have their stipulated effect.

The real reason for their taunts, says our interviewee, was that they feared potential competition from those arriving from other parts of the country.

Lindbergh began to work in Mexico City before finishing his studies, first in the presidential general staff[5] and then for Mexicana airlines.[6] He got both jobs through his father, who had been in charge of the Tijuana airport for eleven years. Paternal influence was, as mentioned earlier, instrumental both in Lindbergh's choice of an aeronautical career and in securing his first job in the United States. During that period, a number of factors came together to act as "driving forces": on one hand, Lindbergh's father came in contact with businessmen from the U.S. looking to set up and run a major helicopter repair shop in Tijuana; and on the other, Mexican regulations required that, to establish their company, they must hire an engineer who had earned his qualifications in Mexico. Lindbergh's father told the businessmen that he had just the aeronautical engineer they needed: his own son.

The Americans were interested in this investment because there was a boom in the tuna fishing industry at that time, and the biggest fishing fleet in the U.S. was between Los Angeles and San Diego, while Mexico's biggest tuna fleet was in Ensenada, Baja California. The fishing boats carried helicopters, which flew out to scout for fish, which is why the company needed both helicopters and the specialists to repair them.

Lindbergh quit his job in Mexico City and returned to Tijuana to seek out career opportunities closely tied to Mexico's northern neighbor. His job at the helicopter repair shop meant interacting with both cultures, as he worked and trained on both sides of the border. Therefore, he moved to Long Beach (California) and lived there for more than a year.

Joining the company as a site manager, Lindbergh not only had a good salary but also participated as a partner, and thus began to learn how to build a business. Although this was a helicopter repair company, he was in charge of certifying U.S. pilots and mechanics to land helicopters on a moving vessel.

Despite the fact that he was from a border town, he had a poor grasp of English and therefore had to learn the language. This chain of events and their consequences had a pivotal impact on his future, as he picked up skills and formal qualifications that would prove crucial to his career. The initial training he received in Long Beach, near Los Angeles, sowed the first seeds of the idea that an engineer's skills are mobile, and therefore that there was no need for him to earn further qualifications. Broadly speaking, the aerospace industry can be divided into two fields: the first is that of critical operations, those that take place under traceability requirements, where responsibility can be tracked back in the event of damages or accidents. These kinds of operations require very high levels of specialized qualifications. The

[5] For the President of Mexico.

[6] A company that went bankrupt in 2010.

second field encompasses everything else, and the complexity of the industry forces engineers to be certified in a range of operations and procedures, both technical and organizational.

This period was brought to an end by a turning point on the broader, macro-economic scale, whose consequences were deeply felt on an individual level: the Mexican debt crisis which caused the strong devaluation of the peso in 1985, as the interviewee remembers with dramatic vividness. It left his business devoid of clients, with a heap of debt to contend with. His partners, horrified by the situation, asked him to either close the business down or go on without them. He decided to go on alone, but only held out another year before closing down, thus concluding a five-year period.

The first important matter to look at in this career path is the context and significance of Lindbergh's initial migration to the United States. It did not, in fact, cause a disruption or radical change in his life (a turning point). He did not have travel thousands of miles, as so many migrants do, or even distance himself from his social environment. All he did was go across the border to a region he was very familiar with. Migrating to the U.S. was not a drastic change for Lindbergh, as he'd had been brought up in a social and cultural environment where "gringo" elements were very much part of everyday life. As he himself says, "we were living like Americans without being Americans." This definition of his border-dwelling identity provides the first insight into the importance of culture and identity in the places where Lindbergh's career and life was to unfold.

The Cross-Border Area and California's Aeronautical Crisis

The next part of the engineer's career trajectory took place in the border area. Like many inhabitants of the region, Lindbergh would cross the border every day to work less than 20 kilometers from Chula Vista, California, and then, after finishing work, he'd come back to Tijuana.[7] After two years of this *commuter* lifestyle, he emigrated with his wife, who was also an engineer and owned an electric motor repair shop in the city.

To find work, Lindbergh made use of his social capital, the networks created during his time at the helicopter company. His second job required the application of new skills, for which his teaching experience at the Technological Institute in Tijuana came in handy; he was now using the knowledge he had acquired while giving lessons in material resistance. Teaching had, indeed, brought him a better understanding of certain engineering topics. Throughout the interview, Lindbergh markedly insists on the importance of training and education, and of educational institutes of any kind, universities or other.

Lindbergh was hired for this new job because he had obtained an internationally recognized work permit. He himself interprets this stage of

[7] A *commuter* is a person who crosses the border on a daily or weekly basis to work in the United States.

his trajectory in the light of his general view of how things arise, an idea he repeatedly expresses: that one needs to *act*, because things do not just happen spontaneously; things happen when one personally takes the initiative.

The job, however, was an associate position, one category down from engineer, with a lower salary. Nonetheless, seven months later, Lindbergh was promoted, and the company raised his salary by about 90%. He told us that he joined the company when it had 8,000 employees in Chula Vista and dominated 100% of the worldwide market. In any event, the company gradually began to struggle as it was faced with more and more competition from companies in other parts of the world, until, in 1994, there was a crisis and the company had to cut back its staff. Like many others, Lindbergh's company left California to escape environmental regulations. These were the contextual elements that contributed to Lindbergh's layoff and also to the increased difficulty of finding a new job in the region. Confronted with a total lack of opportunities, Lindbergh had to return to Tijuana, where he found a job completely unrelated to aviation. It was in a "maquiladora" (manufacturing operation for export) for electronic goods. He quit after six months because he was unhappy with the company's use of certain dangerous solvents, which he deemed hazardous to the health of the employees. The pay was good, but Lindbergh refused to work in conditions harmful to health of workers.

For Lindbergh, this constituted abuse, especially when you consider, as he reminds us, that the workers only earned one or two dollars an hour. After four months as assistant manager of the factory, he quit his job and started looking for work all over again.

Wichita, Kansas: Wow, Amazing...

Lindbergh was hired by Boeing and began the next stage of his career trajectory in Wichita, Kansas. He'd been told about the job by a childhood friend and former colleague at the Chula Vista company, who said someone was looking for a nacelles expert and that they would give software training in an aeronautical software system called Katia. This new job in Wichita entailed a major life change, and his peers teased him about going to a place that had nothing but corn. Nevertheless, Lindbergh says it suited him perfectly because he earned a salary that allowed him to build up savings, and his children began to speak English, with the help of tutors.

Despite the positive outlook given above, it is important to keep in mind that the Boeing job took the form of a subcontractor relationship; that is to say, the company provided no guarantee of a stable work situation. This is a classic example of the growing variety of ways in which workers of any trade are hired today. As a subcontractor, one receives a higher salary, but must forego employment benefits. Lindbergh earned 40 dollars per hour and worked 40 hours a week, with extra hours paid 90 dollars; but he was responsible for paying all his taxes, retirement funds, and health care.

Although this job resembled his previous job as a materials specialist, at Boeing, he received additional training. He attended a range of courses on Japanese techniques such as *just in time* and other, similar ones related to *lean process*, a socio-technical production model that was popular all over the world in the 1980s.

Since the job was initially to last only six months, and there was no guarantee of any work beyond that period, Lindbergh moved to Wichita alone. His wife and children continued living in Chula Vista, California. The children were attending school in Tijuana, where Lindbergh's wife had her electric motor business. After the six months were up, they decided to join Lindbergh in Wichita. This kind of move, and the one that was to follow—all the way to Montreal—was problematic for the family, raising questions about where and when to continue the children's education. But the family took it all in stride, and, during their time in Kansas, Lindbergh's wife secured an income as a translator in an agency she and her husband founded.

Five years later, another crisis hit the industry, leaving Lindbergh out of work again: as soon as the industry is in difficulty, subcontractors are the first on the chopping block.

The move to Wichita involved a slew of legal challenges for the family, since the children did not have U.S. residence permits. That was a real problem when they entered high school, says Lindbergh, because, as he was the only one granted a permit, the children had to pay the full school fees, as foreigners, at a much higher cost than U.S. residents.

This resulted in a serious dilemma when Lindbergh lost his job and failed to find another one. The family considered moving back to Tijuana. Meanwhile, Lindbergh carried on supporting the family with occasional jobs, until one day, his former boss in Wichita called him to tell him there was a job opening at Bombardier... in Montreal.

Before moving to Montreal, however, Lindbergh founded an Autocad editing company in Tijuana. During this period, Lindbergh was living off his savings, as he had no reliable source of income. When his former boss in Wichita offered him the Bombardier job in Montreal with a "pretty juicy" salary, it was a no-brainer especially as the company paid for the move.

Montreal, Open City: Bombardier, the Ups and Downs of the Industry

This was the beginning of a new chapter in Lindbergh's career. He was in charge of a team of five engineers, he had a good salary, and he was excited about his new life in a cosmopolitan city. To top it all off, his legal status had improved: Bombardier issued him a work visa rather than just a work permit, thus paving the way for him to apply for permanent U.S. residency or a green card. In the course of his work, he continued attending courses and managed to certify as a Six Sigma[8] auditor. He took a range of courses on other subjects as well, including aeronautical software.

However, the good times were short-lived, because even at Bombardier there was no guarantee of long-term stability. Yet again, there was an industry crisis looming in the background, set to strike. Two years after the attack on the World Trade Center, the repercussions hit the aeronautical industry, and sparked a crisis.

But that ordeal was still yet to come: the first challenge the family had to face was that of adapting to Montreal. The children went to an English school, and Lindbergh also hired a Moroccan tutor to give them lessons entirely in French so that, little by little, they would learn to speak French as well. Languages were, indeed, a complex matter for the family: Lindbergh wanted his children to learn English and French without forgetting their Spanish in the meantime. To make sure that would not happen, he subscribed to Spanish-language TV channels. Far from being discouraged by the difficulties, Lindbergh and his family fell in love with Montreal. They were fascinated by what they saw as a sophisticated cosmopolitan city.

At Bombardier, Lindbergh was promoted each year until 2005, when he was told his department was to be shut down. Before the Bombardier job came to an end, Lindbergh got in touch with Airbus in Toulouse and also with Rohr, the company he had worked for in Chula Vista, which had since been acquired by Goodyear. This time, he had a much better hand with which to negotiate the terms of the job, since he and his family had already secured Canadian nationality.

Goodyear offered to pay 80% of the costs of moving, and to help him obtain the U.S. residence permit (green card). Armed with a contract from Goodyear and a Canadian passport, he obtained the H-1B work visa "within two and a half hours." 18 months later, he got his green card. At the time of our interview, Lindbergh was still working at Goodyear, living back in Chula Vista, and, as mentioned at the beginning, thinking about retirement.

Contextual Elements, Bifurcations, and the Capacity for Agency

Lindbergh's career path, as hectic, haphazard, and full of changes as it has clearly been, seems to correlate with a certain way of seeing the world. The engineer casts himself as an actor with the capacity to control and steer events. But it must be pointed out that his *philosophy of action* (see introduction) does not quite correspond to the way his career and work life have actually unfolded. His general view of the world is founded on the idea of balance, from a dialectical, dualistic perspective. Human action—in this case that of the engineer—causes states of imbalance in which things move, change, and evolve. He says, "You have to have the right mind-frame as well as the

[8] Six Sigma is a corporate technique that is widely used in corporate management.

willingness to move to a different place." This is a sort of philosophy of action, seemingly implying that he does, indeed, have the capacity for agency.

To this abstract idea, Lindbergh adds something more tangible: an innate and insatiable curiosity about different cities and countries, powerfully manifested in his descriptions of the two biggest cities he has lived in, Mexico City and Montreal. Both are, to him, places of knowledge, of learning, places filled with opportunities, where you meet people, learn languages, experience different ways of life and different customs. Lindbergh says he never wanted to leave Mexico, and yet he never expresses nostalgia – because if he had been nostalgic, he would never have experimented, he would not have done what he did, saw what he has seen; he would not have engaged in the fight: he would know nothing about any of it other than what he heard from others.

Lindbergh appropriates the places he goes to on all levels—intellectual, pragmatic, and even emotional—and he does it in a variety of different ways. He sees Mexico City as the capital of the country he was born in; he sees Montreal as a cosmopolitan area that opens up the door to a new world, where people from different places and cultures peacefully co-exist. The border area, from Tijuana to Los Angeles, is his home base, his most familiar space and the place he can go back to when things go wrong, in a sort of *circular migration* that allows him to draw on his social capital when he needs to. Even Wichita, a city with neither the attractions of the metropolis nor the advantages of the border, is seen in a positive light by Lindbergh, who describes only what he likes about it.

Lindbergh not only accepts the continual movement imposed on him by forces outside of his control, he occasionally even manages to transform the elements of these forces into resources for agency. It is clear that his career path is conditioned by macro-economic and political events on a global level. For example, the aeronautical crisis in California was closely linked to the environmental regulations imposed on the industry and to the cost of land and labor. The attack on the World Trade Center was clearly the root cause of Lindbergh's dismissal from Bombardier in 2005, with its delayed effect on the aeronautical industry. And the first phase of Lindbergh's career was interrupted by the Mexican crisis, with the devaluation of the currency bringing the helicopter company he was working for in Ensenada, Baja California, to bankruptcy. Tying in closely with all of it on a more individual level, there are the specific crises of the aeronautical industry and of the companies Lindbergh worked for, some of them large corporations. The flip side to all this instability, however, is that the job market remains relatively open, and the regulations are more lenient than those of other professions, which are regulated by explicit policies requiring a high level of qualification. Lindbergh describes his experience at Boeing as being truly multinational, adding that, as part of a community of globalized engineers, he had colleagues from all over Asia, Latin America and Europe.

What resources does Lindbergh use in the transition phases between jobs, when he has to make momentous decisions? Equally, what resources does he use in the phases of apparent calm when working for a company? First, there is the use of qualifications, titles, skills, and knowledge that he builds up as he moves through the various companies. This process seems to be more or less expected in the profession—these days, "it's all part of the game". For Lindbergh, this process unfolds in a variety of ways. To begin with, the helicopter company gave him more than a year's training in Long Beach; and then, progressively, in a sort of self-taught manner, he became a specialist in materials, which, oddly enough, combined the knowledge he brushed up on while teaching at the technological institute in Tijuana with the training he received at the Chula Vista company. Both at Boeing and at Bombardier, he learned the industry techniques associated with *lean production*, together with organizational techniques such as *Six Sigma* and Katia, a specialized software system for the aeronautical industry. There is no doubt that these skills, acquired through training and also through practice, are a considerable asset; but they are still not enough to guarantee Lindbergh a stable contract or to prevent his dismissal in times of crisis. This would imply that Lindbergh's capacity for agency in fact, fairly limited. Indeed, that seems to be the case for much of the time that Lindbergh is employed; but, whenever he loses his job, his capacity for agency kicks in and drives him, for example, to found a company, as previously mentioned, and to redirect his career time and again.[9]

Secondly, the engineer makes use of his family environment and adapts it to all the different circumstances of his professional life. In this environment, his wife, an electromechanical engineer, plays a prominent role. She appears at several points of the narrative, contributing to the family income through work, at first independently, with her electromechanical repair shop, then as a translator in the agency founded by the two of them. All of Lindbergh's actions take into consideration how the change in circumstances may affect his children, and he tries to steer things in such a way as to enable the whole family to adapt and to access new opportunities. His decisions are made with a potential future in mind, projective agency (Ebirmayer & Mische, 1998) especially in Montreal, when he secures Canadian citizenship and throws open a whole new world of possibilities. Little wonder, then, that Lindbergh decides to hire a French tutor to further develop his children's linguistic abilities; they already speak good English and he makes an effort to prevent them from forgetting their Spanish. Occasionally, he has to make difficult decisions, such as accepting the Boeing job, which takes him away from his family for six months, as they could not risk moving to Kansas without some indication that the job would be stable. The decision to keep the family in Tijuana until the situation became clearer also reveals a particular mindset – that of action in the midst of doubt.

[9] A constant thread throughout the narrative is Lindbergh's enthusiasm for the cities he knows, what he undertakes, and what he learns.

At other times, when Lindbergh returns to the border area where he has a network of contacts, his capacity for agency is *iterative,* since it leans upon his previous experiences. On these occasions, the capacity for agency clearly takes the form of "defensive or reactive strategies," but these are not the only strategies that can be seen over the course of Lindbergh's career. There are also proactive strategies, such as when he founds the translation agency and the Autocad editing company, or when he takes the firm decision to obtain U.S. citizenship through his experience at Bombardier, even if he already has his Canadian citizenship at that time.

It is Lindbergh's legal situation that presents one of the major obstacles to his career. It is a stumbling block that continually gets in his way. He goes through every kind of legal status over the course of his career: working in the U.S. while residing in Tijuana, working as a subcontractor with a work permit, working as an employee with a work visa, and, finally, obtaining a second nationality, but not in the U.S.—in Canada. This legal achievement is a real game-changer, bringing stability both to his professional life and his home life. Lindbergh's career path presents a stark contrast to the life stories of other engineers who work for companies that continually provide their employees, especially engineers, with the best legal conditions (Carrión & Hualde, 2013).

Nonetheless, Lindbergh has more than one trick up his sleeve. On the one hand, there are his personal convictions and his family strategy, demanding the constant adaptation of his cognitive resources, along with a certain predisposition for continual learning; on the other, it is clear that, as he progresses through the various companies, his social network of friends and acquaintances provides him with opportunities that lead to new jobs, in which the knowledge he has accumulated along the way becomes a key asset. As is normal in any career, there are some people with whom he forms close relationships and others he does not get along with as well; however, on several occasions, it is his friends and colleagues who pull him out of tough times. This allows him to overcome crises, cutbacks, and layoffs, and steer his way through constantly troubled waters.

While there is no clear long-term plan to Lindbergh's career path and he goes along without a specific teleological vision, there are also no real ruptures to speak of; that is, there are no deep, irreversible shifts in his professional career. From the very beginning, immigration is a smooth and gradual transition from life on the border. Later on, although the Kansas and Montreal phases give rise to difficult situations and elements of rupture with the past, Lindbergh almost continuously chugs along with his career in the aeronautical industry, interrupted only by a few transitional periods of unemployment or underemployment, which, strictly speaking, cannot be viewed as genuine ruptures or changes in career direction. However, as far as Lindbergh's family life is concerned, there are indeed some real changes of direction. First, there is the move from California to Wichita; then, the move from Wichita to Montreal; and finally, the move back to the United States to settle on the border. Therefore it seems appropriate to qualify these critical junctures as "passive bifurcations," a term coined by Helardot (2009). The opposite would be an "active bifurcation," occurring, for example, when Lindbergh decides to quit his job at the *maquiladora* because he disagrees with the use of certain chemicals.

In short, the path of Lindbergh's career suggests that he is a world away from the stereotypical idea of a company career and "organization-man" described by Harrison White. Lindbergh's case is in direct contrast: he characterizes the professional worker in times of flexibility, deregulation, and subcontracting, times in which the mobilization of resources becomes a key factor in achieving family goals and, to a certain extent, professional goals. All of this requires a new kind of attitude, driven by a sort of philosophy of change, together with a strong survival instinct. Lindbergh sums up his philosophy as follows: "If you take what you like and try to leave what you don't like behind, then life becomes very pleasant".

Despite all the difficulties encountered along the way, Lindbergh's passion for aircraft has not diminished. His children, however, do not dream of engines and planes: the eldest is a composer; the second, a daughter, is a biologist; while the youngest is studying to be a vet. Lindbergh, far from being disappointed that his children will not follow in his footsteps, considers this a great success, achieved, in part, through his own personal efforts and the combined efforts of the family as a whole. His own plans hint at an upcoming active bifurcation, which will put his "capacity for projective agency" to the test. The return to Chula Vista makes him think that he can recover a few years of the work he has done for the company and add them to those he has accumulated in the current phase, making a total of 12 years, and thus be able to retire early, before turning 65. But that does not mean he has to stop all economic activity, because he would still be able to work as a subcontractor.

References

Ackers, L. 2004. «Managing Relationships in Peripatetic Careers: Scientific Mobility in the European Union» *Women's Studies International Forum* 27 (3): 189–201.

Bertaux D & M. Kohli. 1984. "The life story approach: a continental view". *Annual Review of Sociology* 10: 215–237.

Bidart, C., M. E. Longo & A. Mendez. 2013. "Time and process: an operational framework for procesual analysis", *European Sociological Review*, 29 (4): 743–751.

Borges, G., H. Rosovsky, C. Gómez & R. Gutiérrez. 2013. "Epidemiología del suicidio en México de 1970 a 1994", *Salud Publica de México* 38 (3): 197-206.

Carrión, V. & A. Hualde. 2013. "¿Profesionales sin fronteras? Una aproximación a las trayectorias laborales de los ingenieros mexicanos en Estados Unidos", *Revista Latinoamericana de Estudios del Trabajo,* 18 (30): 71-102.

Demazière, D. & C. Dubar, C. 2009. *Analyser les entretiens biographiques: l'exemple de récits d'insertion,* Québec: Les Presses de l'Université de Laval.

Ebirmayer M. & A. Mische. 1998. «What is agency?», *The American Journal of Sociology* 103 (4),962-1023.<http://www.ssc.wisc.edu/~emirbaye/Mustafa_Emirbayer/articles

_files/what%20is%20agency.pdf> .

Elder, Jr. & H. Glen H. 1994. "Time, Human Agency, and Social-Change: Perspectives on the Lifecourse", *Social Psychology Quarterly* 57 (1):4–15.

Harvey W. S. 2011. "British and Indian Scientists Moving to the United States", *Work and Occupations,* 38 (1): 68–100.

Hélardot, V. 2009. "Vouloir ce qui arrive? Les bifurcations biographiques entre logiques structurelles et choix individuels", In M. Grossetti, M. Bessin, C. Bidart, Bifurcations, Paris: La Découverte: 224-238.

Hughes, E. C. 1964. *Men and their work*, Glencoe, Ill.: Free Press.

Iredale, R. 2001. "The migration of Professionals: Theories and Typologies", *International Migration*, 39 (5): 7– 26.

Kofman, E. 2000. "The invisibility of skilled female migrants and gender relations in studies of skilled migration in Europe", *International Journal of Population, Geography*, 6: 45– 59.

Koser, K. & J. Salt. 1997. "The Geography of Highly Skilled International Migration", *International Journal of Population Geography,* 3 (4): 285-303.,

Kõu, A. & A. Bailey. 2014. "'Movement Is a Constant Feature in My Life': Contextualising Migration Processes of Highly Skilled Indians", *Geoforum,* 52:113–122.

Larsen, J., H. T. Aggergaard, K. B. Allan & P. Smith. 2005. "Overseas Nurses Motivations for Working in the UK: Globalization and Life Politics", *Work, Employment and Society* 19 (2): 349–368.

Lazonick, W. 2007. "Globalization of the ICT Labor Force"_In R. Mansell, Ch. Avgerou, D. Quah & R. Silverstone (eds.), *The Oxford Handbook of Information and Communication Technologies*, Oxford: Oxford University Press:75-99.

Mahroum S.1999. "Highly Skilled Globetrotters ", In OCDE Mobilising Human Resources for Innovation. Proceedings of the OECD Workshop on Science and Technology Labour Markets, Paris: OECD.

Mendez A. (ed). 2010. Processus. Concepts et méthode pour l'analyse temporelle en sciences sociales. Leuven: Academia-Bruylant.

Robinson V. & M. Carey. 2000. "Peopling Skilled International Migration: Indian Doctors in the UK.", *International Migration* 38 (1): 89–108.

Stark, O. & S. Fan. 2007. Losses and Gains to Developing Countries from the Migration of Educated Workers: An Overview of Recent Research, and New Reflections, IZA Discussion Paper 116. Bonn: University of Bonn.

Sullivan, S. 1999. "The Changing Nature of Careers: A Review and Research Agenda", *Journal of Management*, 25 (3): 457-484.

Williams A. M. & V. Baláž. 2005. "What Human Capital, Which Migrants? Returned Skilled Migration to Slovakia from the UK ", *International Migration Review* 39 (2): 439–468.

COLLECTIVE ACTION: THE FOUNDATION OF THE CAPACITY FOR AGENCY IN THE MIGRATORY PROCESS?

Ariel Mendez

February 13, 2015. Djamila's name appeared on the list of practitioners who passed the examination required in articles L. 4111-2-I and L. 4221-12 of the French Public Health code. She was now a doctor and registered with the French National Medical Council. Her husband was so happy that he took a photo of her registration card at the Council and sent it to their friends and family. I met her a few weeks later. During the interview, she took her card out of her wallet: "it's unbelievable," she says, "it took me ten years..." And yet, a few years earlier, Djamila who had graduated with a DEMS (Specialized Medical Studies Diploma) from the University of Algiers, was working as a traveling nurse in a private French clinic. As a surgeon, she found the situation unbearable and incredibly humiliating. The other nurses working with her continually reminded her of her lower status. One day, Djamila reacted a little more brutally than usual to a remark that she had heard practically every day. "Are you a doctor in your country? And now you're a nurse? [...] Don't you prefer being a doctor? Why don't you go home? You'll never be a doctor here." Djamila's answer to her colleague was quite direct: "The difference between you and me is that you're a nurse and for you the elevator is stuck on the ground floor. Whereas I can get in the elevator and one day I'll be on the top floor." The nurse complained to the management and Djamila was fired from her position as a traveling nurse because of issues with her relations with her colleagues.

In 2015, Djamila did indeed make it to the top floor, but the journey to the top was not straightforward. The elevator often stopped and Djamila almost got out on several occasions. But she persevered, and her experience is the proof that a young Algerian woman, without any special resources, can be a success in a closed professional environment. It is a good illustration of the capacity for agency in the process of migration: migrants are not just victims (Agustin, 2003), but also actors in their lives. But her story also highlights the obstacles faced by many qualified foreign workers when faced with unfavorable regulations. It also shows the discrimination suffered by these workers at the hands of their colleagues: non-recognition of their skills and their qualifications, exploitation that is structured by the profession or by the institution itself. One might expect qualified migrants, that is, graduates from higher education or with an equivalent experience (Iredale, 1999) to migrate in favorable conditions. Many of them, however, have trouble gaining recognition for their qualifications and suffer a decline in status when they move abroad.

Djamila's experience is, therefore, exemplary in two ways. It is exemplary in the sense that she can be an example for those who attempt to move abroad and hope for their skills to be recognized in a foreign country; and exemplary in the sense that her experience is not an isolated case. You need only to look in the Journal Officiel for the last names of doctors who, like her, have passed the examination required in articles L. 4111-2-I and L. 4221-12 of the French Public Health Code. Many of them who graduated from a university in a country that is not in the European Union have to fight for recognition of the diploma they earned in their home country to practice medicine in France. Some of them manage to do so through personal means: networks, capacity for work, determination. Others choose collective action. The two forms of struggle are not mutually exclusive, and Djamila is proof of this, since after several difficult years, she decided to become an activist in the SNPADHUE (*Syndicat National des Praticiens à Diplôme Hors Union Européenne*) a labor union whose aim is to defend "the rights of all medical professionals (doctors, surgeons, pharmacists, dentists, and midwives) to practice in the same way as their peers with EU qualifications."[1]

The Meeting (Methodology and Justification)

I met Djamila through her work at SNPADHUE. She was contacted by one of my PhD students, Leila, who was writing a thesis about the access of doctors with non-European qualifications to French public establishments (Mendez & Merzouk, 2013). In France, only qualifications issued from a member state of the European Union (EU) give individuals the right to register for the French Medical Council, which is vital if they want to have official status. For qualifications from outside the EU, registration is possible after a long process during which individuals must work as doctors in a public health establishment without status or salary (Denour & Junker, 1995; Déplaude, 2011). This legally applied reduction in status often goes hand in hand with a phenomenon of symbolic status reduction, during which the migrant doctor feels unfairly demoted and must continually prove his or her right to practice medicine (Lochard et al., 2007). So, to understand the processes through which doctors with non-European qualifications manage to earn recognition for their abilities and qualifications, Leila and I contacted Djamila to request an interview. As part of this doctoral project, over 50 interviews were carried out. Primary and secondary statistical and document sources were studied. The interviews, lasting an hour and a half on average, were conducted with practitioners (anaesthetists, gerontologists, gastroenterologists, psychiatrists, and emergency doctors) working in public hospitals in the Paris, Centre, Languedoc-Roussillon and Lower Normandy regions, with health care professionals with different statuses (doctors, assistant associates, full- and part-time hospital practitioners), and

[1] SNPADHUE website: http://www.snpadhue.com/presentation

representatives of medical practitioners' federations. The semi-guided interviews were carried out with the help of a structured document covering four themes: general presentation of the interviewee; professional career; resources used during their career; perception of their professional situation. All the interviews were fully written out. The documentary data come from reports, articles and/or data from the different organizations concerned (SNPADHUE, the French Medical Council, etc.). The decision to focus this chapter on Djamila is linked to a number of elements:

- Djamila studied in Algeria. Among doctors with non-European qualifications who practice medicine in France, Algerians are the largest group (as of January 1, 2013, according to the statistics drawn up by the French Medical Council, Algerian doctors represented 40% of medical practitioners, far ahead of doctors who earned their certification in Syria (11%), Morocco (10.5%), or Tunisia (4.8%)).

- Djamila's professional experience has been successful. An objective of this study was to highlight the capacity for agency among qualified migrants, and the conditions in which this capacity can be expressed.

- Djamila is active in SNPADHUE, which has played a major role over the past ten years in defending the rights of medical practitioners and the recognition of their qualifications. Djamila's situation is thus particularly interesting since we can use it to compare an individual situation and a work of collective mobilization.

The interview with Djamila took place at the Institute of Labor Economics and Industrial Sociology (LEST) in Aix-en-Provence and lasted for over three hours. Djamila was in the region because she was taking part (as an instructor) in a course for psychiatric nurses. The aim of the interview was to collect as much information as possible about her experience, based on the life stories method (Chaxel et al., 2014) to highlight the process through which Djamila managed fully to practice medicine in France. Methodologically, we based our work on the method of processual analysis developed at LEST (Mendez, 2010; Bidart et al., 2013), to isolate the different sequences and thereby highlight the connections between various levels of context and the driving forces behind developments.

Context

Djamila's experience developed at the intersection of multiple contexts deployed on different scales: micro (individual, family), meso (particularly institutional) and macro (political, economic, social). Djamila is from a family of doctors and health professionals. Nonetheless, throughout her experience, she only benefited to a small degree from this cultural and social capital, because her aunts and cousins were doctors, but not her parents. In Algeria, she had no mentor to help her—a condition for success in a university-hospital career. Her family was a model for her more in terms of professional success, guiding her towards practicing medicine as a private doctor and showing her the opportunities that existed abroad (her brother and sister-in-law are dentists in the United States). Djamila's family and their perspectives strongly contributed to the form taken by her initial project. Her family dissuaded her from giving up psychiatry during her medical studies.

Djamila's experience is also indissociably linked to the Algerian context. Djamila had originally planned to study in France and return to practice medicine in Algeria. But her parents were not wealthy enough, so in the end, she studied in Algeria. After her studies, the political and social situation in Algeria prompted her to leave. Despite her attachment to her country, Djamila left Algeria because of the appalling working conditions in public hospitals, the corruption in the university-hospital system, and the system of co-optation that forced young doctors to work with a mentor if they wanted to have a career. Djamila never mentioned the threat of terrorism as part of her decision.[2] It has even acted as a fundamental element in her determination and her capacity to resist.

In France, the decisive context was the organization of the medical profession and its development. Practicing medicine is highly regulated, and starting in the late 19th century, the first measures were taken to limit it to individuals who had state-recognized qualifications acquired in France (Déplaude, 2011). This is still the case today, and the qualifications issued in France or in a member state of the European Union are the only degrees that allow individuals to register directly with the French Medical Council. At the same time, the French medical environment is characterized by extensive unevenness (geographic distribution, in terms of specialization, etc.). Since the 1980s, hospitals and clinics have filled vacancies with candidates without EU qualifications. While this category plays a full part in the establishments where they work and make an extensive contribution in many wards, the number of reforms, procedures, exceptions, and individual statuses have been expanded because of this over the years. This category must face differences in treatment that are allowed by law (Lochard et al., 2007). In this constrained institutional context, doctors qualified outside the EU have developed strategies to prove their competence and their legitimacy in obtaining a permanent right to practice medicine. At the end of the 1990s, the situation was paradoxical: many public hospitals could only effectively operate thanks to health professionals from overseas who were practicing medicine without any security of employment, since the public authorities

[2] From 1991 to 2002, Algeria was torn by a civil war between the Algerian government and a number of Islamist groups. The conflict resulted in tens of thousands of victims (60,000 according to official records; 150,000 according to independent sources).

had tightened recruitment conditions. On top of this was added the fact that some specialities had been deserted by French practitioners, while others had disappeared altogether, being absorbed into other specializations. This was the case for maxillo-facial surgery, Djamila's specialization, which was gradually absorbed by the ear, nose, and throat (ENT) specialization.

Life Story

Djamila was born and grew up in Algiers. She was the youngest of four children in a family of doctors and health professionals. After passing a scientific baccalaureate, Djamila began studying medicine in 1988 at the University of Algiers without taking the entrance exam, since she had earned a baccalaureate "with honors." In 1995, she earned a degree in general medicine and then studied to be accepted for a hospital internship, which she began in September 1996. She then chose to specialize in maxillo-facial surgery, with a program that lasted for three years. She did not see this specialization as her vocation, however. She was more interested in psychiatry, but the discipline lacked prestige, and was even poorly viewed socially. Her family dissuaded her from taking this path. At that time, she was not sufficiently motivated to combat social and family pressure. Furthermore, surgery provided a chance to work as a private doctor, which was the embodiment of social success for her family.

In 2000, she passed the entrance exam for the DEMS (Specialized Medical Studies Diploma) and qualified as a maxillo-facial surgeon. She was young and enthusiastic. She describes her generation as one of dedicated professionals:

> You won't stop them. It's like with the terrorists: ten years of terrorism, you won't stop us, you won't get to me. If you want to get rid of us, you won't succeed. We learned as we went along. We even reconstructed an ear. We were artists, it was a pleasure for us.

After passing the entrance exam, Djamila did her obligatory national service in public health, before starting to work as a private doctor. In November 2000, she was assigned to a hospital that was actually a former sanatorium from the colonial era. The establishment was managed by the Tizi-Ouzou Hospital, and some specializations were centralized there. Djamila worked in deplorable conditions, without resources, and with a management she describes as incompetent. For her, these three years were an ordeal. She was given a cold welcome from her colleagues (ENT), who saw her as a young specialist arriving from the capital. She could not operate (respirator out of order, surgical instruments that went missing), which led her to send patients to the hospitals in Algiers.

> I'll give you a twisted, rusty teaspoon and ask you to operate with it. It was appalling. Those three years were awful. Without resources, they were like ghettos, free clinics.

She wrote critical reports about the situation, which led to problems with her management. The head doctor granted her one day a week for her studies. She made the most of it to join the training department at the hospital in Algiers where she had occasionally worked as an intern. She was not allowed to treat patients, but it gave her the chance to "keep her hand in."

After her national service, she realized that she didn't have the resources to work as a private doctor, and a university career was closed to her since access was only available through co-optation.

On October 31, 2003, she left the hospital, despite receiving a job offer, and worked for one year in a private clinic to prepare for her departure to France. She had decided to leave Algeria. She wanted to practice medicine in good conditions.

Djamila arrived in France in September 2004. She had no family or professional networks that might help her to get contacts in the medical profession. Before leaving, she nonetheless made the acquaintance of an associate professor at the Ecole des Mines, on the internet. He was an Algerian who had studied in France, and whom she started dating. He helped her out with administrative procedures.

Djamila first tried to gain recognition for her qualifications. She did not yet know that she would have a long way to go before she could practice medicine in France. She sent all her qualifications and diplomas to the Ministry of Higher Education, along with the content of the lessons she had taken. The Ministry replied that her diplomas were considered to be equivalent to French qualifications, but she could still not practice medicine in France. So Djamila had to change tack. She first tried to pass the AFSA (*Attestation de Formation Spécialisée Approfondie*), a specialized exam, in maxillo-facial surgery. The AFSA is reserved for overseas doctors from countries outside the European Union, and who are already specialists in their home countries. Signing up for the AFSA allows them to follow part of the theoretical courses and practical internships linked to specialized diplomas. Djamila had to find a head doctor in maxillo-facial surgery who would accept her as an intern and wrote to the AFSA coordinator in her chosen region.

Her partner found her the list of coordinators for each region. Djamila wrote to the coordinator for the Paris region, a professor in maxillo-facial surgery at Pitié-Salpêtrière Hospital, who gave her the authorization to sign up for the AFSA. She sent out dozens of unsolicited letters to head doctors in maxillo-facial surgery in different hospitals but received few replies. Djamila had no networks, either personal or professional. But she obtained a one-year internship in a general hospital in Meaux. She was recruited as a temporary intern, earning 1,250 euros a month.

Very quickly, Djamila realized that the internship did not match her expectations. Even worse, in France, she found the same situation she had wanted to get away from. For Djamila, the maxillo-facial surgery department in Meaux was "maxillo-facial" in name only. The main activity of the department was stomatology, since the head doctor had a qualification (CES, *Certificat d'études spécialisées*) in the subject. His wife was the maxillo-facial surgeon. She had a private practice, and the head doctor sent hospital patients to consult with her. Djamila, meanwhile, spent her time pulling out wisdom teeth and working long hours.

The year was not completely wasted, however, since after the internship, Djamila passed the AFSA exam. But she wanted to make progress in surgery. She again sent out hundreds of application letters and was given a new internship in Argenteuil, near Paris. Here she also worked as a temporary intern but was not paid. As in Meaux, the maxillo-facial surgery department actually had a different activity, since the head doctor was qualified as a plastic surgeon. Djamila nonetheless saw this experience as an opportunity. At the time, she thought she would learn plastic surgery and then work in Algeria. Her financial situation was difficult. She was living off her savings from the first year. Fortunately, she still had her partner, which helped reduce financial hardship.

Her experiences in Meaux and Argenteuil made her realize that maxillo-facial surgery was on the way out in France. It was gradually being taken over by other specializations, particularly ENT. To maintain their departments, head doctors were developing other activities. For them, temporary interns were a godsend, since they helped the department to continue functioning at a minimal cost.

At the same time as these internships, Djamila signed up at the university. To renew her residence permit, Djamila had to sign up for university courses and prove she had taken them. In the first year, her registration and success with the AFSA enabled her to renew her residence permit. In 2005, she signed up for a first university diploma (the FIEC, *Formation des Investigateurs aux Essais Cliniques des médicaments*), which she passed in 2006. This was a course reserved for foreign doctors aimed at training project managers or clinical research assistants. In 2006-2007, along with her internship in Argenteuil, she studied for and passed a university diploma in "wound-healing/wounds/burns." The courses were expensive—between 600 and 1,200 euros. At this time, Djamila realized that the aim of many courses was to make money for universities rather than provide jobs for students.

After Argenteuil, Djamila was unable to find another internship. She became very depressed. Her dream was to find an internship in a university hospital and work with a top doctor. Instead of this, she was pulling out wisdom teeth and operating on breasts and stomachs in departments that were struggling to survive. She also experienced discrimination and stigmatization. She would have liked to work in a university hospital, but for foreign doctors like herself, the only opportunities for internships were in regional hospitals, like Meaux or Argenteuil. Internships in university hospitals were reserved for French interns. At Pitié-Salpêtrière Hospital, during her first year in France, although she was authorized to attend lessons in surgery free of charge with interns who had studied in France, she noticed that the French interns did not mix with doctors from overseas and behaved differently towards her when they realized that she was a temporary intern:

> And are you a specialist in your country? Yes, I'm a doctor in my country. And then I'd say, and I will be here, too, soon; and they'd ask: Where are you? In Meaux? Ah...

During her vacation in Algeria she looked for a job, with no success. The situation was worse than before her departure, and her personal situation was a failure: she did not have the money to settle in Algeria, and on the medical level, she had made no progress. She realized that she could not go back to Algeria. She felt ashamed because she had the impression that her former colleagues had progressed, while she had regressed. In 2006, she thought about starting her studies all over again in France so that she wouldn't be faced with the issue of fighting for recognition for her qualifications. At the end of 2006, she found a job as a night nurse in an operating room in a private clinic. For her it was humiliating, but she made a good living.

2007 was a dark year for Djamila. She knew she couldn't retreat any further. She couldn't return to Algeria. She felt miserable. At that time, she experienced her first serious depression. She was unhappy in every respect: in love, at work, and financially. She wondered what would become of her.

At the same time, 2007 was also a turning point. Djamila spoke about her dismay to her friend, a temporary intern in psychiatry, whom she had met at a SNPDHUE meeting (she joined in 2005 when she was in Meaux but did not yet have an official position). He told her about a university degree program in general psychiatry run by two very well-known professors and advised her to take it. So Djamila decided to return to her first love and signed up for the university degree program from between 2007 and 2009. She loved the first few courses and quickly obtained some very good results.

She was studying at the university as well as working in an operating room. The situation lasted until Djamila lost her job because, although she was earning a good living, she found the situation humiliating. She still speaks about it with strong emotion eight years later. She was a surgeon who had been reduced to the status of a nurse:

> Not everyone can be a surgeon. You get used to giving orders. You become punchy, pragmatic. When you're a surgeon, you don't have time for politeness. There's a lot of prestige, it has a strong narcissistic aspect. There's a feeling of power. When you're in the operating theatre, the patient is asleep and you say, "Quiet, incision." It's...

The other nurses conveyed her lower status to her even more strongly. The questions were hurtful: "Are you a doctor in your country? And now you're a nurse? Are you planning to go back to your country?" Coming from Algeria only added to the stigma. One day, she reacted a little stronger than usual to a nurse's remark, which led to her losing her job. But for Djamila, the spiral had changed direction. She had gotten into the elevator and it was starting to move upward.

In 2009, her friend, who had recommended the university program in general psychiatry, left the psychiatric hospital in the town of Plaisir in the Yvelines. He knew that the hospital was looking for a temporary intern and advised her to apply. She was recruited, and from June to August she interned there. This was her first experience in psychiatry. She liked the hospital and the work a great deal. She felt recognized.

This first experience in psychiatry was very important. The unit manager was well known for his focus on systemic therapy. He managed the ERIC (*Equipe Rapide d'Intervention de Crise*) group, whose approach consisted in no longer taking a patient systematically into the hospital, but in sending a medical team to the patient's home. In this team, Djamila acquired experience proved later to be decisive.

Djamila found a new partner, a teacher at the university. They were married and she joined him in Rennes in September 2009. In November, she was hired at the Rennes psychiatric hospital as a temporary intern. She stayed there until May 2010. The situation began to develop favorably for Djamila. Her shift to psychiatry, where there is a shortage of doctors, provided her with more opportunities. The fact she had a university degree in general psychiatry and had spent time working in Plaisir, which was recognized for its systemic therapy approach, opened doors for her. The very nature of the specialization meant she could work more independently, since psychiatry is highly codified.

As soon as she arrived in Rennes, Djamila signed up for a degree program in addiction studies in Paris. Now that she was married, she no longer needed to study at a university to have a residence permit. She wanted to dig deeper into her specialization and acquire new skills. The degree in addiction studies was not financed by the hospital, but the department head gave her one day off a week to attend classes. Until May 2010, Djamila went to the university in Paris once a week. She passed the theoretical exams but failed the practical part. This put a stop to her studies. The failure demoralized her. She could no longer put up with her insecure status, being far away, traveling from Rennes to Paris each week… The hospital asked her to stay for another six months, but she refused since she wanted to prepare the PAE (*Procédure d'Autorisation d'Exercice*) exam. In summer 2010, she told her husband she wanted to move closer to Paris, where the best university courses are available. But her husband was teaching in Rennes. On a map, he traced out a straight line between the two cities. The halfway point was Le Mans. The couple moved there in September 2010. Djamila could then drive or take the train to Paris and economically it became possible for her.

Djamila studied tirelessly for the PAE exam. She took it in October 2010 and failed. She knew that her perspectives had narrowed, since candidates only have the right to take it three times. She again looked for a job, but the psychiatric hospital in Le Mans was not recruiting foreign doctors because of the legislation. It was at that moment that the accumulation of her disgust, revolt, and depression prompted her to become an active member of the SNPADHUE.

Djamila wrote to the psychiatric hospitals within 100 kilometers of Le Mans. It is usually forbidden by law for a hospital to recruit foreign doctors, but the Regional Health Agencies of economically deprived regions may grant provisional derogations. Alençon Hospital obtained permission from the Regional Health Agency to recruit Djamila as a temporary intern but, due to her experience in systemic therapy, she was given PAC status, giving her more freedom to practice. The hospital had mobile teams of the ERIC type. She worked there from November 2010 to January 2012 in a team of 12 people under excellent conditions. With the nurses, relationships were more difficult. For them, she had no legitimacy: she was Algerian, her medical qualifications were not recognized in France, and she only had a university diploma in psychiatry. But Djamila continued to study. In 2011, she signed up for a DIU (inter-university diploma) for general assistants in psychiatry. This diploma is recognized as the equivalent of a specialization, since it is a three-year course, and was originally designed for general practitioners working in psychiatric hospitals. She passed it in May 2014. She now had five years of theoretical psychiatric studies behind her.

While she was working in Alençon, Djamila committed to working with the SNPADHUE. She had been a member since 2005 but, like several colleagues she met on the internet, it was the problematic situation in 2010 that prompted her to become more active. Several laws had changed the status of foreign doctors, but in 2010, foreign medical practitioners found themselves in legal no man's land. Individuals who had arrived before June 2004 simply had to take an exam to practice medicine, while those who had arrived after June 2004 had to pass the highly selective PAE. In 2010, hundreds of doctors used up their three attempts, and the law stipulated that on December 31, 2012, all medical practitioners who had not passed the PAE would have to stop working in hospitals. The situation was catastrophic, both for the doctors and for certain hospitals and specializations that had been deserted.

In 2010, Djamila and four of her colleagues formed what they called the "Group of Five." They wanted to change the law for those who arrived after 2004 and who had to take the PAE. But they still had to prevail within the federation because within the SNPADHUE, many members already had a fixed status. Djamila and her colleagues had to win recognition from peers who were in an extremely insecure situation and to mobilize them. But many medical practitioners from overseas did not believe their situation could be improved.

To promote their cause, the "Group of Five" carried out a vast statistical study to highlight the number of foreign practitioners who help French hospitals to function. They criticized the gap between the political discourse and the situation on the ground and revealed the danger of creating medical "deserts." In 2011 a high-profile strike and demonstration took place. In January 2012, the SNPADHUE managed to get the law changed. But this was just a new exemption to the 2004 law, an exemption that was planned to expire in 2017.

As soon as the change to the law was announced, Djamila again contacted the director of the psychiatric hospital in Le Mans. She sent him her CV, her diplomas, and informed him that he could now hire her. She was recruited in January 2012, but more than ever her aim was to work as a doctor. She again took the PAE in October 2012 and this time she passed. The last stage of the process began. In June 2013, she sent her file to the National Administration Center at the Ministry of Health. In November 2014, she was summoned before the Qualification Commission to provide more information about her unusual career from surgery to psychiatry. Her official qualification appeared in the *Journal Officiel* on February 13, 2015. She was now officially authorized to practice medicine.

As soon as she earned her authorization in February 2015, Djamila resigned from her job in Le Mans. A friend told her that there was a vacancy in a psychiatric hospital in the Paris region. In March, based only on her CV and qualifications, she was recruited as a PHC (contractual hospital practitioner) with the chance to move to a permanent position later. This was a major victory for her, achieved after ten years of struggle and effort.

Theoretical discussion

Same Professions, New Boundaries

Djamila's story is fascinating. It illustrates the fact that despite a context or contexts that are *a priori* unfavorable, a migrant can still succeed professionally. It also shows that a qualification is not always a resource; or to be more precise, for qualified migrants, it is a resource that is not always effective and not always the basis for their capacity for agency. Not all qualified migrants can find work related to their qualifications in the host country. This is true of doctors with non-European diplomas in France, but the situation is the same in other contexts and professions, as for Mexican engineers in the United States, for example (Carrion, 2014; Hualde & Carrion, 2016). For qualified migrants, the more the profession is highly structured, the less their qualifications constitute a resource in terms of freedom of movement. The structure of the profession, its closed nature, act like an extra boundary, and in a context like this, qualifications are a source of challenges for many of those involved: for the professionals themselves, who must gain recognition for their qualifications or skills from the public or private institutions (in the health professions, for example) or for the companies employing them (for expatriates who work in multinational companies, for example). Qualifications are also an issue for the diversity of those involved in the migratory process: the public authorities, the authorities controlling flows, professional organizations (which want to protect their profession), organizations employing professionals and that want to take advantage of these qualifications by recognizing them (or otherwise). The migration of qualified workers is thus indissociably linked to a dialectic between closure/protection of the profession, on the one hand, and movement/recognition of skills and qualifications, on the other. Due to this tension, qualifications do not always lead to upwardly mobile careers.

And yet, some people do succeed, by making use of their skills, obtaining recognition for their qualifications, and taking up jobs that correspond to their qualifications. How can we explain this? Djamila's experience is a wonderful success story, even if it took her ten years to achieve it. A processual analysis of Djamila's trajectory helps us to understand its hidden bases and bring out the resources that proved to be essential.

A Capacity for Agency, Embedded in Time

Djamila's trajectory is characterized by an unfavorable context and a lack of resources. Djamila arrived in France without any particular resources (aside from her first romantic partner, who provided her with help in her initial applications and with financial assistance when she arrived), in a French medical system that is characterized by a near-complete closure to outside recruitment. The profession protects its members, and at the end of the 1990s, the authorities tightened the recruitment conditions for doctors from overseas. Djamila was also unlucky in choosing a specialization that was on the way out. To the institutional context was added an unfavorable medical context that did not allow Djamila to work and develop her skills. On the other hand, the unfavorable context of psychiatry would provide her with resources and opportunities.

Djamila's trajectory is in fact organized in three major sequences during which she accumulated resources. After her arrival in France and until 2007, Djamila's aim was to practice medicine as a maxillo-facial surgeon. Her earliest strategies were oriented towards this end: she tried to gain recognition for her diplomas, did a first internship to earn the AFSA, then studied several programs to progress in her field of knowledge. During this sequence, Djamila's project was sorely tested: she did not practice her specialization in better conditions than she had in Algeria, and she was stigmatized, discriminated against by her colleagues. But it was the recommendation of a colleague, a member of the SNPADHUE, which opened up a new sequence in reorienting her project towards psychiatry. This is the first turning point in Djamila's trajectory.

This reorientation was all the more acceptable to Djamila since psychiatry had been her original choice when she was studying medicine. Through the SNPADHUE, even though she was not yet an active militant, Djamila gathered together a network of relations that would play a role in her experience: by suggesting she reorient her career towards psychiatry, by advising her about courses to take, by opening the doors to hospitals. Djamila, who had been at a loss until then, began to gather resources and, more specifically, *relevant* resources. During the previous sequence, Djamila had already tried to accumulate resources (internships, courses), but they had no effective value, because, given the regulatory context (obligation to take the PAE to practice as a doctor) and medical context (unfavorable to maxillo-facial surgery), these resources were of little use to her in achieving her goal. In this new sequence, the project could bear fruit: psychiatry is a specialization that has been deserted and needs doctors. The resources that Djamila had (experience, training) were valued in this new project. In a non-intentional way, Djamila also gained a rather unique experience (of systemic therapy and the ERIC groups), which would become a particularly valuable resource for her future. Nonetheless, despite the increasing value of the resources she could mobilize, Djamila was still faced with the same regulatory context. She practiced medicine with an insecure status and without total freedom of action. Her first failure at the PAE in 2010 made her realize that her project might never come to fruition.

This individual failure, together with the collective context in 2010 (overseas medical practitioners who had not passed the PAE by December 31, 2011 could no longer practice medicine), led to a new sequence: Djamila moved from individual action to collective action. She began to campaign within the union with the aim of changing a regulatory context that was unfavorable to overseas medical practitioners. This commitment to collective mobilization constituted the second turning point in Djamila's career. But at the same time, she continued to gather educational resources (signing up for the DIU in 2011) to expand and give legitimacy to her skills in the field of psychiatry. Her determination paid off, since in 2012 she passed the PAE exam. All the accumulated resources finally took on their full meaning: in 2015, she was finally registered with the Medical Council, and got a job in a Parisian hospital. Once again, her personal network, the skills and qualifications she had acquired in psychiatry and a favorable context due to the shortage of psychiatrists in public hospitals all worked in her favor. All through her career, elements from the macro and meso context worked together, along with a strategy of accumulating resources. If we make use of the categories developed by Longo (2010), the first sequences were sequences of "dissociating" ingredients (they did not cohere together—the project, the resources, the context were combined, but not in a coherent way), while the last two sequences were more sequences of "association," where the project, resources, and context come together in a more convergent way.

Djamila's career illustrates the temporal embedding of agency, as defined by Emirbayer and Mische (1998). In their view, agency is a complex temporal dynamic, shaped by the past and turned towards the future. They distinguish three constitutive elements of agency:

- The iterational element, constructed by the past, based on the schematization of social experience. Through their experience, individuals construct cognitive frameworks that orient their capacity for action.
- The projective element. This involves "hypothesizing" experience. Individuals modify their frameworks by generating alternative responses to the problematic situations they are faced with.
- The practical–evaluative element. This consists in contextualizing social experience and in committing individuals to pragmatic decision-making processes. This process tests routines acquired by repetition and projects, bearing in mind the context.

These three dimensions can be seen in Djamila's experience. Her education, her family, her earliest experiences helped forge a project and produce an outlook in her about what it was possible or impossible for her to do. At the same time, Djamila developed a professional project (to become a maxillo-facial surgeon). But over time, the different contexts put her successive projects to the test: to become a doctor in Algeria, then in France. During these sequences, testing of the project called it into question, causing her to redesign it. But, if these were the only elements, Djamila's career would simply be the result of the impact of the context on her projects. At a given point in her career, however, Djamila "took back control." In 2010, when her situation seemed at a dead end, Djamila made a decision that would radically upend the course of action. As Emirbayer and Mische (1998) underline, "individuals who feel they are stuck in problematic situations can become pioneers and explore and rebuild contexts of action" (p. 1009). This was exactly the case for Djamila. In 2010, the dead end in which she found herself led her to change her approach (she went from individual to collective action) and helped her by acting on the wider context to resolve her individual problem. Finally, perhaps this is what agency is: the capacity for individuals at a given moment to look at their situation differently and identify the tools they can use to change their context. In the earliest sequences of her experience, Djamila placed her situation in a given context, but she only was subject to it, she didn't try to transform it. Starting in 2010, her action consisted in trying to change the context itself by making use of a new tool. Her action with the union shows one thing: being part of collective action makes acting on the context possible. Then the question arises of individual/collective relations and their status in constituting a capacity for agency.

For a Critical Realist Approach to Migration

Following Bakewell (2010), we propose to overcome the antagonism between Structure and Agency and turn towards the critical realist approach in analyzing the professional experience of migrants. Bakewell considers that the opposition between Structure and Agency leads to a dead end in constructing a coherent theory of migration. At the same time, combining them is impossible, not only because of the fact that their epistemological foundations are radically different, but also because they operate on different timescales. The critical realism proposed by authors such as Bhaskar (1978) and then Archer (1982, 1995) seems to resolve this difficulty. For Bhaskar (1978), reality is stratified and made up of three areas or domains: (1) the real, where the structures and "generative mechanisms" reside; (2) the actual domain, made up of "events" taking place in time and space, due to the activation of certain generative mechanisms; (3) these events, once identified, become "experiences" in the empirical domain, which is the one perceived and experienced by individuals. This is the domain that can be known. As for generative mechanisms, they exist even when they are not activated. Activating a generative mechanism, and its manifestation in the actual domain and/or the empirical sphere, depends on these environmental "contingent conditions." Thus, critical realism highlights the crucial importance of context (Pascal et al., 2013). As for the events, even when generated, they may not always be identified and transformed into experiences. Bhaskar (1978, 1989) calls for a procedural model for social action in which social structures pre-exist. Individuals are not passive, since their actions are based on the structures and on generative mechanisms. In this way, the individual takes part in the reproduction and/or changes to social structures. Society defines a framework for the interaction and helps to "socialize" individuals who, through their intentional actions, reproduce or transform social structures. Beyond a procedural vision of the social, Bhaskar also affirms a relational conception of structures.

To take the analysis of migrations further, Bakewell suggests exploring social structures such as labor markets, migrant networks, etc., based on a critical realist perspective to assess generative capacity. In Djamila's case, joining the union movement clearly marked a turning point in her career. So, we could hypothesize that collective action constitutes a relevant generative mechanism in the migratory process. It is always possible, but not necessarily activated. Its activation (commitment to militant action) triggers events that individuals transform into experiences that help them to transform social structures–in this case, the structure of a profession. Of course, it is not possible to generalize this proposition from a single example, and in order to confirm the result, the analysis needs to be extended further. But an in-depth study of Djamila's experience confirms the relevance of qualitative methods in bringing out the generative mechanisms that would otherwise remain invisible.

References

Agustín, L. M. 2003. "Forget Victimisation: Granting Agency to Migrants." *Development* 46 (3): 30-36.

Archer, M. S. 1982. "Morphogenesis versus structuration: on combining structure and action." *British Journal of Sociology* 33(4): 455-83.

Archer, M. S. 1995. *Realist Social Theory: The Morphogenetic Approach*. Cambridge: Cambridge University Press.

Bakewell, O. 2010. "Some Reflections on Structure and Agency in Migration Theory." *Ethnic & Migration Studies* 36 (10): 1689-1708.

Bhaskar, R. 1978. *A Realist Theory of Science*. Brighton: Harvester-Wheatsheaf.

Bhaskar, R. 1989. The Possibility of Naturalism: A Philosophical Critique of the Contemporary Human Science. 1st ed. Atlantic Highlands, NJ: Humanities Press.

Bidart, C., M. E. Longo & A. Mendez. 2013. "Time and process: an operational framework for processual analysis." *European Sociological Review* 29 (4): 743-751.

Chaxel, S., C. Fiorelli & P. Moity-Maïzi. 2014. "Les récits de vie: outils pour la compréhension et catalyseurs pour l'action." *¿ Interrogations ?* 17, http://www.revue-interrogations.org/

Carrion, V.. 2014. La migración de ingenieros mexicanos a Estados Unidos: un análisis de trayectorias profesionales. Ph. D. Dissertation, Tijuna: El Colegio de la Frontera Norte.

Denour, L. & R. Junker. 1995. "Les médecins étrangers dans les hôpitaux français." *Revue Européenne de Migrations Internationales* 11 (3): 145-166.

Déplaude, M. O.. 2011. "Une xénophobie d'État ? Les 'médecins étrangers' en France (1945-2006)" *Politix* 3 (95): 207-231.

Hualde, A. & V. Carrion. 2016. "Los otros actores de la migraci*ón: ingenieros mexicanos que trabajan en Estados Unidos*. " in /////

Iredale, R. 1999. "The Need to Import Skilled Personnel: Factors Favouring and Hindering its International Mobility." *International Migration* 37 (1): 89–123.

Lochard, Y., Ch. Meilland & V. Mouna. 2007. "La situation des médecins à diplôme hors UE sur le marché du travail: Les effets d'une discrimination institutionnelle." *Revue de l'IRES* 1 (53): 83-110.

Longo, M. E. 2010. "Les parcours d'insertion professionnelle des jeunes: enchaînement de séquences singulières." In A. Mendez (ed.) *Processus: concepts et méthode pour l'analyse temporelle en Sciences Sociales*. Leuven: Academia Bruylant: 107-119.

Mendez, A. 2010. Processus. Concepts et méthode pour l'analyse temporelle en sciences sociales. Leuven: Academia-Bruylant.

Mendez, A. & L. Merzouk. 2013. "Les médecins à diplôme non-européen dans les hôpitaux publics français: Entre déqualification et légitimation des compétences." *Coloquio internacional: la fabrica de las migraciones: perspectivas desde México-CentroAmérica y Magreb-Machrek*. Universidad del claustro de Sor Juana, México, 21, 22 y 23 de octubre.

Pascal, A., A. Mendez, L. Gastaldi & K. Guiderdoni-Jourdain. 2013. "Pour un modèle intégrateur de l'entrepreneuriat institutionnel collectif dans une approche réaliste critique. Le cas de la création d'une structure fédérative de recherche." *Communication pour la conférence AIMS*, Clermont Ferrant, 10-12 juin.

CONCLUSION: UNCERTAINTY, ANTICIPATED

Deborah A. Boehm[1]

Uncertainty frames nearly every aspect of everyday life, even as daily interactions are perceived and experienced as mundane or routine. Within the context of migration, such unpredictability can seem inevitable as people cross borders or are unable to do so. This collection powerfully shows us how the outcomes and destinations of migration are rarely assured. Here, uncertainty is to be expected: strategies enacted with a particular goal can bring about another outcome, anticipated events may not come to pass, crisis might result in stability, assumed trajectories lead to the unknown.

A significant contribution of this volume is how the authors so skillfully convey and analyze precisely this tension - the side-by-side character of the ordinary and the extraordinary - showing how the continuity of everyday life intermingles with the (often state-orchestrated) disruptions that accompany global movement. In particular, the contributors explore this contradiction within family networks, as intertwined with the geographies of movement, and, perhaps above all, within migrants' imaginings for the future, revealing common conditions that frame nearly all forms of global movement in the current moment.

By focusing on these everyday experiences - within families, across borders, and across time - the contributors to this volume individually and collectively challenge a number of supposed divides, questioning binaries and permitting their analysis to linger in or even be directly guided by the contradictions themselves. In the context of the ruptures inevitable to migration and border crossings, there is a difficulty in neatly or simplistically categorizing the experiences of migration. In these chapters, we see how the exceptional can blur with the mundane and how the unusual is to be expected.

And, by centering ethnography, a biographical approach, and other methods that uniquely reveal the nuance of everyday experience, this volume challenges another assumed but problematic divide within migration scholarship - the misdirected notion on the part of some researchers that frames quantitative versus qualitative research as "rigorous" versus "anecdotal." As we learn from well done ethnographic research - such as that which is highlighted in this book - a textured understanding of the experience of migration requires interdisciplinary and mixed method study in collaboration with people directly impacted by global movement. A full picture of endurance amid unpredictability relies on research that privileges

[1] Deborah A. Boehm, Professor, Anthropology and Gender, Race, and Identity, University of Nevada, Reno, United States.

the words and experiences of migrants themselves.

The Precarity and Stability of Family

Throughout the volume, we learn how migration is shaped by but also shapes family ties and estrangement. The assumed affections and unions of family life can be strained or severed, while family itself is often formed (or dissolved) through migration processes. In one particularly telling example of this tension in the book, Robin Cavagnoud describes how Daniel, "left-behind" in Bolivia when his mother migrates to Argentina, also develops strong ties to other family members, including his grandparents, aunts and uncles, and cousins. And in Kamel Doraï's chapter we see the dispersal - and coming together - of members of a Palestinian family in and outside of countries they migrated to and were excluded from at different times, including Lebanon, Jordan, and Syria.

Lindbergh's moves to different countries followed employment opportunities, but were especially motivated by his commitment to providing for his family (Hualde); his economic migrations were sometimes built on existing family connections and yet in some instances took him far from loved ones. And, Hélène Le Bail introduces us to Ma Li and Wang Hong, women with family trajectories that included violence but also strength, caring, and connection. In these chapters and throughout the book, "family" is complicated - a source of disconnection, hardship, and challenge, as well as support and protection - and thus analyzed by the contributors in all of its complexity.

(Un)Intended Destinations

Another contribution of the book is the questioning of assumptions, especially by scholars, about predictability in migration flows. While research about migration frequently distinguishes between locations of departure and destination, the chapters demonstrate how problematic such binary categorization can be. As we see throughout the volume, the labels assigned to places are repeatedly blurred. For example, Ayoub and Malika have migrated at different times to different places, with uncertainty framing plans for supposed "settlement" (Décosse); around the globe, the circular and circuitous migration flows of seasonal agricultural workers, as well as laborers in many other sectors, challenge predictability in people's imagined life trajectories. Further underscoring this experience of the unanticipated, Michel Peraldi introduces us to Mano and other "expats" living in Marrakesh, unlikely migrants in many ways who have moved to an unexpected place.

Another set of border crossings that reveals this kind of anticipated uncertainty is Sadar's migration from Iraq to Turkey to Israel, and later to Switzerland, including the once available option of going to the United States for an arranged marriage, a migration that did not in fact take place (Roussel).

And, in Víctor Zúñiga and Betsabé Román-González's research with young people, they reveal the unpredictable locations of Beto, who migrated from Mexico to the United States and back to Mexico; Lulu, who experienced a migration south, from the United States to Mexico; and Flor, a U.S. citizen who has moved back and forth between Mexico and the United States to be with her parents who live in two different countries. Collectively, these migrations cannot be fully anticipated, underscoring how the geographies of migration can be different from those once assumed and how even intended destinations may never be reached.

Anticipated and Unknown Outcomes

And, perhaps above all, the interlocutors highlighted throughout the book live in and through the unknown across time. While some migrations unfold in ways that are especially unpredictable, arguably *all* migrations are shaped by a kind of precarity and uncertainty of what the future holds. Some who cross borders experience the unknown more acutely, such as Albanians moving though - or stalled within - the process of applying for asylum in France as described by Carolina Kobelinsky. And, although her movement across borders followed a very different path to France, Djamila's professional migration from Algeria, followed by a desired but unactualized return there, ultimately results in an unexpected career shift to psychiatry after initial training in another field (Mendez).

In Delphine Mercier's chapter, we learn of the precarious - and unpredictable - trajectory of Suzana and those close to her. The multiple migrations in this one family network include her former partners' migrations to the United States, her own migration to Mexico City, and the internal border crossings of several family members to work in maquiladoras run by transnational corporations. Similarly, Réda's migration trajectory from Morocco to France is uncertain at nearly every stage, including if he would actually be able to migrate at any point; unable to initially go to Europe with his parents and siblings, he later reunites with family and then marries and has children there, creating a future not imagined - even unimaginable - as a young man (El Miri). Futures are envisioned, even if they are unable to be actualized in anticipated ways.

Uncertain States

At the center of this contradiction—uncertainty, anticipated—are the actions of nation-states. In the current moment, the constraints imposed by state governments on the everyday lives of people on the move are deeply felt. From the control of international borders that directly puts human lives at risk (e.g. De León 2015) to policing within nations that targets immigrants (e.g. Inda 2008) to policies and actions that produce "illegality" itself (De Genova 2002), states foster uncertainty as a central strategy in the disenfranchisement of so many. Such forms of state violence can be plotted along a continuum, ranging from "ordinary" and "everyday" violence to physical threats and death (Scheper-Hughes and Bourgois 2004). Even bureaucracies, laws (Menjívar and Abrego 2012), and "the politics of humanitarianism" (Ticktin 2011) can take violent forms. Again, this is a kind of expected uncertainty, although within the sphere of immigration, states generate uncertainty with unusually high stakes. By design, state policies shape people's everyday lives in nearly every social sphere, but for those crossing borders, the effect can be particularly harmful, even deadly.

Yet amid such profound suffering created by state action, the power of states is never absolute. As Roger Waldinger writes in the "Prologue," this volume shows us the "creative accomplishments" people attain within (and against) state structures. Perhaps the most valuable lesson we glean from this collection is the fact that despite the strength of states, the fortitude of people subject to them is also assured, underscoring the resiliency of migrants and their ability to navigate, circumvent, and/or overcome the barriers built by states. Everyday life persists—at least collectively—and the ordinary, seemingly mundane, aspects of human experience endure. Out of the volume's collective approach of uplifting individual stories, a common experience and shared humanity emerges.

And, still, as we learn again and again of the struggles migrants face, a question persists—why should any human being experience the increasing, even relentless, uncertainties of state control? People's physical, emotional - and, indeed, everyday - lives should not be threatened based on a characteristic as arbitrary as the nation within which they are born (Stevens 2011). The contributors to this collection provide strong evidence of human potential to navigate state power, compelling us to consider at what point we must demand something else -something more- from national governments. As Sayak Valencia so persuasively posits, we need "to think beyond the limits of our current options" (2018: 13). It may be that the right to the "ordinary," however one might define it, is among the most pressing of rights in the current moment. Indeed, the right to migrate is intertwined with this very point: as people cross borders despite state power, uncertainty can be expected, but all humans are entitled to construct and proceed with their everyday lives as imagined.

References

De Genova, Nicholas. 2002. "Migrant 'Illegality' and Deportability in Everyday Life." *Annual Review of Anthropology* 31:419-447.

De León, Jason. 2015. *The Land of Open Graves: Living and Dying on the Migrant Trail.* Berkeley: University of California Press.

Inda, Jonathan Xavier. 2008. *Targeting Immigrants: Government, Technology, and Ethics.* Oxford: Blackwell Publishing.

Menjívar, Cecilia and Leisy J. Abrego. 2012. "Legal Violence: Immigration Law and the

Lives of Central Americans." *American Journal of Sociology* 117 (5): 1380-1421.

Scheper-Hughes, Nancy and Philippe Bourgois. 2004. "Introduction: Making Sense of Violence." In *Violence in War and Peace: An Anthology*, edited by Nancy Scheper-Hughes and Philippe Bourgois. Oxford: Blackwell Publishing.

Stevens, Jacqueline. 2011. *States without Nations: Citizenship for Mortals*. New York: Columbia University Press.

Ticktin, Miriam. 2011. Casualties of Care: Immigration and the Politics of Humanitarianism. Berkeley: University of California Press.

Valencia, Sayak. 2018. *Gore Capitalism*. Translated by Erica Mena. Semiotext(e) Intervention Series. South Pasadena, CA: Semiotext(e).